From the Bayou to the Bay

SUNY series in African American Studies
—————————
John R. Howard and Robert C. Smith, editors

From the Bayou to the Bay

*The Autobiography
of a Black Liberation Scholar*

ROBERT C. SMITH

Cover image: San Francisco State University

Published by State University of New York Press, Albany

© 2021 State University of New York

All rights reserved

Printed in the United States of America

For information, contact State University of New York Press, Albany, NY
www.sunypress.edu

Library of Congress Cataloging-in-Publication Data

Names: Smith, Robert C. (Robert Charles), 1947– author. | State University
    of New York Press.
Title: From the bayou to the bay : the autobiography of a Black Liberation
    scholar / Robert C. Smith.
Description: Albany : State University of New York Press, 2021. | Series:
    SUNY series in African American Studies | Includes bibliographical
    references and index.
Identifiers: LCCN 2020024805 | ISBN 9781438482316 (hardcover : alk. paper) |
    ISBN 9781438482323 (pbk. : alk. paper) | ISBN 9781438482330 (ebook)
Subjects: LCSH: Smith, Robert C. (Robert Charles), 1947– | College
    teachers—United States—Biography. | African American teachers—United
    States—Biography. | African American scholars—United States—Biography.
Classification: LCC LA2317.S6235 A3 2021 | DDC 378.1/2092 [B]—dc23
LC record available at https://lccn.loc.gov/2020024805

10 9 8 7 6 5 4 3 2 1

For Omar X, Harry Scoble, Ronald Walters, John Howard, Mack Jones, and Hanes Walton Jr.

Contents

Contents

Introduction

There is arrogance in deciding to write a memoir or autobiography, to assume one's life is worth reading or writing about. I am not arrogant and never expected to write a memoir. As retirement approached after near fifty years of teaching, research, and writing, I told everyone who asked what I was going to do, "Nothing." That it was time to rest, to retire. Virtually everyone—family, friends, and colleagues—told me that was not possible, that satisfaction in retirement required doing something, maintenance of some kind of activity: something to do, something to keep one busy. My colleague Wilbur Rich, who retired from the faculty at Wesleyan after more than forty years of teaching and research, told me that he tried doing nothing for a year or so after retirement and could not do it. "It will drive you crazy," he said, and so to keep busy he undertook a major archival research project. Playing golf, watching reruns of *Gunsmoke* and *Rawhide* and the mindless drivel of cable television news, Wilbur insisted, would not suffice.

My wife Scottie and my daughters Scottus and Jessica also insisted that I should find something to do—fishing, bird-watching, or something; otherwise, I would get on their nerves. Jessica, who was temporarily moving back home, said, "Do something Daddy, otherwise you will be constantly bugging me." Scottie expressed similar concerns, which was odd since for the last five years I had been teaching only one late Monday afternoon class and thus was home virtually all the time. However, I was usually writing so I was doing something and leaving her alone to do what she was doing, mainly talking on the phone and going to meetings. Scottus suggested that I sell the house and move near her so I could babysit my grandson, which was something in my seventies I did not wish to do.

I assumed that family, friends, and colleagues' insistence that a satisfactory retirement required doing something was likely supported by gerontology research. To my surprise, in a quick look at *Wikipedia* I discovered there is no consensus on the keeping busy or "activity" theory of aging and retirement. Rather, some scholars of the aging process embrace what is called "disengagement theory," suggesting it is natural and inevitable for older persons to disengage, to do nothing. Interesting, but I concluded that at least in the early years, why risk it? Why risk going crazy or constantly getting on Scottie and Jessica's nerves? So, for a time at least I decided I would do something to keep busy.

But what? Not golf, fishing, or bird-watching, although we do live in a wonderful bird habitat. Not taking classes in Berkeley's Olli program (Osher Lifelong Learning Institute) for students over fifty, although it often offers classes of interests such as The Beatles, The Sixties, Consciousness, and The Philosophy of Martin Luther King Jr. Also not teaching an Olli class; thus I declined an offer to join the Berkeley Olli faculty to teach a course on conservatism and racism. The Olli offer was alluring; to teach a class one afternoon a week on a subject of interest and importance using two of my own books. But I was tired of teaching, finding it tiresome in my last couple of years of teaching my Monday afternoon seminar. Nor did I wish to undertake a major research project. Thus, I declined an invitation from Polity Press to write a textbook on African American Political Thought, and from Palgrave to edit a Handbook of African American Politics. I planned to continue my work as a general editor of the State University of New York Press's African American Studies series, and to prepare every couple of years a new edition of my textbook *American Politics and the African American Quest for Universal Freedom.* But neither of these required major expenditures of time.

So, what might I do that did not require a lot of work of the kind I have been doing for nearly fifty years? A memoir or autobiography? Although I never anticipated doing one, doing so—writing about myself—would require little research—some but not a lot—and it would be on a subject I know and care about—me. Even if I am not worth reading about—except perhaps by my children and grandchildren—I decided I am worth writing about.

Probably another source of the idea of a memoir was that my last two books—published in the year of my retirement—were quasi-biographies of two of my closest friends and colleagues, *Ronald W. Walters and the Fight for Black Power, 1969–2010* and *Hanes Walton, Jr.: Architect of the Black Science of Politics.* Walters and Walton were preeminent black political scientists of my generation, whose prodigious scholarship and, in Walters's case activism, shaped the parameters of the modern study of black politics.

I knew Ron Walters and Hanes Walton; they were friends of mine. I am no Ron Walters or Hanes Walton. But writing about them in books that combined history and biography helped me develop skills useful in writing about myself in work that is part memoir and part history that uses my experience, my memory, as part of the evidence in an account of the last fifty years of the African American freedom struggle. In a sense, I am going to have a conversation with myself, with my memory, about my experiences in one of the most crucial periods in the history of African people in the United States.

This leads to another rationale. I came of age in the 1960s—the best decade for black people in the history of the United States, and one of the most pivotal decades in the history of the nation. In his 1998 book Tom Brokaw, the *NBC News* correspondent, portrayed the Depression era, World War II generation of Americans as the Greatest Generation. I disagree. I believe my generation—postwar baby boomers who came of age in the 1960s—is the greatest generation. This is not mere generational vanity, as Leonard Steinhorn writes in *The Greater Generation*, "It is safe to say that the World War II era Americans, for all their virtues, wouldn't be so honored today were it not for the fact that their children, Baby Boomers, have spent their lives righting the wrongs that the Greatest Generation condoned, accommodated, or never addressed."

Righting wrongs was the rallying cry of the 1960s generation of protest and reform that brought about fundamental cultural and political transformations resulting in a more equalitarian and culturally inclusive America. The seminal civil rights movement, the campus revolts, the Black Power movement, the making of a counterculture, the ghetto rebellions, the movement against the war on the Vietnamese people, the sexual revolution, women's liberation, gay liberation, the music, the drugs—all in all an exciting, liberating, radical time with heady talk of revolution. For African Americans this was the greatest generation because it broke the back of the centuries-old systems of legal racism and segregation and inaugurated some freedom. My generation was the last to come of age under legal, Jim Crow apartheid and the first to mature in an era where racism was not morally and legally a part of the American way.

The university was an epicenter of the 1960s revolution, and I have spent all of my adult life on the campus, beginning as student in 1965 and thereafter as a professor (my generation of blacks was the first in large numbers to attend, and become faculty at predominantly white universities). The Black Power movement had a profound, transformative effect on my consciousness and understanding. The movement found its first institutional expression on the campuses of predominantly white universities while I was student. We formed Black Student Unions and fought to establish Black Studies programs. Black studies were a major achievement of my generation. Before the black studies "revolution" the curriculum of the humanities and social sciences at US universities was racist and Eurocentric, celebrating a triumphal narrative of Western civilization while ignoring its oppression of nonwhite peoples. Black studies and subsequently Chicano studies, Asian American studies, Indigenous Peoples studies, women's studies, and gay and lesbian studies changed all of this, bringing the perspectives of the oppressed and marginalized into academic study. The results: the American university was irrevocably changed. Mainly because of the debate about black studies the faculties and curriculum became more diverse, universal, and multicultural, reflecting not only black perspectives in teaching and research but the perspectives of other groups marginalized by Western civilization. In telling my story, I tell in part this story of the transformation of the American university.

I have titled my story *From the Bayou to the Bay: The Autobiography of a Black Liberation Scholar*. I was born in 1947 in a small town in Northwest Louisiana, the Bayou state. In 1969 I moved to the San Francisco Bay Area to complete my undergraduate studies at the University of California, Berkeley. After completing the master's in political science at UCLA, I moved to New York City to study urban policy at the New School for Social Research. Subsequently, I earned the doctorate in political science at Howard in 1975. After completing the PhD I wished to return to the Bay Area, but it took fourteen years before I was able to do so, securing an appointment at San Francisco State in 1989. I have lived here since and it is where I expect to spend my last years.

W. E. B. Du Bois described San Francisco as the most beautiful place of human habitation on earth. I have not traveled the world as Du Bois, so I do not know if San Francisco is the world's most beautiful city, but Du Bois did not often exaggerate or engage in hyperbole. I have traveled widely in the US and I can safely say San Francisco is the nation's most beautiful city. The city of Tony Bennett and the Four Tops' (I like the Tops' version better) hills, fog, the bay, the windy sea, the little cable cars, and the golden sunshine . . .

Aside from its natural beauty, distinctive architecture, and pleasant climate, the city is also beautiful to me because of its countercultural tendencies and its progressive, left political traditions. With Oakland and

Berkeley across the Bay, the Bay Area is the most self-consciously radical place in the US. *Left Coast City*, as my San Francisco State colleague Richard DeLeon titled his book about the city's politics. When I arrived in the late 1960s it was the acknowledged forward base camp of the "revolution" we saw coming to America.

John Kennedy was the first president I was conscious of. Born when Harry Truman was president, I had no consciousness of his or Dwight Eisenhower's presidency. Perhaps this was because Kennedy was the first television president and as I recall we got our first television around this time. I followed the 1960 campaign and Kennedy's brief presidency closely (he was murdered on the same day my daddy died). In a sense this book begins with the Kennedy presidency. As I began writing Donald Trump was president. Of the forty-four persons who have been president, Kennedy was one of the three or four most sympathetic to the African American freedom struggle. Trump is one of the three or four most hostile. Despite his many shortcomings and imperfections, the young, intelligent, literate, and rhetorically gifted Kennedy is my favorite president. The aging, boorish, buffoonish, neoracist, white supremacist Trump my least favorite, although Andrew Johnson is a close second. Bracketing my story between Kennedy and Trump is to anchor the beginning with inspiration and optimism and the end with despair and pessimism.

To write a memoir one should have a good memory. I do not. Scottie often reminds me of places, persons, and circumstances I have forgotten. I have not kept a diary and only began to keep files—sporadically—in my undergraduate years. Interviews are not possible because most of the persons I would like to refresh my memories are dead or unable to be located. Thus, this is a difficult undertaking, given the absence of a good record. What I shall attempt to do is to have a broad focus, interweaving my story with significant events of the last half century that I observed or was a part of, events of me in history. In doing this, I check my memory with relevant published sources.

It is almost certain that any person's memory of their life is selective and biased, with an inevitable tendency toward emphasizing the positive and favorable while downplaying the negative and unpleasant. Each for sure is necessary for a good story. I shall endeavor to recall and write about the good and the bad, the favorable and unfavorable. How successful I am no one—not even I—can ever know.

I suppose it's somewhat unfair to ask academic colleagues to evaluate an autobiography since there is much they cannot know. However, several intrepid colleagues were willing to do this work for me, and I am grateful to David Covin, David Tabb, Sekou Franklin, John Howard, and Tiffany Willoughby-Herard for helping me order my story chronologically and substantively, and assuring me it was worthy of sharing with others.

Michael Rinella, my longtime editor for SUNY Press's series in African American Studies, did his work with his usual consummate skill. I also appreciate the contributions of the anonymous reviewers of the manuscript, and the efficient work of the production staff at SUNY Press.

My wife and daughter Jessica read the manuscript and made telling, often acerbic, but useful comments. Nothing I have done in the last half century, personally and professionally, could have been accomplished without the presence and love of my beautiful Bird. My greatest accomplishment was loving and marrying her.

CHAPTER 1

Growing Up Accommodating Segregation with Community and Culture

My place of birth, Benton, is located fourteen miles north of Shreveport, Louisiana's second largest city. In the northwest part of the state, the area is commonly referred to as the Ark-La-Tex, since it borders Texarkana, Texas, and Texarkana, Arkansas. When I was growing up Hope, Arkansas, the birthplace of President Bill Clinton, was the last stop on the Continental Trailways bus line that picked up passengers in the small towns to go shopping in the big city, Shreveport.

Shreveport, with a population in 1960 of 165,000 (40 percent black) was the commercial center of the Ark-La-Tex region. Located on the Red River, the city was named for Army Corp of Engineers captain Henry Shreve who cleared the river of sandbars, which made it navigable. When I was growing up the city was not a port, but it was a major center for the oil industry, had a thriving downtown business and shopping district, was the parish (in Louisiana counties are called parishes) seat for Caddo Parish, and Barksdale Air Force Base, one of the nation's pivotal strategic bomber bases, was located across the river in Bossier City. The city's nationally famous Louisiana Hayride and its local radio station KWKH were major venues for country and western music.

Unlike New Orleans, the state's largest city, Shreveport and the surrounding area had none of the Catholic, Cajun French influence. Rather it was militantly Anglo-Saxon Protestant, with both whites and blacks adhering to a fundamentalist, evangelical Christianity, largely Baptist but with a sprinkling of Methodists. The area in the early 1960s was also militantly racist, with an ultraconservative white supremacist power elite committed to the maintenance of segregation forever. The segregationist order was maintained by "Shreveport's Bull Connor," the public safety commissioner George D'Artois, who was in office from 1962 to 1976. The city gained national attention for its segregationist policies in 1963 when Sam Cooke was arrested for trying to register at a segregated Holiday Inn. The arrest is said to have been the inspiration for one of Cooke's last recordings "A Change Is Gonna Come," which became a kind of rally song for the civil rights movement. In a less publicized earlier incident Cooke and Solomon Burke were detained for trying to use a segregated restaurant, taken to a local fire station, stripped naked, and forced to perform some of their songs.

The repression of the D'Artois police regime was partly in response to the civil rights movement that developed in Shreveport, centered in the black community's vibrant commercial enterprises, churches, schools, and nightlife. The city was home to scores of black small businesses, barber and beauty shops, cafés, mom and pop stores, funeral homes, and nightclubs. Its notorious "Bottoms" of saloons, brothels, and juke joints produced a number of blues singers and guitarists, most famously Lead Belly. The city's black radio station KOKA broadcast a culturally rich diet of rhythm and blues, gospel and blues, and was home to one of the world's greatest disc jockeys, Sunrose, the "Gay Poppa." Its Municipal Auditorium showcased the rhythm and blues performances of James Brown, Chuck Jackson, Solomon Burke, Rufus "Dog Man" Thomas and his daughter Carla, among others.

My sister and nephew (who was the same age as I) and two nieces lived in Shreveport. I took the Trailways bus to the city frequently on Saturdays to hang out, shop, and frequent nightclubs. At night when Trailways was not available and no one had a car, we would walk or hitchhike the fourteen miles to attend concerts at the auditorium. Benton was a town of 1,300 persons (42 percent black) in 1960. It was literally a place with one streetlight at the intersection of the main street and the state highway. Named, for reasons I do not know, for Missouri senator Thomas Hart Benton, the town incorporated in 1836 was the seat of Bossier Parish. As the parish seat, during the day there was considerable activity at the courthouse, sheriff's office, the jail, the school board, and other parish offices.

The town's main street about quarter mile from the courthouse consisted of two general stores (one included a drugstore with a three-stool lunch counter), a five and dime store, a movie theater (closed in the early 1960s), a café, bank, post office, and a gas and service station. The parish library, the town hall, and the office of the town lawyer (also a state legislator and large plantation owner) were nearby. At the edge of town was what was universally referred to as the "Jew store," a small market and grocery store owned by the only known Jewish family in town. Benton had one doctor who practiced from his large main street house, treating black patients in a segregated room at the back of the house.

The major source of employment in the town was a plant that processed logs into utility poles; however, most persons were employed in Shreveport or Bossier City (the parish's largest city with a population of about forty thousand). Most blacks in Benton, aside from the small group of teachers and a few preachers, were employed as maids and janitors, and as field workers hoeing and picking cotton. Blacks also worked as caretakers, janitors, and caddies at the country club located on the outskirts of town.

Blacks owned a funeral home, a weekend café, a beauty and barber shop, and a couple of weekend juke joints. Out in the country, "in the hills," several blacks owned large and prosperous farms where they raised vegetables, chickens, hogs, and cattle. Although the town was generally segregated, several neighborhoods were integrated where a few blacks lived among whites and a few whites lived in predominantly black areas. This was the exception, however; the general pattern was one of rigid segregation enforced by custom rather than law.

I was born in 1947 in Benton, delivered by my sister Thelma and a midwife (Thelma told me that when I was born, she dropped me in a slop jar). I was the last of thirteen children; six of the thirteen died in infancy or at an early age. My mother, Blanch, was born in 1901, lived to 103, and was married at age fourteen. I know little of her parents except for her father Blanch Tharpe, whom she remembered as a mean man who beat her mother, Pocahontas Miles, who was half Indian. I know nothing of their parents, who in all likelihood were enslaved. Growing up my mother never told me a single story about her parents (except a little about Blanch's abuse) or about her childhood. My mother was an only child; her father at some point divorced her mother and married a woman named Pearl. Pearl, who worked as a maid on a plantation when I was growing up, was very close to us as a family, but I did not realize until long after I had left home that she was in effect my mother's stepmother (she, I guess, was roughly my mother's age).

I know even less about my father, his parents, or his growing up. Indeed, it is probably the case that the man I grew up thinking was my daddy—Martin Smith—was probably not my father. Apparently, my mother carried on a long relationship with a man named Larkin Hall who fathered my oldest sister Bernice in 1926 and me twenty-one years later. I vaguely remember Larkin visiting my mother (by the time I was growing up Martin and my mother had separated), his buying me a suit, and my mother insisting that my nephew Lynn, who was then living with us, and I attend his funeral.

I much later recalled being cautioned to stay away from any relationship of an intimate nature with a classmate, Ella Mae Hall, who lived down the street, who was apparently my half sister. At a family reunion after I had moved to California, a lady remarked to my mother, "Have you made sure the boy saw his sister," referring to Ella Mae. Also, on another visit home after moving to California my cousin, Josie Mae, told my wife and me a story of how Martin had caught my mother having sex with Larkin. Saying he started to kill her but thought better of it when he considered that the children needed her. On a trip home on another occasion Mr. Wesley Wright, a neighbor, family friend, school teacher, church leader, and one of the most prominent members of Benton's black elite whom we called professor, told me a rather detailed story that Larkin was my and Bernice's father and there was some kind of inheritance available if we wished to pursue it.

I did not wish to pursue it then or before or ever. While growing up I recall vaguely the gossip that Larkin was my father. I ignored it; I never asked my mother or daddy Martin about it, and neither of them ever raised it with me. If they had I would not have wished to talk about it. To me Martin was my daddy, the only one I had ever known and that was the way it was then and that is the way it is now.

By the time I became conscious my mother and father were long separated. But they were on friendly terms and he often came to our house for dinner; I remember especially how he enjoyed coming for fish dinners. Daddy, who was called "Mot," had a large camel-like hump in his back. I do not know how this happened. One story is that a chimney fell on his back and caused it; however, my older brother, Walter, recalls it may have been the result of a birth defect. Again, I do not know and to my regret I never asked him about it. As with my mother, I never discussed daddy's childhood, his parents, siblings, or the circumstances of his growing up.

When I was a young boy, my daddy was already an old man. He lived on a hill several miles outside of town on a farm where he raised hogs and watermelons. I cherish memories of visiting, where I would cut the center out of watermelons and throw the rest to the hogs. I also recall eating plums from his bountiful trees and having a delicious time eating roasted pigs. My other memory is of Daddy sitting on a bench in front of the drugstore in town during the summer with other old black men and chewing tobacco, smoking cigars, dipping snuff, and talking. I would frequently go to him ask for money to buy candy. After upbraiding me for always begging, he would usually give me a nickel or dime. All and all, I liked my daddy and if I was indeed the bastard son of Larkin and not his, he never gave me any indication of that and treated me always with kindness.

In his last years Daddy lived in a house down the street from us. I believe my mother arranged this so he would be close by and we could look after him. To his regret and I sensed shame, he spent the last months of his life in a nursing home. He died on November 22, 1963; although his exact age was not known, he was likely in his late eighties. My sisters and brothers claimed I mourned the death of the president more than Daddy's.

As I said, I have little knowledge of Mama's past, except that her father was abusive; she had no siblings, married young, and half of her children died at birth or at an early age. Reared by an abusive father, marrying so young and then having thirteen children only to see six of them die must have taken an emotional toll that she may have carried for all the years of her long life. But she shared none of this with me; we, for example, never spoke of the circumstances of the death of her six children. Mama was literate although I recall she said she had only a seventh-grade education. She could read and write very well, unlike Daddy who was illiterate, signing his name with an X.

Mama was universally referred to as Brewster. I do not know the source of this name. Perhaps it was because she was always a "Brewster," someone who did not take any mess from anybody. Married at fourteen, she began bearing and rearing children while engaged in all kinds of hard work, working at a dangerous turpentine plant and box factory and then in cotton fields hoeing and picking. I remember her rising early in the mornings, fixing a breakfast and lunch of biscuits, molasses, and salt pork, and boarding an army-like convoy truck to go to the fields where she labored sunrise to sundown. A good cotton picker, she could pick two hundred pounds a day, for which she was paid a pittance. After machines replaced people in the cotton fields, she worked as a maid for three families in Benton. In the last couple of decades before she retired in her late eighties, she was also janitor at the bank, working weekday evenings cleaning.

Mama rarely made me work in the fields, unlike my brothers and sisters who toiled beside her, hoeing and picking. This may have been because I was the baby and she spoiled me and also probably because I was not good at hoeing or picking. The times I recall hoeing, I would more often chop the cotton than the weeds and in a day I would pick very few pounds of cotton. For a time, I helped Mama at the bank until the bank president, for reasons I cannot recall, forbade me to do so.

Mama never invited or showed affection. I recall picking her up at the airport when she visited Los Angeles and we greeted by shaking hands rather than hugging. My friend Larry Mason, who accompanied me, was shocked by this lack of a show of affection between mother and son who had not seen each other for several years. We never hugged or kissed, she never said she loved me nor I her, we did not celebrate our birthdays or exchange gifts at Christmas. She never encouraged or inquired about my schoolwork, and when I made good grades she did not congratulate me or show any overt satisfaction. Similarly, when I made speeches at church or at school for which I was praised by others, she was silent. I thought nothing of this then. I think nothing of it now; that was the way she was, Brewster.

Mama was a hard but fair disciplinarian. When I did something wrong, something I was told not to do or failed to do something she told me to do, she whipped me—what today would likely be called a beating and child abuse. Her refrain would be, "Boy, go get me a switch, and make it a good one because you don't want me to have to get it." She would then have me remove my shirt and whip me. I did not then or now consider these whippings wrong or malicious because I had almost always done something to deserve them. For example, I recall on more than one occasion taking the money she had left with me to buy ice and spending it on candy or ice cream, and then probably whining there was no cold drinking water.

Although Mama was never cruel or mean to me, she was to others even in her nineties when she would sometimes say cruel or mean things to my sisters and brothers and their spouses or friends, and to people in the neighborhood. Our neighbor across the street, Reverend J. C. Goines, for the last decade of her life refused to speak to her because of the abusive things she said to him in front of his wife, such as "You ain't nothing," "you ain't got nothing." She would also berate people for their weight and their color. She did not like light-skin people, often calling them "yellow gals." She was religious, Baptist, prayed every day, attended church regularly, and for a time was on the usher board. She was a leader in the Lilly of the Valley Society, a self-help mutual aid group that collected small sums of money to assist the poor with health-related and burial expenses. And she often visited and gave to the "sick and shut-in."

She disliked and distrusted white people, routinely referring to them as "peckerwoods." We never discussed this animus, perhaps there was no need to. While acknowledging there were a few good white people, she said most were evil, devilish, and wicked. A specific source of her distrust of whites was clear and came to haunt her in the last years of her life. Apparently, a white man at some point had cheated her father out of his land; so even after she had paid the mortgage on her house, she was convinced there was secret lien on it that would be used after her death to take her property. After we assured and reassured her there was no secret lien, she remained worried because of what she thought had happen to her father. Finally, to ease her mind somewhat I had my friend Larry, an attorney in Berkeley, write her a letter stating, "At the request of your son (who by the way is my oldest and dearest friend) I have reviewed the documents concerning your property. . . . I find there is no lien or hold on said property. . . . However, to further rest your mind and reassure you I have conducted a complete computerized search of all liens and deeds in Bossier Parish since you purchased your home and I again found there are no liens or encumbrances. Nor were any 'secret' or hidden liens found. I hope this answers your concerns and helps to put your mind at ease." I think it did to some extent ease her mind, because she did not speak of it afterward, although she deeded the house to us before she died.

On November 15, 2001, we celebrated Mama's hundredth birthday with a large and lavish gathering of family and friends at the top of the tallest building in Shreveport. Although she was a hundred, she continued to wear high heels to church and other special occasions, and at 101 she fell and broke her hip and was thereafter incapacitated and confined to bed. (To I believe her shame, when I visited I occasionally had to change her diaper, reminding us of the Scripture "once a man, twice a child.") Prior to her fall, she lived alone, taking care of herself with a pistol beside her bed, which she would fire outside just to let would-be intruders know she had a gun and knew how to use it. For a couple of weeks toward the end she was placed in a nursing home, but whenever we visited, she pleaded with us to take her home, that the place was killing her and she wanted to go home so she could "die in her own bunk." So, we took her out of the home and my sister Cleo, a retired social worker who lived in Los Angeles, came home to take care of her for the last year or so of her life. She died in her own bunk on September 5, 2004.

Mama was a Brewster. She bore thirteen children, raised seven to adulthood, and was a workhorse of a woman who, never learning to drive, walked miles on a daily basis until she was in her nineties. I never saw her cry, and she rarely displayed tenderness or affection. She was a hell of a woman, liberated long before I heard the word. She did more to shape my character than any other person and, with the exception of Scottie, my wife of nearly fifty years, has more to do with who I am than any other person.

Mama for many years lived and worked on the Stinson plantation, one of two plantations near Benton probably dating back to the Civil War and Reconstruction. I assume Daddy lived there as well, although as I recall it was said he was often away working on the railroads. By the time of my first memory, we lived in a two-room "shotgun" house in Benton in an area called the Quarters. At that time there were only four of us, Mama, myself, my sister Nell, and nephew Lynn Braggs, who was also born in 1947. (Lynn, who stayed with us from late infancy to the second or third grade, was embarrassed I was his uncle because we were the same age.)

My oldest brother Floyd ran away from home when he was fourteen, and Mama did not hear from him for many years, assuming he was likely dead. She was forever bitter toward him for "running away with Bogey," which must have caused enormous distress. Floyd told me when he was in his eighties that he ran away because Mama's discipline was too harsh, and he did not like the hard fieldwork. He recalled that he spent most of his years away as a hobo, hopping freight trains from town to town. He completed only a few years of school, but he was literate. He spent his life working at odd jobs. A ladies' man, he was married several times and probably often relied on women to support him. Floyd died in 2011. He was ninety-one.

Bernice, my oldest sister, after working for a time as a cocktail waitress in Shreveport, became a local fashion model and beautician, eventually co-owning the most prominent salon in the city. An active member of one of the city's most prominent churches and of the NAACP, she used her position as an independent businesswoman to become a leader of Shreveport's civil rights movement. Briefly married, she had a son Lynn who was also active in the movement and years later became a businessman and campaign strategist in the election of Shreveport's first black mayors. Her daughter Brenda was the first black to attend and graduate from the city's most prominent segregated white high school. Bernice died in 2010. She was eighty-four.

My brother Walter, who was called Buddy, joined the navy and was the first member of the family to move to California. While in the navy he married, which caused bitterness between he and Mama because the monthly allotment check she received as his nearest relative now went to his wife, Earlene. Mama probably badly needed the money and was unrelentingly hostile to Buddy's wife, accusing her of marrying him to get the allotment. Buddy settled in Los Angeles, worked for a time in the area's then flourishing aircraft manufacturing industry, divorced Earlene, earned a degree in accounting, and became an Internal Revenue Service examiner.

My next sister, Cleo, had rickets and underwent numerous surgeries for many years. Extremely bowlegged, she was the first of the family to attend college, graduating from Grambling in the late 1950s. In her sophomore year she became pregnant and her daughter Cynthia stayed with us for several years. After Cleo completed her degree in business administration, she moved to Los Angeles, where she worked as case worker for the Los Angeles County Welfare Department. Cynthia committed suicide in 2004, shooting herself in the head at the age of forty-two. Cleo died of a heart attack in 2017. She was seventy-nine.

When we lived in the two-room shotgun house, all my siblings except Marjorie "Nell" had left. Four of us lived in those two rooms, Mama, Lynn, Nell, and I. I cannot recall how many beds we had but I remember Lynn and me taking turns sleeping on pallets. There was no running water or electricity, and we used a slop jar (a white enamel pot) as a toilet at night and often peed on the ground, although there was an outhouse used by the four families who lived in the Quarters (I was afraid of the outhouse because of the maggots and occasional snakes). For water there was an outdoor hydrant, and for keeping food we had an icebox for which we purchased ice from the iceman a couple times a week. A large metal tub was used for bathing and washing clothes, a woodstove for heating and cooking, and kerosene lamps.

After a couple of years in the shotgun house, Mama made a down payment on one of the first houses in the new Pine Hill subdivision for blacks. With four rooms, this new house doubled our living space. Initially, the house did not have electricity, running water, or indoor plumbing, although we had a butane tank that provided for heating and cooking. Sometime in the late 1950s the town extended the sewer system to the new subdivision so we had running water (prior to that we had to walk a quarter mile or so to get water from a neighbor's hydrant), electricity, and indoor plumbing. Eventually the butane was replaced by natural gas and the dirt roads in the subdivision were paved. About 1960 we got a television; before that, we listened to radio with such favorites as *Amos 'n' Andy*, *Our Gal Sunday*, *Ma Perkins*, *The Romance of Helen Tent*, and *Dick Tracy*. By this time Lynn had moved to Shreveport to live with his mother, and in 1959 Buddy came to take Nell to California to live with him and complete high school. I remember crying uncontrollably the day they departed, but there was silver lining to being left alone—I finally had my own room; prior to Nell's leaving I had slept on a cot in Mama's room.

Nell graduated from Centennial High School in Compton, worked for time as a part-time beautician and as clerk in the Los Angeles County Sheriff's Department while attending Cal State Los Angeles. After graduation, she earned a master's in urban planning from Cornell and returned to Los Angeles, where she worked for years as a planner for the state transportation authority. She died in 2015 of pancreatic cancer. She was seventy-three. About a decade before her death she converted to the Baha'i faith and adopted the name Tahirih, "The Pure One."

I was entering ninth grade when Nell left, meaning for most of my teen years I grew up without siblings. However, I had lots of friends in the Pine Hill subdivision. The Wrights across the road were a family of four boys roughly my age and a girl, and the Tillmans down the road were a family of eight with seven boys and a girl. Except for cleaning the bank in the evenings with Mama and selling *Grit*, the weekly newspaper that targeted rural and small-town America (my customers were blacks and whites), I did not work, thus there was plenty of time for reading, playing games, and doing nothing. I loved to read; in school, in addition to browsing books, I read *Newsweek* and eventually subscribed to *Life*, the weekly news photo magazine. The town library was closed to blacks, but Mama was the librarian's maid, and knowing of my interest she allowed me to browse and take books home. We also subscribed to the *Shreveport Sun*, the local black weekly. I wrote stories for the *Sun*. I do not recall how I came to do this or what I wrote, although I guess it was things about Benton.

There was little work to do around the house. I fed the chickens; collected eggs (a sometime hazardous task, since snakes would occasionally nest with the eggs); and slaughtered, plucked, and dressed chickens (Mama would twist their necks, I used an ax). (There was an unfortunate experience with collecting eggs that has remained with me all my life. Once I got an egg from the nest, cracked it to cook, and found inside a tiny fetus. From then on, I have refused to eat the yolk of an egg.) I also cleaned the house and washed the dishes. I became quite good at house cleaning and liked to see it done well; I carried this habit into adulthood and have been responsible for most of the house cleaning throughout my marriage.

With little to do and many friends, I had ample time to do nothing and play. Doing nothing often involved long walks, since we did not have a car. While walking I would often talk aloud to myself and would also from time to time preach to the trees, which gained me a reputation for being weird. But mostly we played—all kinds of games—horseshoes, marbles, jacks as well as football, baseball, and basketball. We also picked fruits—plums, berries, persimmons, and black walnuts. (Early on I developed the bad habit of eating green plums, which likely contributed to early loss of my teeth.) Even in Louisiana's brutal summers with mosquitos, wasps, ants, and snakes, we played since without air conditioning outdoors was preferable to the sweltering heat inside.

For the ball games we improvised. We built our makeshift basketball court in a back yard and played baseball with tennis balls and bats made of sticks. I was not very athletic, so I frequently would umpire or referee the games. Similarly, with the organized games at school I did not play, but in order to attend out-of-town games I was the linesman and then the trainer for the football team and score keeper for the baseball and basketball teams.

A favorite pastime were dances and parties. I mentioned that Shreveport had an excellent R&B radio station that played all the latest songs. KOKA also had one of the world's greatest disc jockeys, Sunrose, the Gay Poppa. Later, in Los Angles and Washington, I had the good opportunity to hear three other great radio jocks, Magnificent Montague in the mornings on KGFJ, the Los Angeles soul station, and the Real Don Steele in the afternoons on KHJ, the top forty Rock & Roll station. In Washington I listened to the great blues man Jerry "The Bama" Washington on Saturdays on WPFW, the local Pacifica station. Yet, of all these jockeys Gay Poppa was the greatest.

To appreciate a great disc jockey, like a great song, it is of course best to hear him. (There were no female jocks during the time I listened to radio between the early 1960s and 1970.) What made the Gay Poppa great is difficult to describe; he had a distinctive, good preacher-like voice that made his jive talk over the music as much a part of the show as the songs he played. His rapping about the music, young love, partying, and subtle sexual messages made for soulful mornings and evenings during his twice-daily shows.

Music is integral to African American culture, and to the culture of the young. It was certainly important in my coming of age. Music, dancing, drinking, and girls were preoccupations for me and my friends. There were Sam Cooke, the Impressions, the southern soul of Bobby Bland, Joe Tex, James Brown, the Wallace Brothers, Solomon Burke, Otis Redding, Little Milton, and then Motown, Smokey and the Miracles, the Temptations, Mary Wells, the Four Tops, the Supremes, Brenda Holloway, Marvin Gaye, and Junior Walker and the All Stars. The early 1960s were the beginning of the making of music that mattered. Music—Bob Dylan, Curtis Mayfield, the

Beatles, Laura Nyro, Nina Simone, Janis Joplin, Van Morrison, and many others—mattered a lot to me throughout the 1960s, but the beginning was in Benton with southern soul and Motown. Although some critics later disparaged Motown as an inauthentic sound of young (white) America rather than the souls of black folk, comparing it invidiously to Stax's southern soul, to me then and now it was all black, sweet soul music. Insofar as the really authentic black music—the blues—KOKA broadcast a daily blues show at 1:00 p.m. hosted by the boring B. B. "Bird Brain" Davis. We ignored it, dismissing the blues as music for old people. I only started to appreciate the blues after I moved to Berkeley and was reintroduced to it by a white boy.

I was a very poor dancer, danced like a white boy, little rhythm, could not swing, but who cared. I loved to dance and with enough Peppermint Snap (a peppermint-flavored gin) I did so with abandon. We danced at school-sponsored events where radio jocks like the Gay Poppa played the records. We also danced at weekend outdoor house parties, where out of the sight of school monitors we could grind until ejaculation. There was also Big Bill Brewer's Flamingo Club in Bossier City where the Gay Poppa reigned on Friday nights; you brought your own liquor and the place was so crowded that the only dance possible was a slow grind. (I do not recall what the drinking age was then—probably twenty-one—but whatever it was we had easy access to liquor.)

Although we always told lies about "getting some," the truth was, as Richard Pryor said, "It was very seldom you got any parts of pussy" in the 1950s and early 1960s. I never had sex in high school, unlike few of my friends, although you would never know it from the lies we told. The pill and the sexual revolution did not reach Benton while I was there, and the puritanical ethos of the church made having sex appear sinful and dirty, something that only "sluttish," nasty girls did. And then there was the risk and fear of pregnancy. If a girl did become pregnant, she was thrown out of church and would be readmitted only after a humiliating public apology before the entire congregation. I recall only one girl in my school becoming pregnant, impregnated by my best friend Charles "Moon" Lee, which of course made the rest of us envious since we knew that not all his stories were lies. Egregiously, most of us routinely sexually assaulted girls in the crowded hallways by feeling their breasts and vaginas.

I had three girlfriends during high school in the sense of engaging in prolonged kissing. I recall one opportunity "to go all the way" but for some reason did not. My niece Brenda arranged for me to meet a friend of hers in Shreveport. Alone in my sister's bedroom, after prolonged kissing,

I began to undress her (I cannot recall her name) and then and I recall saying, "I don't want to hurt you." I do not know why I stopped my first real opportunity to have sex. Perhaps it was because I really did not wish to hurt her by risking pregnancy. But sometimes I think it may have been because I did not know how to do it. In any event, my first sex would have to wait until California.

All and all, I had a great time growing up in Benton. I was never hungry, never had to work hard, had no childhood illnesses, and lots of friends and fun. All of this in the midst of the racist Jim Crow social structure of early 1960s rural Louisiana, which I accepted and accommodated without thought or protest. As I reflect and try to analyze why (really, we since there was never talk of protest among my peers), I believe it was at least partly because of the central role of the church and our segregated school in sustaining a sense of culture and community.

Religion, a faith in God, has been described as the single most important aspect of African American culture. This "peculiar spiritual quality" of black folk, to use Du Bois's phrase, has been traced to our African heritage. In the culture that emerged during our enslavement this African spiritual inheritance became an Africanized Christianity. Enslaved Africans in America were not allowed to maintain their traditional spiritual beliefs and practices. Instead, they were forced to embrace the religion—Protestant Christianity—of the enslavers. Yet while adopting the basic beliefs, tenets, and teachings of Christianity, Africans turned the rituals of worship into something uniquely African American that over time became one of the foundations (along with music) of our culture. Even today African Americans are a very religious people, whether religiosity is measured by subjective belief in God, frequency of praying and church attendance, or belief in the literal truth of the Bible. Of course, southern white culture is also very religious, but cross-national surveys comparing blacks and whites in the United States with the peoples of Europe have consistently found that African Americans are the most religious people in the Western world. The pervasiveness of religion in the black culture and community of Benton in the 1960s is indicated by the relatively large number of churches. In a town of less than five hundred black people there were four churches, all Baptist, with each having a membership of probably less than fifty (I would guess 10 to 15 percent of the black men in town and a smaller percent of women were not church members).

The church and religion were integral parts of my growing up. As far as I can recall I attended Sunday school, I "accepted Christ" at the age of

twelve, and was baptized in a bayou near the church. I was a member of
the Greater New Zion Baptist Church. Because of the number of churches
in Benton and the surrounding area, the preachers usually pastored more
than one church, therefore worship services were held only once a month.
But throughout the week there were activities at the church, Baptist Training Union, prayer meetings, Bible study, business meeting, and meetings
of the various church auxiliaries such as the choir and usher board. Once a
year each church held a week-long revival meeting, where a guest preacher
would come to town to "revive and save souls." A regular at our revivals
was Reverend C. L. Pennywell from Shreveport. Pennywell in cadence and
delivery is the only preacher I have heard who was nearly as good as Martin
Luther King Jr.

Benton was the headquarters of the Northeast Louisiana Baptist Association. In the late summer it held its annual meeting in town. This meeting
of what we called the "Sociation" was essentially a competition between area
preachers as to who could deliver the most rousing sermon. Held at night,
the event, which attracted hundreds of people, was carnival-like with various
stalls selling various tracts and trinkets and the best barbeque one could
find all year. The "Sociation," the revivals, and the regular church activities
were also opportunities to meet girls and attempt to establish relationships.

I thoroughly enjoyed the rituals of the church; everybody dressed up,
the women in their hats and long dresses, the deacon board to the right
of the pulpit, the women sitting to the left and the men to the right. The
choir in its striking gowns marching in and the opening prayer by the
deacons kneeling around a table were emotionally powerful, as were the
old one hundreds—call-and-response songs sung without music. The old
one hundreds—"Father I Stretch My Hands to Thee," "A Charge to Keep
I Have," "Getting Late in the Evening," "I Love the Lord, He Heard My
Cry," and my favorite, "The Old Ship of Zion"—along with the singing of
the choir and the praying and preaching were means by which the Western
religion was Africanized. If the preacher was good (my pastor Reverend A.
L. Coleman was not a good preacher; as the saying goes, he did not have
any "whoop" but to this day he delivered the best altar prayer I ever heard)
the sermon would be marked by rhythmic "Amen," "Preach," "Come up,"
"Go ahead," and "Tell-um" from the deacons and shrieks and shouts from
the congregation as people shouted and "got happy" in an emotional release
that was African. Under the tutelage of Reverend Paul Davis, the associate
pastor, I read the entire Bible and frequently gave speeches on biblical
themes at my church and other area churches. Occasionally I was mistakenly

referred to as Reverend Robert Smith. Most of the men in the church were not good readers or talkers, so for a time I taught the men's Sunday school class. The class was in the deacon's corner of the main sanctuary and would often end just as members and visitors arrived for the main worship service. The pastor's wife, who was also my high school English teacher, thought it unseemly for visitors to see a boy teaching a man, so she discontinued my teaching. As a result of my Sunday school work, I got the opportunity to make my first trip "up North" to Chicago to attend the National Baptist Sunday School Convention. My only recollection of the trip is that while we were standing on the steps of a church, a group of young men beat and robbed several persons in broad daylight.

I was also a part of the black Knights of Pythias, the fraternal order for young Christian men. I say a part of because I do not recall going through any of the rituals to become a member. Reverend Davis, who tutored me on the Bible, was the group's sponsor, and I recall traveling with him to meetings, particularly to deliver the Knights' "Flower Prayer," an address in honor of women and motherhood. Reverend Davis was widely rumored to be homosexual or gay. (Of course we did not use those terms. We referred to allegedly gay persons as sissies or punks.) Since I traveled frequently with him alone at night, it was suggested he might be molesting me. I do not know if Reverend Davis was gay (he was married), but if he was, he never made any untoward suggestions toward me in word or deed. Homosexuality was of course widely condemned in Benton at that time, and my peers and I considered it wholly unthinkable that a man would prefer to have sex with a man rather than a woman. We would have considered such a person a fool and probably would have beaten him; for sure, he would have been scorned and ostracized.

Although I loved the rituals of the church, participated in its activities, thoroughly studied the Bible, and admired the ethics of Jesus as he spelled them out in the Sermon on the Mount, I never prayed and probably never really believed in God. I certainly was always skeptical about the Virgin Birth and the Resurrection and expressed doubt about these core tenets of the faith in Sunday school. And in my admiration for Jesus's ethics I found some of the teachings difficult to obey or even wish to obey. For example, the injunction in the Sermon on the Mount, "Whoever looks at a woman to lust for her already has committed adultery with her in his heart" (Matthew 5: 28) is impossible to obey unless one is gay. I pride myself in near fifty years of marriage in having never committed adultery, except . . . countless times in my heart. I consider the command in Matthew 5: 44 not only difficult to obey but foolish: "Love your enemies, bless those who curse you, do good to those who hate you, and pray for those who spitefully use and persecute you." These two teachings, among a couple of others in the Sermon, are near impossible, ridiculous, and not required in any way by a rational, humane ethical system.

But probably the most critical source of my skepticism was the realization early on that if God and his son were indeed all-powerful then they must be white supremacist and racists; otherwise, why would they countenance the long exploitation and subordination of black people by white people. However, I did not act on this skepticism and abandon faith until decades later when I moved to San Francisco, the least religious city in America. But, in a sense I have probably always been what Albert Camus described, referring to himself as an "unchristian Christian," one who accepts, and, for the most part, attempts to live by Christian ethics without believing the myths or trying to adhere to its more irrational precepts.

If the church was the center of Benton's black culture and community then the segregated C. H. Irion High was a close second. C. H. Irion, named I think after a black doctor, was actually a consolidated K–12 school, with a couple of hundred students from Benton and surrounding areas. In the early years of my attendance in the elementary and middle grades it was both separate and unequal. Unlike the white Benton High, which had modern brick facilities, a gym, and a football stadium, Irion had only two large frame buildings and no athletic facilities. Our teachers were paid less, the curriculum was not as comprehensive (no foreign languages or advanced science classes), and we always had secondhand books, passed down to us after several years of use by the white students at Benton High. In the late 1950s, however, likely as a result of the *Brown* decision and fearing pressures to live up to the separate but equal doctrine or desegregate, the facilities at Irion were modernized and made substantially equal to the white school. An up-to-date brick structure was built, a library was established, and a gym and football stadium were erected. The curriculum was updated (French was added as a high school course), new books were provided, and teacher pay was equalized as a result of threatened litigation by the state's association of black teachers. Also, in the early 1960s new influxes of young, likely better-educated teachers (mostly women) were added to the faculty. Thus, by the time I entered high school Irion was not only separate but for the first time substantially equal in terms of facilities, curriculum, and teachers, fulfilling finally the 1896 mandate of *Plessy v. Ferguson*.

Our school was "ours," a black space, although one controlled by white people, the all-white school board and administration. I suspect these white overlords closely monitored what was taught in history, literature, and civics, making sure the principal and teachers avoided discussions of black politics and civil rights. I do not recall *any* discussions in classes of Rosa Parks, Little Rock, Martin Luther King, or *Brown v. Board of Education*. Thus, except for what we learned from the media we were completely ignorant of the freedom struggle. Even now as I try to remember, as best as I can recall I had no knowledge of the Montgomery Bus Boycott or of the *Brown* decision. That is—and this is amazing now—I cannot recall knowing while in high school that the Supreme Court had declared my school unconstitutional. There were of course no classes on black history or literature, no mention of Du Bois, Douglass, Nat Turner, or the NAACP. This seems, as I said, amazing now but unless memory terribly fails me, this was the case.

The principal and the teachers I guess were thoroughly intimidated or perhaps they were so completely accepting of the existing order that there was little need for overt intimidation. I do recall that when the white overlords visited, the principal and faculty were nervous, warning us to be on our best behavior. And we were on good behavior as none of us ever protested the lack of blackness in our curriculum. Indeed, the very thought of doing this then now seems absurd. I do recall preparing a speech at school on Booker T. Washington in which I wrote something like "he lectured the white man on brotherhood," and the teachers deleted it because it might have offended the white overlords who were to attend. Washington ("Our country's history knows of two Washington's—one father of his country, the other the up-lifter of his people") and George Washington Carver were the only two prominent blacks celebrated in school.

I enjoyed school and found it interesting. The teachers were good in terms of knowledge and concern. Corporal punishment was a routine part of the disciplinary process (corporal punishment was used for infractions of school rules and by some teachers for failure to perform assignments). I was a good student except in mathematics where I passed largely on the basis of the generosity of the teacher (I was lucky in college in that I was not required to take a single math class, although I took a lot of mind-numbing statistics courses). I was active in the drama club (always playing Jesus in the annual passion play) and often gave speeches at school events. And, as I indicated, while not athletic, I was able to participate in the games as trainer or scorekeeper.

  White overlords notwithstanding, the social and cultural life of the school was black, the girls, the dances, the student clubs and government, and the overall space were black. There were the usual fights and brawls with occasional knives and brass knuckles but no guns, although guns were ubiquitous in black households in Benton. Liquor was easily accessible, we drank a lot, and I started my half-century smoking habit at seventeen, but drugs did not come to Benton until several years after I graduated. In Benton there was no separation between church and school; the two were fused. The teachers in the schools were the sisters and brothers in the church and they combined religious and secular teachings. Even after the Supreme Court in 1961 prohibited prayer in school, we continued to pray and engage in devotional services. Our school day began with the singing of "Jesus Keep Me Near the Cross," then the Lord's Prayer, followed by the Pledge of Allegiance and "God Bless America." These prohibited practices continued in Benton well into the 1980s.

  Growing up in Benton in the early 1960s we accommodated without protest or really any concern the segregation in the town's public facilities— the three-stool drugstore lunch counter, the balcony of the movie theater (Lash Larue, Hopalong Cassidy, Cisco Kid, and Tarzan), the backroom of the café with its one table and jukebox, and the colored day at the annual state fair in Shreveport. We more than accommodated our segregated school; we cherished it and would have no more wished to see it integrated than we would have wished to integrate the church. The schools in Benton were desegregated in 1969. Irion became the elementary and junior high and the white school became the high school. Predictably, the staff and teachers in both schools became overwhelmingly white. So, this black space in Benton was forever lost. I should point out that our likely opposition to school desegregation in Benton would not have been isolated or unique. Polling data in 1954 shortly after the *Brown* decision shows that while 80 percent of northern blacks supported the decision, it was supported by only 46 percent of southern blacks.

  Harold Cruse, among others, argues that *Brown* and the NAACP's "integrationist impulse" that guided its implementation were "theoretically flawed." Cruse contends that it was only the legal requirement of racially separate schools that rendered black schools "implicitly inferior. Remove the legal sanction of imposed segregation, and separateness has the potential to achieve equality in its own right." In his view the NAACP should have simply asked the court to end legal segregation and "left it at that," that is, left blacks the freedom to maintain racially separate "plural" school systems. If the courts and the NAACP had pursued this path rather than the single-minded impulse to abolish all racially distinct schools, then "far more positive social and racial achievement might have been achieved." In a sense Cruse was calling for maintaining separate, parallel elementary and secondary school systems after *Brown* in the same way the southern states maintain separate systems of higher education at historically black colleges. Cruse's argument is alluring but likely impractical, because once legal segregation was abolished it would have been difficult to allow voluntary racial separation at the elementary and secondary levels. Nevertheless, in Benton in my time we would have appreciated the opportunity.

I was graduated second in a class of thirty-nine. Our class song was the Impressions' "Keep on Pushing," which was another rally song of the civil rights movement. Usually scholarships to Grambling or Southern were given to the valedictorian and salutatorian of the graduating class, but for some reason this was not the case in 1965. If scholarships had been offered, it is possible although not likely I would have gone to Grambling or Southern. Not likely, because my sister Nell was insisting that I come to California to stay with her and attend college. This was partly because at that time college in California was free to all residents (it took a year to establish residency). So, I left for California where I attended each tier of the California higher education system: junior college (Los Angeles City College), state college (California State University, Los Angeles), and university (Berkeley and UCLA), all tuition free.

When I left for California to attend college my educational horizons were very narrow. Most Irion students aspired to attend Grambling, Southern, or Wiley or Bishop, two private black colleges nearby in Texas. This was the extent of my awareness of higher education at the time. I had no awareness of Harvard or Yale, Berkeley or UCLA, or even Howard. I had no conception of the career I was to pursue, that is, no knowledge of the life of the mind of a professor. Parochial and naïve, I left behind a system of racial oppression I had accommodated without protest. As I said, I think it was because of the sense of community provided by church and school but I am not sure. I had little knowledge of the civil rights movement that was coming to its conclusion as I was leaving Benton.

The civil rights movement began at about the time of my mother's birth in 1901 and ended about the time of my graduation in 1965. In many ways the origins of the movement are the opposition to the accommodationist politics of Booker T. Washington. For a brief period—a decade or so from 1868 to 1876—the emancipated slaves were allowed to vote, run for and

hold office, and exercise a degree of economic, social, and political freedom. But then through a campaign of citizen and state terrorism, southern
whites took these rights away and the system of apartheid that I grew up
under was imposed. Booker Washington accepted or accommodated this
new system of oppression. In his influential 1895 "Atlanta Compromise"
address, Washington told white America that southern blacks were for a time
prepared to accept their exclusion from the political process, the denial of
civil rights, and the status of a subordinate, segregated community. At the
time of Washington's address his views were likely supported by the black
public and the overwhelming majority of black leaders because there were
really few viable alternatives. In the face of the extreme violence of southern
whites and with little prospect for intervention by the federal government,
blacks had little choice: accommodation or death. All those dead Indians
or the near extermination of the indigenous people who resisted was an
omnipresent lesson.

Although Washington's approach was initially supported by blacks,
as the twentieth century opened a few blacks began to vociferously object.
They were led by W. E. B. Du Bois and William Monroe Trotter, who in
1905 organized the Niagara movement. Although a small group of elite
black men, this was the beginning of the civil rights movement. Four years
later Du Bois and a handful of other black leaders joined with a group of
liberal whites to create the National Association for the Advancement of
Colored People (NAACP), which became the leading civil rights organization
in the nation. Its decades of propaganda, lobbying, and litigation laid the
foundation for the mass protest phase led by Dr. King in the 1950s and
1960s. As I was entering high school civil rights protest were beginning to
dominate American politics.

I was little affected by the movement. I vaguely recall reading about
it in *Newsweek* and *Life* and watching on television the Freedom Rides and
the demonstrations at Birmingham and Selma. But Benton was a Booker
T. Washington town, still accommodating rather than protesting. Several
persons in Benton were named after Washington (it has been estimated that
more black children were named after Washington than any other person in
American history), and the most prominent black high school in Shreveport
was named in his honor. Concerning the NAACP, Deacon Lex Phillips in
my church would occasionally furtively mention the need to support "that N
double A" but if there was an NAACP branch in Benton, it met in secret.

I did not grow up with a sense of inferiority to whites. I did not feel
shame because I was black; I did not think whites were smarter or prettier

than blacks; I was not ashamed of our color, lips, or hair. We did not process our hair; we did not lust for white girls. In other words, I did not grow up with what Frantz Fanon labeled a sense of internal inferiorization. I do not know why. I never thought about it until I studied the phenomenon in college. As I write this, I assume this sense of psychological health in blackness of me and my peers was due to the strong sense of community provided by church and school but I really do not how we escaped it, given the putative pervasiveness of the phenomenon according to Fanon and others.

Growing up I also experienced few racist or racial incidents. I never witnessed or heard of a lynching or other racist violence in the area. I cannot recall racist insults or harassment by whites or the police. Indeed, I can recall only being called nigger once, which was on the occasion of my first arrest. When I was in the eleventh grade our football team lost a game. So, someone came up with the bright idea that we should go on the opposing team's band bus and destroy their instruments. We did, and on Sunday morning as I was preparing for Sunday school a deputy sheriff came to arrest me. As we were driving to the jail, he began to ask questions and I told him he had no right to question me unless my mother was present or maybe, I said, a lawyer. In any event, the deputy slammed on the brakes and turned to me and said, "Nigger, I kick ass." My response, "Anything, you want to know, officer, sir." The only other incident of racial degradation I recall is going to Bossier City to register for the draft. As we were waiting lunch hour arrived; the white boys and the staff went across the street to a segregated café to eat while I sat on the sidewalk hungry. I never forgot the incident, which became especially compelling as I faced the possibility of the draft during the Vietnam War.

I recount this growing up free, at least relatively, of internal inferiorization, and in an environment relatively free of overt racist degradation and violence as possible explanations for my lack of interest or engagement with the civil rights movement. My nonengagement or noninterest is all the more remarkable and in retrospect near inexplicable because my sister Bernice was a leader of the movement in Shreveport and my nephew Lynn was an active participant. Before discussing the Shreveport movement, I now surmise that slavery or at least neo-slavery might have existed near Benton when I was growing up. This recollection came to my mind in the 2000s as a result of conversations with my colleague Ronald Walters, who was working on a book documenting the existence of slavery in parts of the South until the 1960s, *Fighting Neo-Slavery in the Twentieth Century: The Forgotten Legacy of the NAACP*. As we discussed his research it occurred to me that slavery might have existed when I was growing up. There were two large plantations near Benton—classic plantations with the owner's big house surrounded by shacks inhabited by blacks and fields of cotton. And there were what our parents referred to as the plantation children; I remember some of their names—Emile Johnson, Hiram Revels—and looking at the roster of the class of 1965, none of these classmates were on the graduating class list. These classmates were only allowed to attend school part-time, when they were not needed in the fields. I recall now times during the school year when one of the white plantation bosses would come to school and literally take them out of class.

While I was watching the civil rights movement on television, it was live fourteen miles away in Shreveport, although one would not have known this by listening to KOKA. It, like most of the southern black-oriented radio stations at the time, ignored the movement in its programing and sparse news coverage. The recognized leader of the Shreveport movement was Reverend Harry Blake, pastor of a prominent Baptist church in the city, field secretary for Dr. King's Southern Christian Leadership Conference, as well as president of the local NAACP branch. Another leader was Dr. C. O. Simpkins, a dentist, and a number of other preachers including C. C. McClain and E. Edward Jones. As in the movement generally, women in Shreveport, especially beauticians, played important leadership roles. In addition to my sister Bernice, who was a beautician, others included Mamie Love and Ann Brewster. Brewster mysteriously died and there were suspicions she might have been murdered because of her civil rights activism.

As in other southern cities, the movement in Shreveport engaged in demonstrations to desegregate public accommodations, to hire blacks as salespersons in the department stores, to require equal treatment and courtesies in the stores, voter registration, and litigation to desegregate the schools. In general, the protests were not successful, and they were met by brutal police repression. Reverend Blake was beaten by police commissioner D'Artois and left lying in the street. As I mentioned, the beautician Brewster may have been murdered and Dr. Simpkins's home was firebombed. Fearing for the safety of his family, he left the city for a time, although he returned and was subsequently elected to the state legislature. In 1962 Dr. King visited the city to rally the movement. One of the proudest possessions of Bernice was a photo of her with King and his associate Reverend Ralph Abernathy. Although the Shreveport movement did not succeed in desegregating the city, it was one of the multiple local movements that eventually ended segregation throughout the nation. Fifty years later when I returned for my class reunion, Reverend Blake was still active in the antiracism struggle in Shreveport.

President Kennedy is referred to by one civil rights historian as a "bystander" on civil rights. I was a bystander as the movement unfolded in Shreveport. Mama was opposed to my involvement as well as the involvement of Bernice and Lynn, saying, "That boy King is not going to do anything but get himself killed along with a lot of other folk." So, she insisted I stay out of it. I did stay out—but it was not because of her command, because I disobeyed her on other things and if had wished I would have gone to Shreveport to join the protests. So, my failure to participate was part of my Booker T. Washington accommodationism. That is, I accepted and was largely satisfied in my separate subordinate community. Fear about my safety may have been a concern but I cannot recall that as a factor. It was simply accommodation.

John F. Kennedy is a starting point for my memories of American politics, the presidency, and African American politics, subjects that have occupied my attention professionally for the last fifty years. I have studied the Kennedy presidency more thoroughly than any other, writing two book chapters on his presidency and *John F. Kennedy, Barack Obama, and the Politics of Ethnic Incorporation and Avoidance*. My focus on Kennedy was not because he is my favorite president, nor because his presidency is the first in my awareness. Rather, it is because Kennedy's presidency coincides with the apogee of the civil rights movement, and the study of the movement and its outcomes has been a principal focus of my scholarly work. Kennedy was a moderate, pragmatic liberal and a reluctant civil rights warrior, a bystander on civil rights, as the historian Nick Bryant titles his book on Kennedy and the civil rights movement. But his presidency was the beginning of the 1960s era of progressive reform, a period of reform as noble as any in American history. Kennedy helped to inspire, and eventually lead these reforms. I recall watching his 1963 civil rights speech on television, which is the most eloquent and morally unambiguous address on race of any American president. In terms of legislation, none of the reforms were enacted during his thousand days in office. That was the work of his able vice president. But Kennedy's impact was important to me; his youth, his vision of service, of a country conquering new frontiers, and his eloquent and reasoned words—what might be called his systematic eloquence—were early symbolic catalysts for my 1960s awakening.

CHAPTER 2

The Awakening

Malcolm, Black Power, and Black Studies

Graduation was on a Friday night. On the following Monday I was on a Trailways bus headed for Los Angeles. In 1965 it never occurred to us that I would fly; blacks in Benton did not begin to travel by air until the later 1960s. I spent the last night with my best friend Charles "Moon" Lee, drinking Peppermint Snap and playing again and again James Brown's "It May Be the Last Time." This was a big hit for Brown, although it was the B side of his "Out of Sight," one of the few times the B side of a record also became a huge hit. Even more than fifty years later it is melancholy to remember that night and that song, and the line "Shake hands with your best friend, you may never see him again." I never saw Moon again. Two months later while working in a Boston factory he fell into an oil vat and was burned to death. His remains, the little that was left of him, were returned to Benton for burial. I did not return for the funeral. I did not wish to; I could not bear to think of him dead. I only wanted to remember the last night, the Peppermint Snap and our drunkenly shaking hands over and over again.

I sent Moon's mother a long, handwritten letter expressing my sadness and great sense of loss. Moon and I had talked about returning to Benton at the end of summer and attending Grambling. Although it is not likely I would have, the thought at the time was on my mind. I cannot recall whether I wrote her that she was a grandmother, although I certainly should have. At the time of Jack Ann's (Moon's girlfriend) pregnancy, I recall Moon's mother was bitter, resentful, and in denial that he was the father. I, as much as anyone, knew he was the father and I hope I told her

31

so in the letter. When I returned home several years later, I was pleased to learn that she acknowledged the child and was supporting him and taking part in his rearing.

Lynn and I visited Thelma in Los Angeles during the summer of 1962 or 1963. I, however, did not see or learn much about the city, my most vivid memories being Disneyland, the ocean, and fighting over who would get the last of Thelma's chili beans. Los Angeles in the 1960s was described as one of the best cities for blacks in the nation. Visitors from the East and Midwest, used to the tenements and high-rise slums of a Chicago or New York, would often remark upon seeing the neat little suburban-like bungalows of Watts and South Central, that there were no ghettos in Los Angeles. As Lou Rawls had famously sung of Los Angeles, "Out West, it was the best." Although blacks in Los Angeles in the 1960s had somewhat higher education and income levels than in most American cities and the architecture and the landscape (not to mention the weather) was more alluring than a Philadelphia or Detroit, the city, as the Watts riot would show two months after my arrival, was no racial promised land.

For sure the kind of overt, individual racism that characterized Benton and the rest of the South was not present, and the schools, buses, and places of public accommodations were not segregated. While not the promised land, for a country boy from the South who was forced to ride in the back of the bus as I departed Shreveport and who had a vivid memory of sitting hungry on the sidewalk in front of a segregated café a year earlier, this was clearly a better place.

Although overt individual racism was absent in Los Angeles, institutional racism, as I would soon learn, was widespread in housing, employment, and police practices. (In 1965 the phenomenon of institutional racism did not have a name. It was first named and conceptualized by Stokely Carmichael and Charles Hamilton in their 1967 book, *Black Power: The Politics of Liberation.*) As the Magnificent Montague put it, when he arrived in 1965, "LA was so barren, so segregated that the most popular deejay was a white man named Hunter Hancock." Blacks in the City of the Angels as I soon came to learn were in some ways as segregated as they were in Benton and Shreveport. Unlawfully enforced restrictive covenants and racism in the housing market confined most blacks to Watts and South-Central Los Angeles, although some parts of South Los Angeles—Baldwin Hills, Crenshaw-Adams, and Leimert Park—were affluent residences of lawyers, doctors, and entertainers such as Ray Charles.

The depths of California racism were shown in 1964 when near two-thirds of its voters approved Proposition14, which overturned the Rumford Act, legislation prohibiting racial discrimination in the sale and rental of housing. Supported fulsomely by Ronald Reagan in his successful campaign for governor in 1966, Proposition 14 was declared unconstitutional by the California Supreme Court. The court's decision notwithstanding, racism in the California housing market—at least in Los Angeles and the Bay Area where we have data—is widespread as I write fifty years later.

Overall, in 1965 Los Angeles was a segregated city. Blacks lived in South Central, Latinos in East LA, and whites in West Los Angeles and the San Fernando Valley. The city's transportation system relied on cars and the extensive network of freeways. That is, there was no effective system of mass transportation. The slow and unreliable buses were the only means of transportation for people without cars, putting poor people at an enormous disadvantage in accessing employment and the city's far-flung consumer markets. I lived with this disadvantage for almost two years before I learned how to drive and was able to buy an old Ford Falcon.

Another racially oppressive aspect of the city was its racist, often brutal paramilitary police department headed by William "Massa" Parker, its chief from 1950 to 1996. The police force was too small for a city the size (in geography and population) of Los Angeles. It therefore relied on mobility and heavy-handed tactics to police the city, especially the black community, where its reputation for brutality was extensively documented after the Watts riot and thirty-one years later after the 1996 Rodney King rebellion. Of all the cities I have lived in in the last half century—Oakland, Berkeley, New York, Washington, Houston, White Plains, Silver Spring, and San Francisco—only in Los Angeles did I fear being pulled over by the police. Politically, although African Americans were a relatively small part of the city's population in 1965, in 1963 Gilbert Lindsay was appointed as the first African American city councilman. Subsequently elected, Lindsay was joined on the council by Billy Mills and Thomas Bradley. Thus, when I arrived in 1965 blacks constituted three of the fifteen members of the city council. However, the city was governed by a rough-hewn reactionary racist mayor, Sam Yorty. In 1973, after losing to Yorty four years earlier in a racially rancorous campaign, Bradley was elected mayor.

Nell and her husband Robert "Bobby" Lewis lived in a two-bedroom apartment in the Crenshaw-Adams area. The second bedroom was mine, and the neighborhood was a comfortable lower-middle-class area. Nell worked as a clerk in the Los Angeles County Sheriff's Department and as a part-time beautician. I do not remember much about Bobby. He was a light-skin, handsome, Billy Dee Williams–looking man, who, I believe, worked in the aircraft industry. He introduced me to the music of Bob Dylan and the Rolling Stones and to KHJ, the top rock station in the city and its afternoon deejay the Real Don Steele.

The only other memory of Bobby is during the Watts riot when he took time from work and he and his friends engaged in systematic looting. The riot was televised so Bobby and his friends could see where the police were not present, and they went to those areas and collected all kinds of goods, small appliances, jewelry, and clothing that they later sold or gave away. I was later to come to understand the riot as a rebellion against systemic racial oppression, but while Bobby and his friends may have had some inchoate sense of their behavior as political, it was likely about making some money. Christmas in August, as many blacks exclaimed at the time. I got along well with Bobby, but in 1966 around the time of the birth of their son Martin, my other siblings in Los Angeles told me Nell and Bobby were having trouble in their marriage and it might be better for them if I moved in with Cleo to give them a chance to work things out. I moved in with Cleo, who lived in South Central, for about six months. After Nell and Bobby divorced, I moved back to live with Nell and her son.

After the divorce Nell had several boyfriends, the most memorable of which was Claude (I don't think I ever knew his last name) from Eutaw, Alabama. A big red-skin man, Claude was slightly disabled, walked with a cane, always had a half pint of whiskey, and told the most outrageous, often ribald stories. A male chauvinist, he dismissed the emerging feminist movement as foolishness, saying over and over again, "I could never stand a sassy woman." He also told stories of how in Alabama he had routinely killed and buried random white men (whom he invariably referred to as "peckerwoods"). This is what he said the so-called black militants should do if they were serious and not just all talk.

I started classes at Los Angeles City College (LACC) in the summer of 1965. Located in West Hollywood on the site formerly occupied by UCLA, the college faculty and students were almost all white. Although this was my first encounter with white teachers and students, I recall no concerns or trepidations coming from a supposed inferior, segregated rural southern school about my abilities to be competitive. There was no need for concern, since I did very well in my two years at LACC. In retrospect, it was probably a good idea that Nell decided to have me first attend junior college rather than Cal State or UCLA. LACC was an excellent school, with a fine, memorable faculty. I remember classes in speech, Western civilization, and an English literature class, where the professor had us study the Beatles and Bob Dylan as part of the canon. I can recall the name, however, of only one of my LACC professors, Gordon Bruno, who in my near ten years of higher education is undoubtedly the most memorable and provocative.

Bruno, a sociologist, was the first radical critic of US society and American foreign policy I encountered. Probably in his midfifties, he would always come to class with a stack of books and when students challenged some of his more radical ideas, he would exclaim, "Read, read. I read." It was in Bruno's class in 1966 or 1967 that I heard the first condemnation of the US war on Vietnam, which he described as an imperialist war in which the Vietnamese people were the victims of US aggression. This did not have a major impact at the time as I was then indifferent or vaguely supportive of the war. But I always remembered Bruno as the person who first told the truth about the war and US foreign policy.

Christopher Columbus Allen, my second-best friend in Benton, also moved to Los Angeles after graduation to stay with his sister and he attended LACC and subsequently Cal State, LA, with me. "Al," as he was called, and I partied together in Benton and often hitchhiked to Shreveport to see concerts. At LACC we hung out together, searched for black girls (there were very few at LACC) and parties. Al majored in accounting and was one of the most apolitical persons I have ever known. He became an accomplished accountant working for Price Waterhouse and Motown in its Hollywood office. But after a time in LA, he decided that he wished to be a pimp. He read Iceberg Slim, bought a Cadillac, dressed in fancy clothes, and eventually became what we called a "Popcorn Pimp," with several ladies who worked for him. Before Al's pimping days, we spent a lot of time singing Sam Cooke's "Another Saturday Night," "feeling in an awful way" because we had "no chicks" to go out with. After a year or so we discovered the LA party circuit, the fraternity house parties, and the LA and Hollywood club scene.

In my last year at LACC, I met Brenda, who transferred with me to Cal State, LA. She became my girlfriend and it was with her that I had my first complete sexual relationship. It was apparently hers as well, and for a couple of years we made good loving at her house and later at her off-campus apartment. We were close enough that I gave her my high school class ring. And then without notice she disappeared. I searched for her, inquired of her to her mother and friends, but I never learned what happened.

At LACC I also met Larry Mason, who until his death in 2004 was my dearest and most abiding friend. Larry was the most honest and thoroughly decent person I have ever known. He moved to LA from San Bernardino, about fifty miles west of LA. Shortly after enrolling at LACC, he rented an apartment in Baldwin Hills where we hung out, smoked reefer, and listened to music (Larry introduced me to marijuana). He transferred to Cal State with me and along with Dwight LeeRay we transferred to Berkeley. A more mundane outcome of meeting Larry was that he had a car, which meant Al and I did not have to rely on buses to go to parties and clubs. It was almost two years before I learned to drive and was able to buy a car. I briefly took professional driving lessons and my brother Buddy tried to teach me, but I really learned by secretly taking Nell's car. When she learned of this, she encouraged me to practice on early Sunday mornings, when there was relatively little traffic, which made it the best time to learn how to navigate LA's complex freeway system.

I was graduated from LACC in 1967 with an associate of arts. I did not attend the graduation ceremonies, nor did I attend the ceremonies when I was graduated at Berkeley, UCLA, or Howard, although the Berkeley case, as I will recount, is special since for my class of 1970 the ceremony was not held until 1990. LACC was an excellent educational experience, testimony to the value of the junior college as a good starting place for students with little money or those who might need some preparatory or remedial work before going to university. However, socially and politically it was a barren place. There were very few black students; I did not associate with white students and was not engaged in campus social or political life. I simply finished my classes and took the bus home. Consequently, I established lasting relationships with only three persons, my girlfriend Brenda, Larry, and Gordon Snorton, the "party man."

Parties and music are integral to the culture of the young and of African Americans. For about a year Al and I spent a lot of Friday and Saturday nights without music and partying. This changed when we met Gordon, who somehow always had a list of the weekend parties. At that time, all over black LA people gave house parties, where you could get in free or for a modest sum (ladies were usually always admitted free). In addition, the Omega and Alpha fraternities sponsored Friday or Saturday night "frat house" parties, where ladies were always admitted free and men for a small charge. After our first year Al, Larry, and I were on the weekend party circuit, meeting girls, dancing, and grinding. Although I loved the frat house parties, I declined the invitation of the Omega brothers to pledge.

This was because the thought of going through the deliberately degrading and humiliating hazing process was too much. I also did not like the authoritarian nature of the pledging process, and although I did not know it at the time, hazing could be dangerous and even deadly.

Musically for me the mid to late 1960s was the golden age of Motown. Although we danced to other music—Sam and Dave's "Soul Man" and "Hold on, I'm Coming," the Olympics' "Philly Dog" and Aretha's "Respect"—the music of those years was mainly Motown: the Four Tops' "Reach Out to Me" and "Bernadette," Junior and the All Stars' "Road Runner," the Temptations' "Getting Ready" and "Ain't too Proud to Beg," the Isley Brothers' "This Old Heart of Mine," Stevie Wonder's "Uptight," and Marvin Gaye and Gladys Knight's versions of "I Heard It through the Grapevine." And for the slow grind, Smokey's "OO Baby, Baby," Martha and the Vandellas' "Love Makes Me Do Foolish Things," along with the Dells' "Stay in My Corner," the Neville Brothers' "Tell It Like It Is," and Marvin and Tammi's "Your Precious Love." After the start of the Black Power movement the music began to matter politically, but from 1965 until 1967 it was just "Sweet Soul Music" for dancing, bumping, grinding, and getting on down.

In addition to the frat and house parties, we partied at local clubs, including the black Club 54 in South Central and the famous Whiskey a Go Go in Hollywood. There were also the great deejays, Magnificent Montague in the mornings on KGFJ, the black R&B station, and in the afternoon the Real Don Steele on KHJ "Boss Radio," the top-forty rock and roll station. Montague and Don Steele were great personality deejays; listening to them was often as entertaining as the music. Montague with his signature "Burn, baby! Burn!" (during the Watts riot, "Burn, baby! Burn!" was often chanted by the rioters, forcing Montague to abandon the moniker and eventually change it to "Learn, baby! Learn!") and Don Steele with his maniac chatter and rhyming introduction of the records. Don Cornelius's *Soul Train* was also part of the music, dance, and party scene of the time. Watching the show on Saturday mornings was a prelude to the night's parties as we copied the fashions and dance steps of the "Soul Train Gang." Cornelius was, in dress and in talk the essence of cool, who we often tried to imitate. Broadcast from Los Angeles, Al and I made many unsuccessful efforts to audition to get on the show.

I arrived in Los Angeles in May of 1965. In August the Watts riot happened. Although I did not know it at the time, the Watts revolt was important in my political awakening as a black man committed to revolutionary change. It was a turning point for the civil rights movement and the African American freedom struggle. The riot in Watts was up until that point the most violent black rebellion in American history. Over five days, a forty-five-square-mile area was burned, more than a thousand people injured, and thirty-four killed. Three thousand police and the National Guard were used to suppress the rebellion, and black areas of the city were occupied by the military for two weeks. Although rioting did not occur where I lived in Crenshaw-Adams, it too was occupied by the military. I did not at the time appreciate the radical, historical significance of the riot. I recall in my Western civilization class the professor asking me as the only black in the class what was it all about, and then telling us it was just a bunch of hoodlums and criminals. I agreed with this assessment, not because the professor said it but sincerely. This was the prevailing explanation of the riot at the time, the so-called "riff-raff" theory advanced by the commission the governor appointed to investigate the riot and in some of the early scholarly commentary. Harvard political scientist Edward Banfield, for example, wrote that Watts was not a political act of rebellion but rather a case of young men "rioting mainly for fun and profit." Within a year this view had been rejected, replaced by a riot ideology that defined Watts and the subsequent riots as political acts of revolt, rebellion, or revolution. I fully subscribed to this ideology.

In the fall of 1967, I transferred to Cal State, LA (California State University, Los Angeles) and began working in the afternoons on the loading docks of the Central Los Angeles post office. I had worked before as a carpenter's helper and as a stock clerk at one of the area aircraft manufacturing plants. This work was uneventful, except some of the whites at the aircraft plant resented the fact I, "the college boy," had the clerk's job where I spent most of my time reading while they toiled on the assembly line (my brother Buddy who worked at the plant may have got me the job).

The work at the post office was more interesting. First, because most of the dock crew was black or Mexican American and this provided my first opportunity for sustained interactions with working-class blacks and Chicanos, as Mexican Americans in Los Angeles were then beginning to be called. But by far the most consequential outcome of my work at the post office was meeting Omar X. Omar, who was also a student at Cal State, is the person who opened my eyes to blackness and the individual most responsible for my transformation from a Negro to a conscious black man.

I cannot recall whether Omar was a native of LA, but he carried himself as good old boy from down home who had become wise to the ways of the white man up North. Although he replaced Davidson with X,

Omar was not a member of the Nation of Islam (Black Muslims) but he admired the Black Nationalist philosophy of the group. He often said he admired the Nation but did not care for any religion (what he called "spook talk") and in any event he could not give up the pig (eating pork). Omar was a Malcolm X man, and he was responsible for getting me to read Malcolm's autobiography, which like for many black men had a transformative effect. He also encouraged me to read *Malcolm X Speaks*, George Breitman's collection of Malcolm's speeches, and shared with me tapes of Malcolm's speeches. As a result, I too became a Malcolm man. When I left Louisiana, I was more or less a Martin Luther King man. Although I do not know if I personally would have had the wherewithal to practice his philosophy of nonviolence, and I rejected his love-your-enemies teaching, I had embraced his strategy of nonviolence because it appeared to have worked in places like Birmingham and Selma. I also admired his Christian ethic and I loved to hear him preach (I thought then, and now, he was the best preacher I ever heard). Although, like Malcolm, I thought that violence under some circumstances might be necessary to overcome evils, but certainly nonviolence was preferably if possible.

In any event, when I arrived at the post office, I certainly had more admiration and respect for King than Malcolm. Frankly, I knew very little about Malcolm and what little I knew I did not like. I did not like that he was not a Christian; I did not like that he advocated violence; I did not like he preached hatred of whites; and I did not like that he had mocked the death of President Kennedy as "chickens coming home to roost." These were of course to some extent distortions of Malcolm's views, but they were the views I held of him when I left Louisiana. I recall when I heard of his murder on television my response was, "So, what, he who lives by the sword, dies by the sword." All of this changed when I got to know Malcolm the man and studied his ideas. The autobiography had a huge impact on me, as it did on my generation of blacks generally, especially men, who came of age in the 1960s. Malcolm impressed me first because he told the truth, the truth about white people, white racism, and white supremacy. He also told the truth to and about black people, our often willingness to accommodate rather than resist, our obsequiousness and timidity, and our failure to respect ourselves, our blackness, and our African heritage. In other words, he articulated the anger and frustrations of my generation in a militant, uncompromising way that was exhilarating to us, all the more so because it appeared to frighten white people. His white biographer, Bruce Perry, nicely captures his appeal: "Malcolm X fathered no legislation. He engineered no stunning Supreme Court decisions. He scored no major electoral triumphs. Yet, because of the way he articulated his followers' grievances and anger, the impact he had on the body politic was enormous."

Malcom became totemic for us. Large photos of him adorned our walls, his speeches were played over and over, and this famous quote became our mantra: "We declare our rights on this earth, to be a man, to be respected as a human being, in this society, on this earth, in this day; which we intend to bring into existence by any means necessary." I recall once in a class at Cal State a professor disputed a Malcolm argument by pointing out that according to *Webster's* dictionary Malcolm had incorrectly defined a word. The student (black) pounded his desk and shouted, "Webster be damned, I am talking about Malcolm."

Related to and as important as Malcolm and Omar in my black awakening was Stokely Carmichael and the Black Power movement. The Black Power philosophy as explained by Carmichael and Charles Hamilton in their 1967 book *Black Power: The Politics of Liberation in America* was in many ways based on or rooted in the ideas of Malcolm, although inexplicably Malcolm is nowhere cited in the book. Among the ideas of Malcolm incorporated in the Black Power philosophy were his insistence on the right and imperative of self-defense against attacks by white racists, his identification with Africa and the Third World, the valorization of the African heritage, his call for the abandonment of "Negro" in favor of black or Afro-American, his call for autonomous all-black organizations, and his call for black control of the economy and politics of the black community.

Little did I know in June 1966 when Willie Ricks and Carmichael chanted black power in the Mississippi Delta, they were launching a movement that would profoundly shape my political consciousness and identity for the rest of my life. Little did I also know that study of the movement and its consequences would dominate my work as a scholar. My first professional paper at a political science conference was "Black Power and the Transformation from Protest to Politics" delivered in 1979 at the Southern Political Science Association in Gatlinburg, Tennessee. This paper became my first article in a political science journal. This article is the most widely cited and likely influential of the more than fifty I have published. Among the first papers I delivered at the National Conference of Black Political Scientists was "The Impact of the Black Power Symbol on American Politics" in Atlanta in 1980. My most influential and widely read book, *We Have No Leaders: African Americans in the Post–Civil Rights Era*, is a detailed analysis of the consequences of the defeat of the radical wing of the movement and the institutionalization of its reform faction. And my book published in 2018 is a Black Power study, *Ronald W. Walters and the Fight for Black Power, 1969–2010.*

After the civil rights movement, the Black Power movement is the most important development in the twentieth-century history of African American politics. It had profound and enduring consequences for the cultural, ideological, and structural relationships between blacks and whites. The movement also altered the internal ethos and organizations of the black community, reshaped its identity and consciousness, and for a brief period gave rise to genuinely revolutionary ideas and organizations. Together with the civil rights movement, Black Power served as an inspiration and model for movements among other Americans, including Latinos, women, and homosexuals, which contributed to a shift toward what is now called identity politics. A major impact of the movement was also in the white community. Partly in response to the radicalism and militancy of some Black Power activists and the violence of the ghetto rebellions, white public opinion became more conservative on civil rights and other issues related to race. The increasing conservatism of whites helped to build support for the openly racist campaigns of George Wallace and the subtly racist campaigns of Richard Nixon, Ronald Reagan, and Donald Trump.

I immediately embraced Black Power in the summer of 1966. While I did not have a clear sense of what the slogan meant—nor did Carmichael or anyone else at the time—its rhetorical militancy was alluring. That the political establishments, black and white, were hostile to it made it all the more alluring. I also liked Carmichael. Indeed, he immediately became and is today one of my heroes. Charismatic and rhetorically gifted, he was a symbol of blackness. Although he initially defined Black Power as reform, as ethnic interest group politics, within a year he began to view it as a rev-olutionary challenge to the racist, capitalist, imperial American system. In 1969 he embraced a version of Pan-Africanism that called for the unification of all of Africa under an Africanized communism. I rejected this ideology as utopian. His embrace of this utopian vision of Black Power made him largely a symbolic presence in African American politics for the next three decades of his life until his death from prostate cancer in 1998. I heard him speak once at the massive "Free Huey" rally in 1968 at the Los Angeles Sports Arena. The limits of his utopian Pan-African ideology notwithstanding, Stokely remains a hero as symbol of resistance and blackness.

As a result of Omar, Malcolm, and Stokely, by the time I arrived at Cal State, LA, in the fall of 1967 I had become a black man committed to the liberation of black people. I had undergone what the distinguished Africana psychologist William Cross, in his first published paper, called the five-stage Negro to black conversion process. At the first stage, "Pre-Encounter," I was politically backward, "dependent on the assimilation-integration paradigm." Stage two, "Encounter," was meeting Omar, "a friend who is more advanced in his blackness and who may 'turn a person on' to his own blackness." The third "Immersion-Emersion" stage is reading black literature such as Malcolm, adopting an Afro hairstyle, dropping the word Negro in favor of black. The fourth "Internalization" stage is the psychological internalization of this new black value system, and the final "Internalization-Commitment" is when I became committed to blackness and the liberation struggle.

Cross's five stages are a rather crude categorization of a complex continuous process. However, it captured well my personal development and growth in blackness. When Cross published the article he was, like me, a graduate student—in psychology—at Princeton. Like me he was very much informed and influenced by the Black Power movement. He subsequently had a distinguished career on Cornell's Africana studies faculty. In his seminal 1991 text, *Shades of Blackness: Diversity in African American Identity*, he credits Black Power with improving black identity, consciousness, and self-esteem. However, in an important finding he shows that the idea of Fanon and others that all blacks suffered from internal inferiorization was not accurate. Rather, he concluded that some blacks of all social classes were able to grow up with a positive sense of "blackness" and group identification. (In 2016 I was pleased to publish in the SUNY series in African American studies, *Meaning Making, Internalized Racism, and African American Identity*, edited by Professor Cross and the young scholar Jas Sullivan of Louisiana State University. This wide-ranging collection of essays further documents the diversity in how blacks have made psychological sense of being black in America.)

Cal State, located in East Los Angeles, in the late 1960s had the largest percentages of minority (black and Chicano) students of any campus in the state. Unlike LACC where I encountered few blacks, at Cal State there was a relatively large and diverse black community. There were recent migrants from the South like me, poor and working-class blacks from South Central, and the children of LA's black bourgeoisie. And there were all kinds of beautiful black women in all colors, from those "who were darker than blue to the high yellow girls at the surface of our dark deep well." And then there was Sophia, the first sexually liberated woman I met. The daughter of a doctor, she was a strikingly beautiful woman who resembled Marilyn McCoo of the

Fifth Dimension. I first met her at the Black Student Union (BSU) table in the campus quad, where she asked what the organization was about. Little did I suspect—although I certainly wished—that she would become my lover. That came about because she was the roommate of a friend, Margaret. Margaret and Sophia were happily apolitical, and in my visits, I would often talk about the BSU, Black Power, and the liberation struggle. Sophia listened and tried to show interest, but this was more because, as she later said, she wanted to screw me than any real interest in my talk of black liberation. So, I became one of her many lovers, and she had many. While I was seeing Brenda at the time and trying to start a relationship with a student from Arkansas, Sophia had at least three lovers. She treated sex like a man. That is, she enjoyed it and therefore she had no inhibitions about doing it with men she was attracted to, including white men. In her attitudes toward sex she was akin to Spike Lee's Nora Darling in the 1989 movie *She's Gotta Have It.* Although I was seeing other women and we agreed at the outset of our relationship that both of us should continue to do so, after a time I became jealous and wanted a more monogamous relationship—on her part. She refused and continued her liberated ways, while I continued to want her to be my woman alone.

The sexual liberation of women gained some acceptance on the campuses in the late 1960s, overturning the ancient tradition that for women sex was not something to be shared and enjoyed but something to be hoarded and doled out like a scarce commodity. The widespread availability of the pill at this time made this change more feasible, but it was more than this. It was a change in attitudes and values that made women having and enjoying sex as acceptable as it was for men. Sophia epitomized this sexual revolution. The relationship with Sophia continued after I left for Berkeley in 1969, with her occasionally visiting. When I returned to LA, we attempted to continue the relationship, but for some reason our friend Margaret objected and set in motion a process—which I discuss in chapter 4—that resulted in my meeting and marrying my wife Scottie.

Black Power was a widespread movement of cultural awakening, revitalization, and expressions that affected everything from names, fashions, the arts, hairstyles, to music. Many blacks changed their names to reflect African or Islamic heritages. Lew Alcindor became Kareem Abdul Jabbar, Cassius Clay became Muhammad Ali, Don Lee became Haki Madhubuti, Ron Everett became Maulana Karenga, Stokely Carmichael became Kwame Ture, and Leroi Jones became Amiri Baraka. At Cal State my coauthor of the black studies proposal was Mwalimu Abdulhamid Akoni; two of the major leaders of the BSU were Jomo Kenyatta (J. K.) Obatala and Ayuko Babu. With a name like Robert Smith one might have thought I would have considered a name change, but it never occurred to me, although on two occasions in Los Angeles I was arrested and detained on murder charges in cases of mistaken identity with another Robert C. Smith of my race, age, color, height, and appearance.

The major name change brought about was collective. Both Malcolm and Stokely had called on blacks to abandon Negro because it was the oppressor's designation of us in favor of black or Afro-American. Black became the preferred choice because it had been a term of denigration by white supremacists, and shame for some blacks, thus, to use it was to reject the white supremacist denigration and reclaim the name as a point of pride. Thus "Black Is Beautiful" and "I Am Black and I Am Proud." It was a struggle to get whites as well as some blacks to embrace the name, a struggle of nearly two years. At Cal State we black students would sit together in the back of classrooms and when professors or students used the word Negro, we would bang the desks and shout "Black, Black."

I tried with the help of Afro-Sheen and the Afro pick to grow a big Angela Davis–type natural, but my hair was too kinky. So, once I moved to Berkeley, I stopped getting haircuts altogether, although this may have been as much a result of the influence of the counterculture as Black Power. From the 1970s until the Million Man March in 1995 I did not get a haircut. I had my hair cut bald for the march and have not had another cut since then. In my seventy-plus years I also have never shaved, although with my kinky hair one would never know it. I attribute my never shaving less to movements—black or countercultural—and more to simply never seeing the need to do so.

I wore dashikis (I still do occasionally), bell bottoms, Nehru jackets, and sandals. These were movement-inspired fashions. We referred to our fellow blacks as brothers and sisters—I still do—and gave the clenched-fist Black Power salute as we greeted on campus and the streets. These symbolic expressions of Black Power were reflected and reinforced by the poetry of Haki, Sonia Sanchez, Baraka, and Ted Joan, among others. They were also reflected and reinforced by the music of the era.

For the most part R&B and soul music stayed away from politics, the civil rights movement, and the larger freedom struggle. The music of the early 1960s was so politically barren that we often read political meaning into songs that had little or nothing to do with politics or the movement, such as Sam Cooke's "A Change Is Gonna Come," Little Milton's "We Gonna

Make It," Aretha's version of "Respect," and most ridiculously Martha and the Vandellas' "Dancing in the Street." This mythmaking about the political significance of music that was politically insignificant was part of the 1960s generation's quest to make the music matter when it did not. After the culturally transformative effects of the Black Power movement for a time the music did politically matter.

In his 1976 Stanford dissertation my former San Francisco State colleague Robert Walker showed that between 1966 and 1969 there was an inordinate increase in message music. Walker downplays its significance but there was also an increase in message music by white rock and roll, and rock artists, reflecting the influence of black movements, the antiwar movement, and the counterculture. Even the ever cautious and commercial Berry Gordy acquiesced to Motown's production of political music, recognizing that while controversial it could be commercially successful. One can see this in the music of the Temptations as they moved from "Get Ready" and "Ain't to Proud to Beg" to "Cloud Nine," "Ball of Confusion," "Message from a Black Man," and their little noted but powerful lamentation about young black men and the drug trade "Take a Look Around." Marvin Gaye's masterpiece *What's Going On*, the album with its inner-city blues, antiwar, and environmental themes, was message music at its best, and it rivals in creativity the Beatles' masterpiece *Sargent Pepper's Lonely-Hearts Club Band* as one of the greatest albums ever.

The music of the Black Power era reflected in a new, bold, and inspiring way the newfound black identity and consciousness. It also helped to shape as well as reflect the pride and militancy of the era, and to motivate some to become involved in the struggle. It was certainly an inspiration for me. Bob Dylan and Curtis Mayfield are quintessential examples of makers of music that mattered to me.

Bob Dylan received the Nobel Prize for literature in 2016. Curtis Mayfield should receive it posthumously. The music of both is poetry of a high order that made significant contributions to understanding their times. I first was introduced to Mayfield's music in Benton and it became a soundtrack of my coming of age, influencing attitudes about women, romance, religion, protest, and blackness. My memoir of Mayfield begins with his songs celebrating black women, love, and romance: "I'm So Proud," "Gypsy Woman," "Woman Got Soul," and "Love Is the Place." Then the protest songs and music of the struggle: "Keep on Pushing," "We're a Winner," and "The Got Dang Song." Then the religiously inspired: "Amen," "People Get Ready," and "Come Free Your People." Finally, songs of blackness: "Choice of Colors" and "We People Who Are Darker than Blue." The Dylan memories begin with his seminal, subtle protest songs: "Blowing in the Wind" and "The Times They Are A-Changing," and then the explicit songs of black protest: "Oxford Town," "Pawn in the Game," and "The Death of Emmett Till." The antiwar music: "Masters of War," "God on Our Side," and "A Hard Rain Falling." The subtle songs of drugs and getting high: "Rainy Day Women" and "Mr. Tambourine Man," and last the songs about women: "Like a Rolling Stone," "Ain't Me Babe," "Positively Fourth Street," and "Just Like a Woman."

The music by Dylan and Mayfield helped to shape my consciousness, attitudes, and values as no music has done before or since; it is part of the past that has no future. I have told my daughters when I die to tell family and friends who wish to remember me to drink some Jack Daniels and play some Dylan, Curtis, and the great blues master Bobby Bland.

I cannot conclude this memoir of music without discussing jazz. At Cal State and Berkeley, the cultural nationalist and some of my more culturally advanced friends (so they thought) contended that the only music that mattered was jazz. They argued jazz as performed by Archie Shepp, Charlie Parker, Eric Dolphy, and especially John Coltrane was the blackest of music and, if properly appreciated, the only black music with revolutionary potential. Frank Kofsky in *Black Nationalism and the Revolution in Music*, a book widely read at the time, linked Malcolm and Black Nationalist ethos to jazz, as did Amiri Baraka. Perhaps they were correct, but I did not like, perhaps a better word is, appreciate, jazz. I found the generally long albums boring, and I guess I was too dense to appreciate its blackness and revolutionary potential. I listened to a bit of Ramsay Lewis probably because Sophia liked him and to Charles Lloyd and even attended a Lloyd performance. But to the jazz elitist Lewis and to some extent Lloyd were not authentic; they were popularizers. As I indicated and will later discuss, at Berkeley I did develop an appreciation of what I take to be the blackest music—the blues—but jazz to me, like the symphony and the ballet, was long, tedious, and boring.

Aside from the cultural, Black Power was first institutionalized on predominantly white college campuses—which in the 1960s saw for the first time the enrollment of a critical mass of black students—with the establishment of racially separate and autonomous black student unions, caucuses, associations, or societies as they were variously called. Later, black members of Congress, mayors, judges, journalists, social workers, political scientists, and other black professionals established racially exclusive organizations, but we were the first.

The first BSU was established at San Francisco State in 1966, and soon thereafter at Cal State. When I arrived on campus in the fall of 1969 the BSU was a well-established, respected, influential, and ably led organization. Like elsewhere in the nation, the black establishment in Los Angeles had opposed the formation of the "separatist" BSU as a case of "racism in reverse." The local NAACP, Urban League, and city councilman Billy Mills opposed any organizing on a racially separate basis. The leaders of the BSU ignored them.

Among the BSU's leaders when I arrived in addition to Omar were Ayuko Babu, who later became the founder in Los Angeles of the Pan-African Film and Arts Festival; J. K. Obatala, the writer and first head of Black Studies at Cal State, Long Beach; Abdulhamid Akoni, the lay historian and first head of Black Studies at the University of California, Santa Barbara; and Earl Ofari Hutchinson, who subsequently became a Los Angeles civic leader, author, political commentator and radio talk show host. Women played essential leadership roles on the BSU Central Committee, most notably Sandra Scott and Clotilda Blake. Other influential members I recall were my friend Larry, Lloyd Walters, Ron Finney, and Hiram Channell.

The BSU declared it "functioned as the government of black students on campus" and unsuccessfully petitioned the university to grant course credit to its officers as was done with the officers of the general student government. The BSU held weekly meetings, sponsored lectures and poetry readings, held intensive reading and study groups, and sponsored demonstrations and rallies on campus and in South Central. On campus we had a "Black House" for office space and meetings (a large photo of Malcolm greeted persons entering the building), and in South Central we had an off-campus facility where we sought to bring the campus to the community in terms of student recruitment and community service. Harry Truly, a sociologist and the only black I recall on the faculty at Cal State, attempted to organize a Black Student Alliance, a coalition of all BSUs in Southern California. His vision was this could eventually expand throughout the state and perhaps the nation. Students so organized he thought might become a potential revolutionary force. Most BSUs in Southern California did form an alliance, but little progress was made in creating a statewide let alone a national coalition.

The Black Student Alliance was part of the umbrella Los Angeles Black Congress, a coalition of all the major civil rights organizations in the city, from the relatively conservative NAACP and Urban League to the radical US organization and the Black Panthers. Anticipating the 1972 National Black Political Convention at Gary, Indiana, the LA Black Congress was ably led by Walt Bremond. It was an effort, like the later national effort, to bridge the growing ideological differences in black politics. Like the Gary convention, the Congress could not bridge those differences as over time it came to be increasingly dominated by Ron Karenga and his authoritarian US organization. But for a time, it offered the potential for unifying an increasingly fractured Los Angeles black politics, publishing the newspaper *Harambee*, which for a time was coedited by Elaine Brown, the future head of the Black Panther Party. I occasionally attended Congress meetings as a representative of the Black Student Alliance, which is probably where I first saw Angela Davis after she arrived in Los Angeles from San Diego. Also, the BSU held its regular Sunday Central Committee meetings in the Congress building on Florence and Broadway.

The members of the Central Committee had frequent reading and study sessions. Among the persons we read were Malcolm, Fanon, Lenin, Che, Nkrumah, Harold Cruse, and Carmichael and Hamilton's *Black Power*. All members of the committee were required to be familiar with Mao's *Little Red Book* and its teachings on the "Pitfalls of Liberalism":

> To let things slide for the sake of peace and friendship when a person has clearly gone wrong, and refrain from principal argument because he is an old acquaintance, a fellow townsman, a schoolmate, a close friend, a loved one, an old colleague, or subordinate.

> To indulge in irresponsible criticism in private instead of actively putting forward one's suggestions to the organization. To say nothing to people to their faces but to gossip behind their backs, or to say nothing at meetings but to gossip afterward.

> To show no regard at all for principles of collective life but to follow one's own inclinations.

> To indulge in personal attacks, pick quarrels, vent personal spite, or seek revenge instead of entering into an argument and struggling against incorrect views for the sake of unity or progress or getting the work done properly.

> To hear incorrect views without rebutting them . . .

> To be among the masses and fail to conduct propaganda . . .

> To regard oneself as having rendered great service to the revolution, to pride oneself on being a veteran, to disdain minor

assignments while being quite unequal to major tasks, to be slipshod in work and slack in study.

To be aware of one's own mistakes and yet make no attempt to correct them, taking a liberal attitude toward oneself.

These principles we studied to build group solidarity. The Central Committee discarded Robert's Rules of Order and attempted to make decisions on the basis of what we took to be traditional African decision-making by consensus after all were heard.

The BSU had frequent campus rallies to mobilize black students and to make our positions known to the administration and white students. One of our more sensational demonstrations was a reversal of stereotype; a group of us gathered in the main campus quad and ate chicken and watermelon. Poetry readings and lectures were sponsored. I recall off-campus poetry jams with local poets and such luminaries as Baraka and Sonia Sanchez. Adam Clayton Powell after his ouster from Congress came and gave a militant Black Power address. Muhammad Ali gave an antiwar, Black Power speech to a large mixed-race audience. Ali told a humorous story about ice cream and white supremacy. He said that whenever he ordered a double dip of chocolate and vanilla the vanilla was always placed on top. After a time, he said he grew tired of this racism and began to demand, "Put my chocolate on the top." Several of us tested Ali's theory by ordering chocolate and vanilla cones and found he was correct. So, we too said, "Enough of this racism, put the chocolate on the top."

But for sure the most contentious lecture was given by Alex Haley. Haley, coauthor with Malcolm of the autobiography, was then working on what was to become his acclaimed book and television miniseries *Roots: The Saga of an American Family*. We did know this and did not care. We invited him because we wanted to hear about Malcolm. Haley was about fifteen minutes into his talk about his research for *Roots* when Dwight interrupted, accusing him of giving a "long, pedantic, esoteric" lecture that nobody wanted to hear. A visibly angry Haley shouted, "Do you know what those words mean?" Dwight responded, "Yes, do you?" And the lecture ended in acrimony as we told Haley we invited him to hear about Malcolm not his roots.

We also held several "Free Huey" rallies on campus, after Black Panther cofounder Huey Newton was sentenced to prison for killing an Oakland policeman. His imprisonment became an international cause, and Free Huey rallies were held around the world. In addition to our rallies, we proposed a resolution calling on the student government to call for Huey's freedom. It refused, which resulted in my writing my first op-ed, which appeared in the campus paper, titled "A Statement from a Black Colonial Subject to the White Colonial Masters—HUEY NEWTON MUST BE SET FREE NOW." After making the case that blacks constituted a domestic colony "in the midst of the world's greatest imperialist power," I argued that Huey was a political prisoner, a revolutionary "charged with defending the integrity of his people and unless he is tried by his people (the poor blacks of the Oakland ghetto) his trial will be a farce." I ended with revolutionary rhetoric: "Finally, if you kill Huey the days of postponements (legislative acts), the delays (court decrees), the negotiations, the dialogues, the resolutions are over. The die will be cast, the Rubicon crossed, and the black liberation struggle will enter its final stage—the stage of absolute violence against the oppressor. Huey Newton must be set free NOW!" The BSU also supported the massive Free Huey rally in 1968 at the Los Angeles Sports Arena, which featured as speakers leading black and brown revolutionaries of the era—Stokely, Rap Brown, Karenga, and Reies Tijerina. Larry and I attended amid a heavy police presence and fears of a police attack.

Perhaps our most audacious community mobilization was the "Peoples' Tribunal" to try a Los Angeles policeman who we believed murdered Gregory Clark, a young black man. Clark was stopped by the police because "he didn't fit the car" (a late-model Mustang) he was driving, and after some kind of dispute he was shot in the back of the head and killed. The key organizer of the tribunal was Earl Ofari (he didn't use Hutchinson at the time) who probably then was the BSU vice president and was flirting with communism as the appropriate ideology for black liberation (in 1972 he published in *The Black Scholar* "Marxist-Leninism: The Key to Black Liberation"). As I recall Ofari took the lead in investigating the killing of Clark and came back to us and said, "It's a clear case, and we should put the honky on trial for murder." We distributed leaflets and posters with the officer's picture throughout South Central with the caption "Wanted for the murder of Brother Gregory Clark." After several weeks, we convened the trial on a Sunday afternoon in a South Central park. After the evidence was presented the crowd of perhaps a hundred shouted "guilty." We left it to the people how to carry out the sentence of death.

As the Free Huey rallies and the Peoples' Tribunal show these were exciting times with much talk of revolution in the air, and the Black Panther Party was the most exciting organized expression of the revolutionary fervor. The Panthers were initially a self-defense organization, established in the Bay

Area in 1966 to protect blacks from police brutality. But within a year of its founding it had declared itself a revolutionary Black Nationalist organization. Adopting a version of Marxist-Leninism, the Panthers, headquartered in Oakland, proclaimed they were committed to the overthrow of capitalism as the key to black liberation in the United States. In 1967 in Los Angeles there were two rival Black Panther parties. One was headed by John Floyd and the other by Bunchy Carter and John Huggins. The Huggins-Carter party was approved by the main Panther organization in Oakland. Elaine Brown recalls in her memoir, *A Taste of Power*, at a Black Student Alliance poetry reading amid threats of violence Huggins declared in the presence of Floyd that no other group in LA could use the name except his group sanctioned by the Oakland headquarters. Floyd subsequently abandoned the name and potential violence between the groups was avoided.

Violent conflict within the Los Angeles black liberation movement did eventually occur between the Huggins-Carter faction of the Panthers and Karenga's US organization (both Huggins and Carter gave BSU-sponsored lectures at Cal State). After the Watts riot Karenga and his US organization became major players in LA's radical Black Nationalist politics, espousing a form of cultural nationalism based on what Karenga contended were distinctive African traditions. Karenga posited his version of cultural nationalism as an alternative to the Panthers' revolutionary nationalism. This led to bitter recriminations between the groups as they vied for supremacy in the radical wing of LA black politics. I never liked Karenga. First, I thought his idea of cultural nationalism based on supposed ancient African traditions was nonsense. Second, at the Black Congress where Karenga sometimes presided, he exhibited an authoritarian leadership style that I found offensive. Third, although I never considered joining the Panthers—partly perhaps because of fear and partly because I could not submit to the discipline required of members—I was nevertheless more enamored and intellectually impressed by their revolutionary nationalism than Karenga's cultural nationalism. Finally, I thought Karenga and his group of armed followers often tried to intimidate opponents in sometimes thuggish ways. Ironically, when I returned to LA for graduate study at UCLA, in my last year one of Karenga's top aides, Clyde Daniel-Halisi, also became a student in the Political Science Department. We became friends and I found him intellectually curious and hardly a Karenga sycophant. He later became professor and chair of Cal State's Black Studies Department.

Although we engaged these off-campus Black Power groups and they impacted our work, the major work of the BSU was Black Power on campus.

Like countless other BSUs across the country at this time, we advanced four *demands* in pursuit of campus Black Power. I emphasize demands because BSUs almost always presented their proposals as demands, often as "nonne-gotiable demands." The four demands were: (1) the hiring of black faculty and the creation of a black-controlled Black Studies program, (2) racially exclusive or separate cultural spaces, (3) the establishment of EOP—Educa-tional Opportunity Program—to recruit more black students, and (4) special tutorial and financial assistance for black students. We achieved each of our demands at Cal State, although we were not successful in our demand for decision-making positions on the committees that admitted black students and hired black faculty.

Our core demand was Black Studies, staffed and controlled by black people. We saw black studies as means to establish bases of Black Power. Recognizing that knowledge, like wealth, political offices, and group solidarity, was a base of power we saw the development of black studies as a power base in the liberation struggle. We saw it also as a way to reclaim our history and culture, which were also a part of the liberation process.

The first Black Studies program was established at San Francisco State in 1969 after a five-month, often violent strike led by the campus BSU and a coalition of minority (Chicano, Asian American, and Native American) students united as the Third World Liberation Front. The San Francisco State strike, its broad coalition, and the establishment of Black and Ethnic Studies programs became a model and inspiration for activists on hundreds of campuses throughout the US. Four hundred miles up the coast from Los Angeles, the movement at San Francisco State was covered extensively on Los Angeles television. It was a direct inspiration for us, and a delegation from Cal State visited the campus to consult with our comrades on strategy and tactics. We brought James Turner to campus as consultant. Turner, along with Nathan Hare, Molefi Asante, and Ronald Walters, is a pioneering black studies scholar; he led the successful student protests at Northwestern University and was later the long-serving director of Cornell's Africana Studies program, where he wrote important epistemological and theoretical papers defining the Afrocentric parameters of the discipline (on his contributions see Scot Brown, *Discourse on Africana Studies: James Turner and Paradigms of Knowledge*). Turner visited for several days, gave a couple of public lectures, met administration officials, and offered guidance on how to structure our program organizationally and in curriculum design. While at Howard in the 1980s, I had the good opportunity to renew our relationship when he invited me to visit and lecture at the Africana Studies

Center. In addition to Turner, we also brought Sidney Walton to campus to consult on curriculum development.

I kept a file on my black studies work. It was good I did because if I had relied on memory, I would have thought I was chair of the Black Studies Committee, but Omar was the chair. In addition to Omar and me the other members of the committee were Ted Egans, Ellis Jackson, and Abdulhamid Akoni. I cannot recall Ellis or Egans but Akoni I remember very well as we coauthored the October 1968 proposal accepted by the university as the basis for the creation of the program.

Akoni was probably in his midforties, and while he was studying for the BA in history, he was widely recognized in Los Angeles Black Nationalist circles as an accomplished historian of the African and African American experience. I do not recall whether he had published any of his work, but he was highly sought as a lecturer on black history in the community. As evidence of his credibility as a scholar after he earned his undergraduate degree, he was appointed the founding director of the Black Studies program at the University of California, Santa Barbara.

In addition to coauthoring the proposal, drafting syllabi, and holding countless meetings with members of the university academic planning committee and Anthony Moye, the dean of the College of Liberal Arts, I authored an op-ed for the campus paper where I made the case for black studies. Titled "Black Studies: Its Need and Substance," the article first argued that as a result of racism and white supremacy "historically there had been systematic exclusion of non-white Americans from the intellectual and cultural concerns of American educational institutions." The core of the argument was written in the language of Black Power:

> Black people have begun to question the relevance of an education that ignores their existence. They have begun to say that perhaps colleges and universities as they are presently operated are at least irrelevant, and sometimes even destructive to black students in terms of new recognition of unfulfilled needs of the black community. Black people have begun to define the concept of "black consciousness." They have begun to say that perhaps the recognition of themselves in terms of their historical presence is the primary interest of black students today. That is, black people did not come from the West, they came from Africa. They came here not as immigrants but as a domestic colony. But in college—when they are allowed to go to college—they are

taught little or nothing about African history, their own history in this country, the literature of black people, African languages, black art and music or the development of their own culture.

Finally, I wrote, "I believe that the Black Student Union proposal for an academic area in Afro-American Studies is a good first step toward this goal and the development of a concentrated, well-rounded field of study leading eventually to Bachelor's and Master's degrees."

This article was written to influence student, faculty, and administration opinion. Watching the events at San Francisco State some faculty and some in the administration (especially Dean Moye) recognized perhaps something should be done to meet our demands in order to avoid the kind of disorders taking place at San Francisco State and other universities around the country. Not only were campus administrators concerned, so were local and state authorities. As part of its COINTELPRO program of surveillance and repression of potential radical and revolutionary groups, the FBI targeted BSUs across the country. J. Edgar Hoover ordered informants and possibly agent provocateurs be inserted in many BSUs and worked with local authorities on surveillance and disruption of the groups. (In 1979 I filed Freedom of Information requests with both the CIA and the FBI requesting any files or documents they had on me. The FBI indicated it had nothing on me. But the CIA indicated it had two documents on me generated by the FBI, which I would have to obtain from the FBI. The FBI continued to claim it had nothing. I did not pursue the matter because I was told it would involve costly litigation.) I became aware of the authorities' surveillance of our BSU when my sister Nell, an employee of the LA County Sheriff's Office, told me an informant in our group was supplying detailed accounts of our meetings. She did not tell me the name of the person; I cannot recall if she knew. I also cannot recall if I shared this information with anyone at the time, although I would guess I told Omar and Larry. But perhaps not, since revealing it would have caused suspicious tensions and dissension within the group.

This occurs to me because when we decided to engage in disruptive protest to press our demands, I thought at the time the persons who pressured us to do so may have been agent provocateurs. Those brothers whose names I even now recall, but will not name, were not active members but began to come to Central Committee meetings pressing us to stop talking and writing and take some action to force the administration's hand. So, we did. About a half-dozen male members went to the admissions office and scattered files. Three—Wilfred Tennyson, Henry Parks, and Omar—were arrested, charged with vandalism, and threatened with suspension and possible imprisonment. Although I was among the group, I was not arrested. Instead, the protest led to my first television appearance as I was designated the spokesman to appear in the media to defend the action. In addition to the charges against the three members, the BSU was placed on "conduct probation" and threatened with suspension as a recognized campus organization.

Shortly after the admissions office protest the BSU issued its formal demands to the administration. The first of the eleven demands included the dropping of charges against our three members and rescinding the BSU's conduct probation status. The remainder dealt with the specifics of establishing the Black Studies program. On the organization of the program we insisted "that in order to prevent racist participation and contamination of Afro-American Studies, there be active participation of the Black Student Union in all decision-making processes involving Afro-American Studies—especially with respect to selection of instructors."

It is likely the admissions office protest had little impact on administration's decision to yield to our demands. Rather, the administration likely responded, as I said, to avoid San Francisco State–type disorders. A second reason it responded when it did was the assassination of Dr. King. All across the country in the aftermath of the killing of King in April 1968 and the nationwide uprisings that followed, university administrators acceded to black student demands. On the night of King's murder, I was at work at the post office. When we learned of his death, Omar went to the microphone and announced the blacks were walking out. My recollection is that most of the nonblacks—mostly Chicanos—joined us. (Of all the major US cities, Los Angeles was one of the few that was quiet that night. There were no riots or disorders.) Omar immediately decided to ask for a meeting of the Central Committee, and we spent the night drafting demands to present to the university president. This was the first time the university president had agreed to meet with the BSU. I believe the events of April 1968 were instrumental in his decision to personally embrace our demand for black studies.

Although we did not establish a Third World Liberation Front as at San Francisco State and Berkeley, we did establish on campus one of the first black-brown coalitions in Los Angeles. The Chicano Students Association was led by Carlos Munoz, who joined with us to create the Minority Studies Committee to push for the simultaneous creation of black and

Chicano studies; both proposals were accepted by the administration at the same time. Munoz went on to become an important scholar of Chicano politics and professor of ethnic studies at Berkeley.

In October 1968 we submitted our formal "Proposal for the Creation of an Administrative-Academic Entity in Afro-American Studies Including Justification, Philosophy, and Goals, with Suggestions Concerning Fiscal Feasibility and Staffing." We justified the new program as providing "an intellectually exciting academic experience" that would help to develop "a constructive black consciousness by black students" and educate all students "in the historical significance of the experience of black people." For those earning degrees "by virtue of having studied black music, black history, black art, black psychology, economics of the ghetto, city planning, and special problems relating to the black community, Afro-American Studies majors who become social workers, teachers, and library assistants, for example, would be able to meet the special needs of black people, lessen racial ignorance and prejudice among white people, and work responsibly to build a sense of community among and between black and white people."

In terms of the broader impact of the new discipline, we concluded, "The goal of the Afro-American Studies program is the revitalization of American education. The program will be designed to bring to the educational process and the media of communication a more comprehensive understanding of Afro-Americans and humankind." Finally, we insisted that "inasmuch as the college's efforts to establish the program were initiated by a student group, the Black Student Union, and since through student efforts the program has been brought to this point of being able to offer classes as soon as the program is formalized by the college, it is only reasonable to predicate success of the Afro-American Studies program on the students continuing to have an effective voice, and *meaningfully* active participation in all decision-making relating to the Afro-American Studies program, now and in the future."

For the first year (1968–1969), we proposed a faculty of 6.8 FTE including the coordinator or director, and a total budget of $11,731. By the year 1972–1973 we projected a budget of $16,820 and a faculty of eleven. Along with the proposal, we included syllabi for the following courses: Afro-American Culture, Afro-American History, Personal and Social Development of Afro-Americans, Swahili, The Economics of Racism and Poverty, Urban Black Politics, History of Afro-American Music, and the Politics of Black Power.

Ironically, the month of black studies approval at Cal State was melancholy for me, because it occurred when I was disengaging from the BSU, a disengagement that was partly responsible for my decision to transfer to Berkeley. As I have said, there were tensions in Los Angeles' black radical community between Karenga's US and the Black Panthers. A part of tensions related to the ideology of the groups but also to personalities and turf. A part of the turf conflict involved differences over the ideology and resources of the emerging Black Studies programs in the Los Angeles area. At UCLA this struggle over the resources allocated to the Black Studies program resulted in a shoot-out in which US members killed Panther Party members John Huggins and Bunchy Carter. Although it was later learned that the conflict between US and the Panthers was deliberately exacerbated by the FBI, the tensions between the groups were real and the UCLA killings were a tragic, perhaps inevitable, outcome.

Carter and Huggins had lectured at Cal State, and I may have actually met them, I cannot recall; but their deaths deeply disturbed and to some extent frightened me because the killings were meaningless and sad, and partly also because I disliked US, and the faction of the Cal State LA BSU aligned with it had won the recent BSU elections and taken control of the organization. It was clear that as a result I would no longer be welcome in the organization, certainly not in a leadership role. In December 1969 I submitted to Omar a letter resigning from the BSU Black Studies Committee. I wrote:

> It became clear to me a few weeks ago that, as a result of the BSU's election, some members of the new leadership do not wish that I serve on the committee. It became clear that I, and the opinions that I express on this and other matters was a source of division about the program within the Union. Furthermore, the black students on this campus in the fall 1968 elections chose new leadership—leadership which holds opinions that I am in fundamental disagreement with—; therefore I feel that it is only fair that I (a person closely associated with the previous administration) should give the new administration an opportunity to staff this very important committee with persons of its own choosing. I have waited until this time to resign because I wanted to leave the program on a sound foundation. I feel the acceptance of the proposal in a manner of speaking does that.

I ended the letter with the revolutionary bravado and hyperbole typical of the times:

I have worked for the last two quarters on this program, and I have found it to be a difficult but rewarding experience that I shall never forget, and I shall remain forever grateful to the Black Student Union for giving me the opportunity to work on this program. In my judgment, this program is of utmost importance to Afro-America because as another member of the committee has said, "It has the potential, if correctly implemented and administered, of completely disrupting this society." I am sure we will agree that this profoundly racist society must be disrupted if the race and mankind is to survive. Indeed, a program of this kind could go a long way toward solving the most acute problem of the black revolution—the crisis of the black intellectual, and the absence of a definitive theory of revolution and as Lenin said many years ago "without revolutionary theory there can be no revolutionary practice."

At the time of these events I had learned—I cannot recall how—of Berkeley's affirmative action program to recruit black students. Affirmative action—the diverse set of programs and policies designed to remedy historical racism, enforce the Civil Rights Act of 1964, and to create a diverse university and workplace—was just beginning in 1969. President Nixon had not issued his executive order requiring affirmative action by recipients of federal funds and the first Supreme Court decision was a decade away. Yet Berkeley on its own began an apparently aggressive effort to recruit black students. This was probably in part a legacy of the King assassination and the wish of some white liberals to atone and do something to quiet the rising revolutionary fervor of young blacks by co-opting them into elite institutions. Berkeley, the most prestigious public university in the state and one of the most prestigious in the nation, certainly needed an affirmative action program since in the 1966–1967 year, of its twenty-six thousand students only 236 (0.9 percent) were black.

So, after a year and a half at Cal State, LA, I, a fully awakened black man, moved to the Bay Area for the first time, where I imbibed its revolutionary ethos, its counterculture, its protest proclivities, and its great climate and beauty.

CHAPTER 3

Berkeley

Revolution in the Air

Dwight, Larry, and I hitched a U-Haul to my old Falcon and drove the four hundred miles from Los Angeles to Berkeley. The drive was too much for the old car, and by the time we reached Berkeley it was nearly completely worn-out, and I abandoned it—literally—on the streets of Berkeley shortly after we arrived. Larry had warned that the Falcon probably could not make it all the way and we asked Dwight midway through the trip to attach the U-Haul to his car, which he drove up, but he refused. This was typical of Dwight who, in contrast to Larry, was a selfish, self-centered, almost amoral person.

I cannot recall but it may have been Dwight who found out about Berkeley's affirmative action program. A native of Los Angeles, Dwight was a tall, light-skin brother who was something of a lady's man. At Cal State he was thoroughly apolitical, taking no part in the BSU, where in contrast Larry was an active member. In any event, we were bound together by our decision to transfer to Berkeley. We moved into a two-bedroom apartment a short distance from the campus. Interestingly, the apartment was located on Dwight Way, which likely inflated Dwight's already considerable ego. We shared the apartment for less than a year and then moved into a large three-bedroom house, also within walking distance of the campus. In the last several months Dwight and Larry moved in with their girlfriends and I moved into a one-bedroom flat, where I stayed until graduation.

The three of us were political science majors, but Dwight, like Larry, was mainly interested in philosophy. In some ways he was the convener of our late-night weed and wine philosophy discussions, where we read and debated Camus and Sartre, Heidegger, Kierkegaard, Hegel, Marx, Kant, R. D. Laing, Herbert Marcuse, and Dwight's favorite, Nietzsche. Although apolitical, Dwight participated in virtually all of the Berkeley protests for the hell and fun of it. During the People's Park protest, a photo of him throwing a tear gas canister at the police appeared on the front page of the *Los Angeles Times*. After graduation he earned a law degree from Hastings in San Francisco. But he never practiced law because he became consumed with thinking that he had solved the assassination of President Kennedy. This was a weird, unexpected departure for him, but he spent years trying to sell his conspiracy theory of the murder of the president. He even wrote a self-published book on the subject, which I read but whose title or contents I cannot recall.

Berkeley is today internationally known as a citadel of radical, progressive equalitarian politics in the United States, the "Peoples' Republic of Berkeley" as we sometimes call it. This was not always the case. For a long time Berkeley was a rather conservative and racist place. Indeed, the city was just beginning to become the radical place it is today when I arrived in 1969. In 1948 Berkeley's white majority elected Byron Rumford, an African American, to represent it in the state legislature and in 1961 Wilmot Sweeney was elected to the city council. Berkeley's liberals pointed to these elections as evidence of the city's liberal equalitarianism. But schools and housing were segregated, there was widespread discrimination in employment, downtown merchants and places of public accommodation refused to hire blacks and many did not welcome blacks as patrons. The city employed few blacks, usually as garbage collectors and street sweepers. In 1963 voters in the city rejected a fair housing law and nearly recalled the school board over its plan to begin desegregation of the schools. Although in 1960 they were nearly a fifth of Berkeley's population of one hundred thousand, blacks in the city lived in an isolated area of the flatlands where they were nearly as segregated and impoverished as blacks in Shreveport.

This situation began to slowly change in the midsixties when a coalition of blacks and white liberals, influenced by the civil rights movement, elected a majority to the city council. This liberal majority began to advance reforms in employment and schools. These changes were accelerated in the late 1960s as a result of student radicalism and the emergence of the Black Panthers in nearby Oakland. In 1967 white radicals formed a coalition with blacks and elected Ronald Dellums to the city council, and in 1970 Dellums was elected to Congress. Dellums was symbolic of the city's transition from liberalism to radicalism. A self-conscious radical, he was a militant opponent of the war on Vietnam, a declared socialist, sympathetic to the counterculture and an admirer of the Black Panthers. He epitomized the Berkeley radicalism of the 1960s—the Afro-wearing, bell-bottomed radical. When he announced for Congress, we did not think he could win but nevertheless eagerly volunteered for the campaign and were surprised when he defeated the liberal incumbent with 55 percent of the vote. He went on to serve a quarter century as the most radical member of Congress, and a term as mayor of Oakland

The Berkeley campus of the University of California, with the possible exception of San Francisco State, was the most self-consciously radical university in the country. The seminal Free Speech movement of 1964 was the spawning ground for campus protests; many Berkeley students were volunteers in the southern civil rights movement and in protesting racism in the Bay Area. Students from Berkeley in 1960 participated in the violent protests in San Francisco against the McCarthy-like hearings of the House Un-American Activities Committee (HUAC). Some of the earliest teach-ins and protests of the war on Vietnam took place at Berkeley. And, just before I arrived on campus, minority student protests to establish Ethnic Studies programs had resulted in disorders that required for the first time the dispatch of the National Guard to the campus.

The Berkeley campus was often referred to as the capstone of the California higher education system. In 1960 the state adopted its master plan for higher education. It created a three-tier, tuition-free, system that has served as a model for other states and nations. The first tier is the now ten-campus University of California (UC) system, in which the top 12.5 percent of students (based on grade point average and SAT or ACT scores) are admitted. The UC campuses are authorized to offer the PhD and are designated as major research universities. The middle tier is the now twenty-three-campus California State University (CSU) system, which grants admission to the top third of the state's students. Viewed primarily as teaching rather than research institutions, the CSU campuses are allowed to offer the master's but not the PhD. The final tier is the more than one hundred community or junior colleges, which are open to any high school graduate. Upon successful completion students are guaranteed admission to one of the UC or CSU campuses. As I said, this then tuition-free system of higher education has been a model for other US states and many nations. Berkeley in 1969 was the flagship campus of the system, and was recognized, then and now, as one of the top ten universities in the world and the best public university in the nation.

The tumultuous strike at San Francisco State to establish Black Studies is the best known of the black student rebellions of the 1960s. But the Third Word Liberation Front strike at Berkeley, which occurred at about the same time, was equally if not more tumultuous and violent, and like the San Francisco State strike resulted in the creation not only of a Black Studies program but a "Department" of Ethnic Studies. The BSU at Berkeley (called the Afro-American Student Union) submitted its demands for the Black Studies program in April 1968. Andrew Billingsley, an African American professor of sociology, was appointed by the chancellor to review the proposal. Toward the end of the year he submitted recommendations for the creation of a department, although it did not include the student demands for community involvement and student participation in decision-making.

Meanwhile in August the Mexican American Student Association (MASA) in support of Caesar Chavez's striking farmworkers asked the university to stop buying and serving grapes. The administration agreed but Governor Reagan intervened and forced the university to resume serving. Several MASA students were arrested for protesting this decision. In January 1969 black, Latino, Native American, and Asian American students created the Third World Liberation Front (TWLF). It issued a set of demands that included the establishment of a Third World College to include autonomous departments of Afro-American, Mexican American, Native American, and Asian American Studies; minority control of minority-related programs; and the admission, with enhanced financial and academic assistance, of more minority students. In support of these demands (including amnesty for the students arrested during the grape protests) the TWLF called a strike and set up picket lines at all major entrances to the campus. The police attempted to break up the demonstrations, periodic violence ensued, and the governor dispatched the Highway Patrol to the campus. The police arrested protesting students and the administration prohibited on-campus rallies in support of the strike. Violence escalated between striking students and the police, tear gas was used for the first time on campus to disperse students, and Reagan dispatched the National Guard to the campus. During this period more than 150 students were arrested.

Shortly after the Guard arrived, the administration in a compromise with the TWLF agreed to create a "Department" of Ethnic Studies with "sufficient flexibility to permit evolution to a college." The department included four separate degree-granting programs in black, Mexican American, Native American, and Asian American studies. This was an unusual arrangement—a department with four separate, autonomous degree-granting programs—but it was enough for the TWLF to accept and end the strike. In the fall of 1968, the budget for the department was approved, Professor Billingsley was appointed department chair, and Ron Lewis was appointed coordinator of the Black Studies program. When we arrived on campus in the spring of 1969 the program in African American Studies was going forward with plans to begin offering the first classes in the fall of the year. I was a part of the inaugural program in Black Studies, taking two classes in Afro-American politics in fall and winter quarters of 1969–1970.

I essentially ignored the study of political science as offered by Berkeley's nationally renowned faculty. I took the required three courses in methods offered by Professor Michael Shapiro. I also took a class in Non-Western Thought taught by the Indian scholar J. Das Gupta, and a course on Marxism offered by A. James Gregor. Although not a Marxist, Gregor's class and his book *A Survey of Marxism* were a good introduction to Marxism as philosophy, history, and science. But mainly I took courses in black studies and the experimental college. In the experimental college (instituted to provide innovative, radical alternatives to the traditional curriculum) I took a class on Soviet Social Thought taught by the iconic Bay Area radical William Marx Mandel. Mandel, a likely communist, was an iconic figure in the radical politics of the area largely because of his testimony in 1960 at the San Francisco hearings of HUAC, where students from Berkeley and elsewhere engaged in a violent confrontation with the police. Inside the hearing, Mandel engaged in a famous, tumultuous confrontation with the committee. In 1953 he had appeared before Joseph McCarthy's committee, where he compared the Wisconsin senator to Hitler. In his San Francisco HUAC appearance, he dismissed the committee as a "Kangaroo Court," "a collection of Judases," and as the "honorable beaters of children," while steadfastly refusing to answer whether he was or had been a member of the Communist Party. This plus his antiwar, antidraft activism made him a revered figure among Berkeley's radical students (although not a student and forty years old, Mandel was member of the Free Speech movement's steering committee). For years he hosted a weekly Marxist-oriented program on KPFA, the Berkeley Pacifica radio station. It was a good and memorable experience to study with this embodiment of Bay Area radicalism.

In the experimental college I also took a class from the radical graduate student James Glass called Liberalism and the Concept of the Psyche. This class was largely about the repressive—particularly the sexually repressive—nature of liberal society. We read the Freudian left—Wilhelm Reich, Geza Roheim, and Herbert Marcuse—including R. D. Laing's psychoanalytic theory of schizophrenia in modern society, *The Divided Self*, and Norman O. Brown's call for sexual freedom and "polymorphous perversity," *Love's Body*. Glass went on to serve on the faculty of the University of Maryland, College Park.

But by far my main course of study was African American politics in the classroom, in campus politics, and on the streets of Oakland and in the politics of the Black Panther Party. In its first classes in the spring of 1969 the Black Studies program offered a two-quarter sequence in African American politics taught by Donn Davis, a graduate student in political science. Davis's class in the first quarter focused on the history of black political thought, reading such figures as Martin Delaney, David Walker, Edward Wilmot Blyden, and Henry Highland Garnett. The second quarter focused on movements—the abolitionist movement, Reconstruction, the Niagara movement, the civil rights movement, the Black Power movement, and the Black Panthers as a case study. Davis, after earning the PhD, became an aide to Congressman Dellums in Washington and later a colleague on Howard's political science faculty.

Davis's classes provided a good foundation for historical and theoretical understandings of contemporary black politics. The case-study-like work on the Black Panthers reflected Davis's admiration and support of the Panthers. Davis was an informal advisor to the imprisoned Huey Newton and a friend of his brother Melvin Newton, and party members attended the class and sometimes gave informal lectures. Located several miles from the campus, students sometimes visited the Panther headquarters. Eldridge Cleaver, newly released from prison and author of the acclaimed *Soul on Ice*, had been named the party's minister of information. He had also been appointed to teach a class in the experimental college, but Governor Reagan intervened, and the class was canceled. Cleaver nevertheless appeared on campus several times to give informal lectures and speeches. I was not impressed by his speeches or his book. I found *Soul on Ice* hyperbolic and banal and its fixation on his craving for white women and discussion of rape as a revolutionary act offensive. His lectures and speeches often mocked Reagan and were characterized by profanity and frequent references to "pussy power," which was his injunction to women to withhold sex from men unless they were committed to the revolution. I suppose his most important contribution at the time was his call to white students to rally to the party, abandon their privileged positions, and join with blacks as vanguards of the revolution.

Aside from Cleaver, party members were frequently on campus distributing leaflets and selling Mao's *Little Red Book*. I was impressed by the dedication and courage of the members, many no older than I, and their bravado was enchanting. During 1968–1969 there were frequent raids by the police on Panther offices, including the 1969 raid on the Chicago office that resulted in the murder of Panther leaders Fred Hampton and Mark Clark. Fearing there might be an attack on the party headquarters in Oakland, the Panthers asked Berkeley students to take turns staying overnight in the building as a deterrent to an attack. The assumption was the police and FBI would be reluctant to attack and run the risk of killing students. I spent one night in the Oakland headquarters. I would have spent more but the Panthers' preference was for whites—especially white women—on the assumption that white women would be a greater deterrent than black men.

In addition to taking black studies classes I was a reader in the program for a professor of literature. Unfortunately, I cannot recall the professor's name or much about the course. As a reader I became (along with the teaching assistants and others) a member of the program's steering committee. The steering committee was supposed to be the mechanism for student participation in decision-making but the coordinator Ron Lewis (who I think was a PhD student) rarely convened the committee.

Like at UCLA and Cal State, Berkeley Black Studies was marked by ideological disputes, turf conflicts, and threats of violence. Unlike in Southern California where the conflicts were rooted in the struggle for ideological primacy between US and the Panthers, in Berkeley the conflict was largely about student participation in decision-making and the willingness of the coordinator to involve the program in community organizing and activism. The African American Studies coordinator was not a radical or revolutionary. Rather Ron Lewis was an academic traditionalist who was skeptical of community engagement and worried that such engagement might put the status of the new program in jeopardy. That is, he argued that if the program were to evolve into a department, it would have to adhere to the norms of traditional academic departments. A number of students who had participated in the TWLF strike disagreed and eventually set about to remove Lewis as coordinator.

Larry and I joined the protest against Lewis. The protest was led by Buddy Jackson and Horace Upshaw, who were members of the TWLF steering committee, and participants in the strike and in the initial organizing and staffing of the program. Dissatisfied with Lewis's leadership, we organized a group portentously and pretentiously called the Committee on Liberation or Death (COLD). In our manifesto we declared:

Allowing that "colonialist oppression" and "institutional racism" provide the basis for the unique thrust of self-determination and autonomy as it relates to Black people and Black Studies, it does not seem unreasonable to expect that a leader (in this case, the coordinator) chosen by his constituency will maintain that aggressive and uncompromising stance when it comes to dealing with the problems of Black people. . . . Leadership of the Black Studies Department, particularly one that is "community oriented" must provide leadership in tackling the problems of the Community: job discrimination, police brutality, abuse by welfare agencies, racism, etc. This must be done by speaking out on community problems whenever the opportunity presents itself, expanding our sphere of influence beyond the campus, and actually educating the community. It means involvement.

Although not ideological in the sense of the conflicts at Cal State and UCLA, tensions were high and there was the threat of violence between COLD and factions supporting the coordinator. At a mass meeting at a local black church where I gave a speech advancing the COLD position and calling for the firing of Lewis, Horace and Buddy came to the meeting armed. Fortunately, there was no violence at this meeting or at any other time during the conflict. Eventually, the conflict withered away because COLD members lost interest or were graduated. In the end Lewis was not fired, and his ideas about the narrowly academic focus prevailed as was eventually the case with virtually all other Black Studies programs.

The Bay Area was the seeding ground and the place of flowering of the 1960s counterculture. The counterculture, largely the makings of young whites, to some extent has roots in the Beat culture of the 1950s. It represented a challenge—to an extent the mocking—of established values in terms of clothing, hair, drugs, sex, and communal living styles. A distinctive music is also associated with the counterculture. In the Bay Area the Haight Ashbury section of San Francisco and Telegraph Avenue, the main entrance to the Berkeley campus, were the centers of the 1960s counterculture. When we arrived in 1969 the counterculture in the Haight was already in decline due to the influx of heroin and increases in crime and sexual assaults.

The year 1967 was described as the "summer of love" and of "flower power" in San Francisco. Scott McKenzie's "If You Are Going to San Francisco" encouraged young people from across the country to come to the city, many literally arriving with flowers in their hair. Many settled in the cheap, often communal housing of the Haight. For a year or so, at least according to legend, the Haight was a place of love, peace, music, psychedelic drugs, free love, and all-around good vibrations. Legend or not, by the time we arrived the area was an international tourist attraction, but it was characterized by crime and drug addiction. Larry, Dwight, and I sometimes visited the Haight, but generally we found it was a caricature of the hippie promised land of McKenzie's song. In any event, we did not have to go across the Bay to partake of the counterculture; it was vibrant on Telegraph Avenue every day as we walked to campus.

Telegraph Avenue was lined with cafés, bookstores, movie houses, and in 1969 with hippies, peddlers, pushers, dropouts, and young people high or getting high. Walking the avenue, one could sometimes get a contact high from the aroma of weed and the ever-present incense. Many of the young played guitars and other instruments; the Hara Krishna were often on the avenue; the San Francisco Mime Troup would sometimes perform nearby; and "Holy Hubert," an evangelist, was a near-daily presence preaching damnation or salvation. Like the Haight, there were very few blacks on the avenue. While Larry, Dwight, and I spent a bit of time hanging out and observing the scene, we were mainly observers, not participants, viewing the avenue and the counterculture generally as a "white thing" for middle-class kids who for a time could afford to "tune in, turn on, and dropout." For us it was an interesting distraction having little to do with black people or the liberation struggle.

To some extent the music associated with the counterculture I did engage or, more precisely, my musical preferences while at Berkeley became whiter, shifting somewhat from R&B and soul to rock and other music performed by whites. Also, as a result of interaction with a white student I developed a lasting love of the blues. A part of the attraction of the counterculture music of the late 1960s was drug related, specifically LSD. Although one could appreciate the music, including what came to be known as acid rock, without use of psychedelic drugs, they were often joined. I probably used LSD a half dozen times while at Berkeley. And often the "trip" was accompanied by listening to acid rock or visiting a psychedelic club, which as I recall was located in the then largely black Fillmore District in San Francisco. The ambiance of the club was captured nicely in the Temptations' "Psychedelic Shack." The purpose of the club was to simulate the LSD experience, with loud music, strobe lights, weird multicolored décor, and the music of the Jefferson Airplane, Santana, Jimi Hendrix, Big Brother and the Holding Company, and the Chambers Brothers. This psychedelic experience was my most frequent and closest encounter with the counterculture.

Overall, the music of my time in Berkeley became more diverse, and white. We listened to Laura Nyro, Joe Cocker, Van Morrison, Janis Joplin, and a bit of the Grateful Dead. I still danced to Motown and soul at the few black house parties in the Oakland Hills (there were no black fraternities at Berkeley), but at this time probably my favorite group was the Fifth Dimension, many of whose songs were written by Laura Nyro and whose music was more white than black—a kind of light white soul. A most memorable musical experience was a concert by Nina Simone at the campus Greek Theater. The legendary Simone was one of the few black artists who sang music that mattered even during the civil rights era. I also can recall an example of music during this time that changed my life. After listening to the Chicago Transit Authority's "Does Anybody Really Know What Time It Is?," I gave my watch to my nephew Greg and have not had one since.

But the most profound influence of Berkeley on my musical inclinations was the development of an appreciation of the blues. In Benton I had dismissed the blues as backward, country, old folk's music. That changed in Berkeley ironically as a result of a white student who lived in my apartment building. I cannot recall his name, but he was a blues devotee with extensive knowledge of the history of the music. He played it constantly. Listening to him talk and play the blues made me a devotee from that time until now. I also frequented with him local blues clubs where blues records were played along with live performances by local artists (Oakland and the Bay Area have a fairly rich blues tradition). He had an excellent collection of rare blues records and tapes, including such contemporary artists as B. B. King, Bobby Bland, Howling Wolf, Muddy Waters, and Sonny Boy Williamson, as well as the classic, originators of the tradition like Son House, Charlie Patton, Bessie Smith, Ma Rainey, and Robert Johnson. I did not have the foresight to make tapes from his collection, but I came away with an understanding of the blues as perhaps the blackest of the music of black people. (Although I did not make tapes of the music in Berkeley, in a class at San Francisco State in the early 1990s I mentioned my love of the music. A student in the class—white—came up afterward and told me he had an extensive blues collection and was willing to make CDs for me. He did and I now have a good collection, ranging from the classics to contemporary artists.)

Apart from drugs and music, the counterculture was known for its liberated sexuality. The music certainly became more sexually uninhibited, as in the Doors' "Come on Baby, Light My Fire," the Beatles' "Why Don't We Do It in the Road," the Isley Brothers' "It's Your Thing" and "Love the One You're With." But sex was not a part of the culture I engaged. If you can believe it, this was partly for political reasons, in the sense as a committed Black Nationalist I did not wish to be accused of "Talking Black and Sleeping White." There were few black women at Berkeley, thus if one were to have sex, it would likely to be with white women since we rarely socialized beyond the campus. Both Dwight and Larry dated white women, eventually moving in with them. In Larry's case the relationship was an enduring one because although he and Linda never married, they were together for decades and she was at his bedside when he died. Dwight's relationship with Louisa was not as enduring, perhaps in part because of his descent into madness and homelessness (see chapter 9).

For me the year and a half at Berkeley was sexless, although I did have a relationship with a shy sister but she was not sexually liberated. Sophia visited once but except for that I was sexless in spite of being in one of the most sexually liberated places at one of the most sexually liberated times. It is point of pride, perhaps misplaced, that I have never had sex with a white woman.

By 1969 Berkeley was the epicenter of student protest in America. A number of Berkeley students (including Mario Savio) in the early and mid-1960s had joined SNCC in the civil rights protests in the South. Earlier students had been part of the group protesting the HUAC hearings in San Francisco. The Free Speech movement at Berkeley in 1964 led by Savio was seminal in the emergence of campus protests at Berkeley and elsewhere. Berkeley students participated in civil rights protests against racist employment practices in Berkeley, Oakland, and San Francisco. And shortly before I arrived black and other Third World students conducted one of the most disruptive protests in campus history. But from 1967 until the decade's end the war on Vietnam was the central concern of protests at Berkeley.

By the time I arrived on campus I had long since embraced the antiwar views I first heard in Gordon Bruno's class at LACC in 1966 or 1967. The sources of my opposition to the war and support for the Vietnamese in their struggle for liberation from Western domination were multiple. Muhammad Ali's refusal to be drafted and his powerful declaration "Ain't no Viet Cong ever called me nigger" were influential. SNCC's 1966 statement opposing the war, the first by a civil rights organization, was also influential as was Dr. King's speech a year later opposing the war. Articles in *Ramparts* magazine in words and pictures displayed the horrors of the war. Senator Wayne Morse's acerbic questioning of administration witnesses during the Senate Foreign Relation Committee hearings showed how little they comprehended

Vietnamese history or international law as it related to the conflict. Bertrand Russell and Jean-Paul Sartre, who I thought were the world's greatest living intellectuals (I had read and understood Russell's masterful *History of Western Philosophy* and read without much comprehension Sartre's *Being and Nothingness*), in 1967 organized a war crimes tribunal where the US was found guilty of violating the UN Charter and numerous human rights conventions. Thus, at Berkeley I was eager to join in protests against the war, which I considered racist, colonialist, illogical, illegal, and immoral. I wished for victory by North Vietnam and the "Viet Cong" (the US's derogatory name for the South Vietnamese National Liberation Front) and vowed I would go to prison rather than be drafted into the army.

Antiwar protests in the Bay Area took many forms: rallies on campus, large rallies in San Francisco at Golden Gate Field; efforts to block troop trains carrying soldiers to the Port of Oakland for transport to Vietnam; and protests at the Oakland Army Induction Center. Most of these protests were peaceful, but the demonstrations at the Army Induction Center and the troop train protests were often met by violent police repression. A major target of near-daily protests on campus was to get the administration to ban ROTC (Reserved Officer Training Corp) from the university. It was in protesting ROTC that I engaged in my most foolish and foolhardy act of protest by attempting to firebomb the ROTC building. This occurred during the protests of the US invasion of Cambodia, when there was a heavy police presence on campus. Nevertheless, a white boy (whose name I cannot recall or how I became associated with him) made Molotov cocktails (he made them) and we planned a night-time firebombing. Looking back, I cannot understand why I agreed to something so stupid. Because of the heavy police presence, we did not actually attempt the firebombing but hovered around the building for a couple of hours before we gave up. (I now think it would have been a mistake to ban ROTC from the campus because it is probably useful to have some military officers trained on liberal arts campuses rather than solely at military academies.)

The major and for me the most consequential protest on campus was after the invasion of Cambodia—consequential because without those protests, I may not have been graduated. But the most violent campus protest at Berkeley during my time was not related to the war. Rather it was the confrontation over People's Park in the spring of 1969. People's Park came to be viewed as struggle against property rights and for counterculture free expression and lifestyles. The three acres that became the park were owned by the university, which had planned to use it for student housing or athletic facilities. A lack of funds delayed construction and the land was essentially abandoned. In the early spring of 1969, it was occupied by hippies and Berkeley street people, who pitched tents, planted gardens, and turned the area into a countercultural space open to all wished to live there and create a community. At first the university ignored the occupation but, amid complaints about loud music, drug use, sex, and unsanitary conditions, it decided to oust the residents and put a fence around the area. This resulted in the bloodiest confrontation in campus history.

I might have visited the park a few times, but it had no particular attraction either as a countercultural expression or as the site of people versus property struggle. This changed when the university attempted to close the park. At the time I had finished all of my course work except French 4, which was required for graduation. However, having taken French in high school and at LACC it was clear I could not learn French or perhaps any foreign language. Barely getting a pass in French 3, I thought the chance of passing French 4 was zero, so I stopped attending class. I do not know what I planned to do since the class was required, but I guess I intended to ask for a waiver since otherwise I would graduate with honors.

Having no classes to attend I became a full-time protester, protesting everything: the war, ROTC, the park. The daily protests about the park eventually resulted in brutal repression by the campus police and Alameda County Sheriff's deputies, using tear gas and batons to disperse protesters. On May 15, "Bloody Thursday," the deputies fired shotgun pellets, killing James Rector who was a bystander. This only intensified our anger and we escalated our protests with attacks on police cars, burning garbage dumpsters, and hurling tear gas canisters back at the police. Larry, Dwight, and I, among the few black protesters, marveled that amid this chaos there was no looting, although there were ample opportunities to do so. We saw this as a striking difference between middle-class white students and poor blacks in the ghetto.

As the violence escalated Governor Reagan dispatched the National Guard, which occupied the city for more than two weeks. During the occupation in an act that I found unbelievable the Guard used a helicopter to tear gas us as we gathered peacefully in Sproul Plaza. Shocked, we nearly trampled each other as we ran to escape the choking gas from the air. A week or so later twenty-five thousand people marched through the streets of Berkeley demanding withdrawal of the Guard and the reopening of the park. After the Guard departed the violence subsided and the university agreed to reopen the park. People's Park became an iconic place in the annals of protests at Berkeley. Fifty years later it is a place of crime and drug use, and the university is once again considering constructing housing on the site for students and Berkeley's homeless.

In the wake of People's Park and its challenge to property rights a rent strike was organized. The ostensible purpose of the strike was to protest increases in rent, but many of the organizers said the long-range goal was to abolish private property. At the time I was living alone, Larry and Dwight having moved in with their girlfriends. With time to spare, I eagerly attended the organizing meetings, joined the tenants' union, and was among the five hundred or so persons to withhold rent. From March until I departed in June, I lived rent-free. This was an act of protest that paid real as well as symbolic benefits.

Two areas of protest emerged at Berkeley in my last year that shaped the course of the future in the next half century. In late 1969 homosexual students and others formed the Berkeley Gay Liberation Front. Although the Black Panthers embraced the gay liberation movement, I viewed it as a distraction from the black liberation struggle and I continued to believe homosexuality to be morally wrong and repugnant.

The women's liberation movement emerged also at this time on campus. I have a distinct memory of witnessing in lower Sproul Plaza what was probably one of the first bra-burnings in the nation. Like the gay movement, I dismissed the women's movement as another distraction from the black struggle and viewed the effort by some feminists to link the oppression of women with the oppression of blacks as ridiculous. My view at the time was nicely stated in a widely read article published by my future colleague at the college at Purchase, Linda La Rue. Published in the May 1970 issue of *The Black Scholar* devoted to "Black Revolution," Linda's article stated, "Any attempt to analogize black oppression with the plight of the American white woman has the validity of comparing the neck of a hanging man with the hands of an amateur mountain climber with rope burns. . . . The depth, extent, the intensity and importance—indeed the suffering and depravity of the real oppression blacks have experienced—can only be minimized in an alliance with white women who heretofore suffered little more than boredom, genteel repression and dishpan hands." Linda wrote this article when she was a graduate student at Purdue. By the time she joined the Purchase faculty she had substantially modified these views and embraced women's liberation as cause for black as well white women, although she remained skeptical about an alliance between the two movements.

In April 1970 President Nixon escalated the war on Vietnam by ordering an invasion of the neighboring country of Cambodia. This escalation of a war we thought was, however slowly, coming to an end enraged students throughout the United States. There was turmoil on college campuses like never seen before or since. In a sense there was a nationwide student uprising; hundreds of campuses went on strike and many were shutdown, some for the remainder of the academic year. ROTC buildings were burned on many campuses (this was the time of our abortive attempt to firebomb Berkeley's ROTC), and students at the University of California, Santa Barbara, burned the Bank of America building. The Guard was dispatched in more than a dozen states and it and the police often responded violently—at Kent State University in Ohio resulting in the killing by the Guard of four students.

Meanwhile, Governor Reagan declared, "If it takes a bloodbath, let it begin now." In the midst of these nationwide disorders and an already tense campus, the Berkeley administration closed the university and announced that all students scheduled for graduation in June would be graduated without having to complete course work. The closing of the university and the preemptive graduating of all students was an extraordinarily fortunate event for me because it resolved my French 4 dilemma. Thus, I can give Richard Nixon part of the credit for my earning, perhaps a better word is getting, my degree from Berkeley.

The repression of the Cambodian protests frightened and disillusioned us; that, along with the killing by the police a week later of two students at historically black Jackson State University in Mississippi, suggested the government was prepared to use any means necessary, including Reagan's bloodbath, to crush the revolution. Looking back fifty years later the idea that we could make a revolution seems little more than utopian wistfulness. How could we possibly have believed that students and blacks could mount a revolution against the most powerful state in the world? But many of us for a time did believe it. From 1968 until the early 1970s talk of revolution was in the air. We saw the ghetto rebellions—especially the Detroit rebellion—as a possible harbinger of urban guerilla war. We watched the movie *The Battle of Algiers* about the successful use of guerilla tactics during the Algerian Revolution for lessons that might apply in the US (*The Wretched of the Earth*, Frantz Fanon's theorizing of the Algerian Revolution, was the bible of the Panthers and other would-be black revolutionaries). We antici-pated well-trained veterans of Vietnam might return to constitute the core of a black liberation army. We rejoiced in the statements of support from

Fidel and Chairman Mao, especially Mao's 1969 statement in "support of the Afro-American struggle against Violent Repression" (I have a copy of the statement on the wall of my study today). We were enchanted by the revolutionary talk of the Panthers, Stokely, Rap Brown, and Angela Davis. In other words, talk of revolution was in the air.

While our talk of revolution was largely just that, talk, the possibility of revolution was also talked about in the highest circles of US police, military, and intelligence authorities. J. Edgar Hoover wrote a memorandum about the possibility of a "real mau mau in America" or the beginning of black revolution. US Army intelligence worried that troops might have to be brought from Europe or Vietnam to suppress the revolution many senior officers anticipated, and police in cities around the country began to establish military-style "tactical" units equipped with armored vehicles and assault weapons. These were not just idle musings. The FBI and the army implemented systematic plans to destroy whatever revolutionary potential there might have been at the time.

Even sober, mature scholars were taken with the talk. In his 1968 book *The Impossible Revolution? Black Power and the American Dream* the sociologist Lewis Killian concluded that while revolution was clearly impossible, it nevertheless might be attempted by blacks despite the overwhelming odds and terrible consequences. Even so restrained a scholar as Yale's Robert Dahl was moved in 1970 to publish *After the Revolution?* because he had "noticed that during the course of the last few years, revolution has swiftly become an in word in the United States." Dahl wrote that revolution in the US was "utterly impossible," but he concluded that the prominence of use of the word was "cathartic" for many.

But for us the most widely read scholar of revolution was Herbert Marcuse, the famous neo-Marxist professor at the University of California, San Diego. We read and discussed Marcuse endlessly, and I had a chance to meet him in October 1969 when COLD cosponsored a campus rally with Marcuse and Angela Davis as the speakers. The purpose of the rally was to protest Davis's dismissal from the UCLA faculty. Davis, a PhD candidate and student of Marcuse, was hired to teach philosophy at UCLA. However, once it was learned she was a member of the Communist Party, Governor Reagan convened a meeting of the Board of Regents and demanded her dismissal. Her firing made her a hero to blacks and the Left, so we invited her and her mentor to the campus. I was an escort for the event and had the good opportunity to meet and briefly talk with Marcuse. The 1970 Berkeley "Blue and Gold" class yearbook has a photo of me on the crowded podium with Marcuse.

Both Marcuse and Davis saluted the Berkeley students for their years of creative protests and called on us to fight for control of the university as base for revolutionary change in an alliance with black and brown peoples in the ghettos. It was great to see and hear Marcuse after spending so many hours discussing his work. His *Eros and Civilization* with its call for a liberated sexuality as key to human freedom was liberating and an important text for the counterculture. But by far his most important book for us was *One-Dimensional Man*. Ironically in this text he made the case that revolution was likely impossible in advanced industrial societies because of their ability to "deliver the goods." That is, by constantly creating false material needs, industrial societies integrate individuals into the system through technology, advertising, and mass media manipulation of their thinking and behavior. The results are a one-dimensional society in which the very ability to conceive revolutionary thought and action is near inconceivable.

In the midst of this generally pessimistic outlook, Marcuse held out the possibility that blacks in America, what he called "the substratum of the outcasts and the outsiders" who exist outside the one-dimensional society, might constitute a revolutionary force. However, even with the revolutionary potential of blacks he concluded, "It is nothing but a chance." It was this chance on which we based our revolutionary hopes. These hopes were dashed by Kent and Jackson State, and our realization that the government was prepared to kill us, to have Reagan's bloodbath. In a sense this was the revolution's Waterloo. People began to retreat, to look inward, to think of other ways to pursue liberation both individually and collectively.

Music, a song, symbolized the end of revolutionary expectancies. The Beatles, the most popular and creative of the 1960s rock groups, in 1968 released "Revolution," which said not only would there not be a revolution but mocked the very idea itself. Given our admiration and respect for the Beatles, "Revolution" was a disappointment. Indeed, many of us saw it as a betrayal and an especially bitter one because it said what we knew to be the painful truth. The song's call for passivity and affirmation that everything will be alright was followed by "Let It Be," where the Beatles sang to let the problems of the world—racism, war, oppression—be and there will be an answer without revolution or destruction. The Beatles' music of acquiescence and passivity was answered by the Rolling Stones in the same year with "Street Fighting Man." The most political of the Stones' recordings, it called out a revolutionary summons to the streets: Some radio stations banned the song, but for those with revolutionary expectancies, "Street Fighting Man" gave us a bit of solace.

With French 4 behind me, I was graduated with honors in 1970, although not completely honorably because I had plagiarized papers for two of the classes in which I got an A, including Glass's course on liberalism and the psyche and a class on the politics of the novel, for which the paper submitted was taken almost verbatim from an article in *Black World*. Plagiarism is the most serious crime in the academic community. The three times as a professor I have caught students plagiarizing I automatically gave them a failing grade and in one case recommended suspension. Yet, I committed this grave offense without any thought.

Having abandoned the idea of a diplomatic career, I had decided to become a lawyer with visions of contributing to the liberation struggle like the legendary William Kunstler or Charles Gary, the Black Panthers' lawyer. I was considering applying to the UCLA law school, but when I shared my plans with Professor Gregor, my advisor, he persuaded me to pursue a career as a scholar. I remember him saying, "You don't want to go to law school; the books are too heavy." More seriously, Gregor said being a scholar gave one *freedom*. He then described his Tuesday-Thursday afternoon teaching schedule and "June, July, and August." This two-day teaching schedule and the summers off gave professors the kind of freedom lawyers could only imagine. The freedom to pursue the life of the mind and if one wished (after tenure, he emphasized) one could do anything including opening a flower shop or becoming a political activist. Further, he contended, one could contribute more to the black struggle by writing articles and books than writing legal briefs and arguing cases in court. In addition, I noticed he drove a fancy sports car and heard he lived in a large house in the Berkeley hills. Not bad for a job in which one had to show up only twice a week. So, I applied to the UCLA graduate program in political science with the ambition to become a scholar of the politics of black liberation and contribute to the revolution by writing books and articles that mattered.

There was, however, one big stone ahead of me, the draft. Undergraduates were granted deferments from the draft, but students in graduate and professional schools were not. In December 1969 President Nixon issued an executive order instituting a lottery as the method of drafting persons. It was based on random drawings using one's birthday. In the first drawing my number made me immediately eligible for the draft upon graduation. I knew I could not accept the draft. First, under no circumstances would I go to Vietnam. Moreover, I thought the US military was largely a force for evil, an aggressive, imperial force for the subordination of Third World peoples. Finally, I did not like authoritarian institutions, whether armies or fraternities, and did not accept the army's hazing process—basic training—anymore than I did fraternities.

I was only several pounds above the weight that disqualified one for the military. So, I spent several months haphazardly trying to lose weight, but I could not. Not having the resources or inclination to avoid the draft by going to Canada, I had resigned myself to likely spending time in prison. Thus, as I prepared to return to Los Angeles, I was apprehensive and melancholy. I was accompanied on the drive (in my new green 1967 Mustang, which I had recently purchased with a student loan and savings from the rent strike) by Larry and his girlfriend Linda. As we enjoyed the beauty of the coast near San Luis Obispo, we passed a joint. A highway patrolman apparently observed us and pulled me over and arrested us for possession of marijuana. At that time possession of marijuana was a felony, and felons were automatically barred from the draft. I found this supremely ironic; here I was a resident of Berkeley, an epicenter of draft resistance and pot smoking, and no one had told me that to avoid the draft all I had to do was blow some smoke in a cop's face.

We were tried by a judge in San Luis Obispo and sentenced to a fine (I cannot recall the amount) and probation. We were told that after a period of years if we were not arrested the conviction would be expunged. Another good by-product of my arrest in San Luis Obispo: on one of the bus trips there I met a sister (I believe her name was Jacki) who was a student at the University of California, Santa Barbara, and she became my lover. However, in terms of lovers I was interested in getting back to LA to renew my relationship with Sophia, hoping I could get her to give up her liberated ways and become my woman and only my woman.

CHAPTER 4

Los Angeles Redux

UCLA and Bird

Located in affluent Westwood, near Beverly Hills, the UCLA campus in location and ethos was in 1970 far from Berkeley's counterculture, Telegraph Avenue, and People's Park. Neither a hippie nor the odor of weed could be found, and the campus was not noted for protests against the war on Vietnam or anything else. In general, of the nine campuses in the University of California system UCLA ranked second in status or prestige after the Berkeley campus. But nationally the campus was better known for its great basketball teams than for its academic excellence. The great Kareem Abdul Jabbar had completed his legendary career at UCLA the year before I arrived.

I entered graduate study with a kind of a chip on my shoulder about political science. At Berkeley the graduate students had prepared and distributed a pamphlet "Political Science at Berkeley: An Invitation to a Discussion" that was critical of what they saw as the conservative, politically irrelevant nature of the discipline. These concerns were raised by students who felt political science had little to say about the pressing issues of the day—racism, war, oppression—because it was too focused on the narrow science part of political science rather than the political. The students wrote:

> We argue that there is a malaise not just in the political science department at Berkeley, but also in the general political science discipline in America. It is seriously flawed, and its flaws are intimately related to the political system which it seeks to describe. . . . In other words, political science has come to define what is amenable to "scientific" inquiry, that is anything

which normally, routinely and generally affects government. These phenomena can be quantified and separated supposedly from the personal biases of the observer. Herein lies the essentially conservative tendency of political science: It is incapable of formulating a vision of what might be. It cannot transcend the description of routine occurrences.

At this time political science, like economics and sociology, aspired to be a science along the natural science model. The proper role of the social scientist in this view was to conduct value-free research, with an emphasis on the empirical testing of discrete hypotheses. A unified science of politics, it was argued, could eventually be constructed on the basis of this kind of small-bore empirical work. Like the natural sciences, this work would preferably be quantitative and published in specialized peer-reviewed journals. For me and the Berkeley graduate students this was nonsense. Political science in our view was the least scientific of the social sciences because it inherently relates to values—the creation of Aristotle's good society. The empirical testing of narrow hypotheses in an attempt to construct an objective, unified theory of politics intentionally removed values from the work.

The rejection of this approach to the study of politics was certainly my view as a student interested in the study of politics in order to contribute to the liberation of black people. I had no interest in contributing to the development of a unified theory of politics, which in any event I thought was a hopeless endeavor. The notion of a value-free social science was also anathema to those of us in black studies, who viewed our work in the new discipline in explicit value-laden, ideological terms—to contribute to the liberation of black people.

It was with these ideas that I started graduate work at UCLA. At that time the possibility of a unified theory of politics—Group Theory, System Theory, Cybernetics or Communications Theory, or Structural Functionalism—was at high tide in the discipline. The UCLA program required familiarity with each of these theories as reflected in the writings of David Truman, David Easton, Karl Deutsch, and Gabriel Almond. These grand theories of politics some fifty years later have little to show in terms of accomplishments and are rarely read or even acknowledged by young scholars in the discipline. The failure of these grand theories to yield much in terms of explaining and understanding the major political events of the time eventually yielded to this reality. In other words, the discipline came to see that the study of politics was not testing hypotheses in order to validate some grand theory of politics, but rather it was about using the scientific method to understand and explain existing political phenomena in their historical and structural contexts, looking toward contributing to normative or ideological understanding of the conditions of a good and just society. This was my view when I entered graduate study and it is my view fifty years later.

This is not to say there was nothing of value in the theories of politics I studied at the time. To the contrary, I found aspects of Truman's group theory useful and in *We Have No Leaders*, my major work, I used Easton's systems theory as framework for exploring the outcomes of the black freedom movements of the 1960s. The theory focused on how political systems respond to social movements or threats of revolution in order to maintain their existing values, structures, and power relations, which was helpful in modeling the outcomes of the civil rights and Black Power movements. But this was not an endeavor to test hypotheses in order to validate the theory but rather to use the theory as one means to explain and understand an important political development.

In addition to its misguided attempt to develop grand, unified theories of politics, political science in the early 1970s was just starting to pay attention to the problem of race in America, after a long sordid history of racism followed by a period of neglect. The civil rights movement, the Black Power movement, the ghetto rebellions, and black studies forced race onto the agenda of the discipline. But since it had so long ignored the subject, its existing research was largely irrelevant to understanding black politics, which meant that most universities, including UCLA, found themselves scrambling to get an academic handle on one of the most pressing problems confronting the nation. This usually involved a professor or two with some interest in the topic retooling in order to develop the capacity to do research and develop courses. At UCLA, which unlike Berkeley did not have a functioning Black Studies program, it was Professor Harry Scoble who had the interest and designed the course.

Like the undergraduate program at Berkeley, UCLA's graduate program required a three-course methods sequence, philosophy of science, major theories or conceptual frameworks in political science, and methodology with an emphasis on the quantitative. At Howard there was a similar three-course sequence, which reflected the discipline's focus on science as its core in which all students were to be trained. Prior to the advent of the "behavioral revolution" in political science, courses in Western philosophy were the required core. In the 1950s and 1960s there were bitter battles in the discipline between the traditionalist advocates of philosophy as the core and the behavioralist advocates of the scientific approach, but by the early 1970s the battles were over and the philosophers had been vanquished.

In addition to the core courses, I took other classes that were largely pedestrian: Political Behavior, Urban Politics, the Congress, and Non-Western Political Thought. The non-Western thought class was taught by Professor Richard Sklar, a specialist in African politics. Sklar's course was memorable, mainly because my first published work, a comparison of Marx and Fanon's theories of revolutionary violence, was prepared as a paper in his seminar. But by far my major work was with Scoble. I was the only black in the class that began graduate study in the department in 1970, and perhaps because of that Scoble took a special interest in me. In my first semester he asked me to be his teaching assistant in the black politics class, partly I guess because I was black but also perhaps because of my unique knowledge of the subject based on my courses at Berkeley. This began a relationship of collegiality and friendship that lasted until Scoble's death. He was the first white person to become a close friend.

Scoble's major area of research was interest groups, but after the Watts riot he developed an interest in black politics and, subsequently, political repression as a state response to dissident movements. His interest in both subjects came about in part as a result of his work on the research staff of the commission appointed by the governor to investigate the rebellion in Watts (the McCone Commission, after former CIA director John McCone who chaired the commission). Disappointed with the commission's "riff-raff" theory of the riots, Scoble was one of the first scholars to argue that the riot represented a political uprising or at least an uprising with political significance. The work on the commission staff led him to a serious interest in black politics and to offering UCLA's first class on the subject, an undergraduate upper-division course. In addition to working as his teaching assistant I took his class on political repression. This experimental class evolved from his study of the Black Power movement, especially the Black Panther Party. Using a modified version of Easton's system model, Scoble advanced the theory that all political systems engage in political repression—what he called "the negative sanctioning" of ideas, individuals, and organizations considered "outside the mainstream." This was as true of democratic states like the United States as it was of authoritarian ones like Soviet Russia. I used Scoble's theory of repression as part of the theoretical framework in We Have No Leaders.

Shortly after I arrived at UCLA, Scoble and his first wife divorced and a year or so later he married a much younger woman and moved to the University of Illinois at Chicago Circle. Partly out of his work on political repression Scoble and his new wife, Laurie, created the Human Rights Internet, a research and advocacy organization devoted to inserting human rights concerns into US foreign policy and to encouraging political scientists to research human rights issues. The Internet sponsored panels on human rights at political science conferences, published an occasional newsletter, and developed linkages with Amnesty International and other nongovernmental organizations. In 1978 as chair of the lecture committee of the social science division at the college at Purchase I arranged for Harry to visit to lecture on human rights. It was indeed a pleasure to host my old mentor to discuss human rights and US foreign policy as President Carter was making human rights an important part of US foreign policy.

As discussed later, Harry likely played a role in my advancement to doctoral studies at UCLA, and he was important in my decision to leave UCLA and complete the doctorate at Howard. Until his death he was an abiding friend, writing numerous letters for me for faculty positions. When I applied at Yale, he not only wrote a fulsome letter but called colleagues on the faculty to put in a good word for me.

Harry was a good drinking man, and the last time I saw him in the late 1970s was the last time I got drunk. He was then living in Washington in a large house that served as both residence and office of the Internet. My wife and I joined the Scobles and his old UCLA colleague David Sears and his girlfriend for an evening of food, drink, and conversation. There was more drink and conversation than food and by the time we left after midnight I was barely able to stumble to the car, where I fell asleep as Bird drove us home.

I made one other friend at UCLA, Gerald Bender, who was an advanced doctoral student specializing in the study of the then Portuguese colonies of Angola and Mozambique. Gerry offered advice on how to navigate the program and later, like Harry, wrote fulsome letters of recommendation. My relationship and friendship with Gerry I thought was fairly straightforward. To him it was more complicated as he told me in a 1972 letter:

You know, Bob, I have taken a special interest in perhaps a dozen or so students who've come through UCLA and while it is always personally rewarding to see some people go on and do well or see your own convictions confirmed by others (which happened in your case), you are only the second person that has bothered to thank me. . . . In our relationship things were even more complicated than they normally are given our society and the inevitable way they complicate any relationship between black and white. There were times when my own neurosis cautioned me to avoid you for fear anything I might do good or bad would be interpreted as one more bleeding heart and therefore why even try. After trying to get as close to my superego as I am capable, I convinced myself that was never the case, but on the other hand I was never sure as to how you interpreted it and, therefore, I maintained my doubts. I believed at the time and still believe you were worth every moment of time I expended on your behalf and whatever time I spent worrying about the neurosis I referred to above. I really believe you deserve every possible break, as I put it in one of my recommendations, I believe you are capable of teaching (if you choose) at any university (including the ivy league). Anyway, this may sound a bit incoherent to you but it is a rather long way of telling you that I do appreciate your kind words and I certainly hope not only the best, but I am prepared to do anything within my powers to help you realize your future goals.

I found the time at UCLA largely uneventful. As I said the classes were generally pedestrian, but I did well in them and a couple of them were foundational for subsequent work. I did not get to know any of my white classmates. They did not seek me out, nor I them. I simply completed my evening seminars and returned home. As the only black student, I did not feel any sense of racism in the department from faculty or students. However, as I was about to leave the department Clyde Daniel-Halisi, the Karenga associate I referred to in chapter 2, a first-year graduate student in the department, circulated a letter suggesting racial bias in the department and asked me to share my experiences.

The letter raised questions about the small number of blacks in the PhD program, the small number who had received the PhD, the "academically conservative" nature of the department, and black students being "hassled out of the department because of racial discrimination." I do not have a record of my response to the letter. I am sure I would have responded, but there is nothing in the files. While I shared the letter's concern about the small number of blacks in the program and the even smaller number completing the PhD, as well as the department's academic conservatism, I would not have agreed that in my experience blacks were hassled out of the department because of racism. In my experience the opposite was the case.

The UCLA graduate political science program involved admission initially to the MA program and upon successful completion advancement to doctoral study. However, if the results of the MA examination were unsatisfactory, one was granted a terminal MA and denied admission to the doctoral program. Initially I was informed that my performance on the MA examination was unsatisfactory and I would not be allowed to advance to doctoral studies. Sometime later the decision was reversed, and I was informed that I could go on to doctoral work. I was never told formally or informally by the department chair or any other faculty member the basis for the reversal. I assume it was because I was black, and the department decided it did not wish to deny advancement to its only black student (the examinations were evaluated blindly, so initially the committee would not have known my identity). I also assume Bender and Scoble may have intervened on my behalf, although neither ever mentioned this to me. Nevertheless, I consider this another instance of my benefiting from affirmative action, where race was taken into consideration in order to give me an advantage.

In any event, this did not matter because by the time I sat for the examination I had already decided to leave UCLA to go to Howard to complete the doctorate. Scoble and I independently came to the conclusion I should go to Howard to study with the young Ron Walters, who had just become chair of the Howard Political Science Department. I was attracted to Walters because of his black liberation scholarship in *Black World* and *The Black Scholar*, and Scoble was impressed in conversations with him about his plans for a comprehensive black politics field at Howard. Since there were no graduate courses in black politics at UCLA, Scoble said if I were really interested in serious study of the field, Howard was the place.

Walters was a pioneering black studies scholar, the founding chair of Brandeis's Black Studies Department, and he was to become the leading black liberation scholar-activist of his generation, and a friend and mentor. But at the time he was a young neophyte scholar trying to start a fledgling new field. In addition to the allure of Walters and the new black politics field, I thought it would be useful and interesting to study black politics in the nation's capital at the most prestigious black university in the nation and in a city with an emerging black population majority.

One of the best decisions of my career was to go to Howard to study with Walters. The best decision of my life was to marry Scottie Bess Gibson. I returned to Los Angeles with the idea that Sophia and I might begin anew our relationship, and she would enter into a monogamous partnership. This idea was wistful. At the time of my return she was attempting to maintain a monogamous relationship with another man, and while I was disappointed, I understood and accepted her decision. Moreover, while I liked and admired Sophia's free spirit and sexually liberated ways, I also knew that I did not wish to be her man alone. This hypocrisy she would not have accepted, nor would I have wished her to accept it. So, although we occasionally dated, it was more like old friends than lovers. Our friend Margaret, her former roommate, however, thought we were establishing a more permanent relationship, and for some reason she objected. In order to disrupt the relationship, she told me about Scottie, her coworker at the telephone company where they both worked as PBX operators. She told me Scottie was a nice girl from Louisiana who had recently moved to LA and that we should have a lot in common.

Scottie often reminds me that, on our first meeting, I picked her up and brought her to my house (actually Nell's house since I was still living with her) and on the way stopped at a liquor store and asked her if she wanted a beer but told her I had enough money for only one. This was not exactly an auspicious start to the relationship but after a time we began to date, although I was also seeing two other women.

Tall, thin, brown-skinned, with luscious lips, Scottie was an attractive woman. Unlike the other women I had dated who were either Los Angeles natives or longtime residents, Scottie, coming from rural Louisiana, and I shared cultural affinities. She was born in 1952 in Pioneer, a hamlet of about a hundred people in Northeast Louisiana near the Mississippi state line. Compared to where I was born, Scottie's area was much more impoverished and racially oppressive. It was also more isolated, more rural, and underdeveloped. The road, for example, leading to her house was unpaved. On my first visit in the aftermath of a heavy rain I drove the car into a ditch from which her father had to pull me out with a mule.

Scottie is the eleventh of thirteen children. Unlike with my mother where half of her children died, most of her siblings survived. A brother was killed in a gun accident at a young age, another was murdered after we were married, and an older sister who briefly lived with us died of a blood disorder also after our marriage. But even today she has nine siblings.

Scottie's father and his brothers inherited a large amount of land from their father and were small independent farmers. Scottie's daddy Willie "Luke" Gibson and his children raised vegetables, pigs, chickens, and a little cotton. This plus odd jobs allowed the family to be self-sufficient. Luke, as he was universally called, prided himself that neither his wife—Ethel Lee—nor his daughters ever had to work for white people.

Scottie's school was desegregated in 1969, so she spent her last years of high school in a nonsegregated environment. Immediately after graduation she moved to Los Angeles to live with her oldest brother, Buddy, a construction worker. Shortly after her arrival she found the job at the telephone company in Santa Monica, with plans to attend Pepperdine University, which was then located nearby in South Central.

Scottie was not a prude, but neither was she sexually liberated. She had the traditional attitudes of small-town, rural southern young black women about sex, thus it was months before we made love. Although I was occasionally seeing other women, I viewed Scottie as my woman. We saw each other weekly, often spending long nights at the Santa Monica beach, where she shared an apartment in nearby Venice. Yet, I had given no thought to marrying Scottie or anyone else. This all changed as a result of the intervention of her brother Buddy.

Buddy did not like me. Although I was a graduate student at the city's most prestigious university, he viewed me as a sandal-wearing, dope-smoking, nappy-headed hippie, who never combed his hair and was likely trying to take advantage of his sister sexually and financially. He did everything he could to break us up, going so far as forbidding her from seeing me. Ironically, it was his heavy-handed attempts to break us up that resulted in our coming closer together and eventually marrying.

On a Saturday night Scottie and I went to visit my friend Al who lived in a motel. Somehow, for reasons that are still unclear to me, Buddy found us at the motel and assumed we were there to have sex. Outraged, he told Scottie he was going to send her back to Louisiana. Although we agreed he could not force her to return, we thought it best she did in order to make a clean break and then come back and we could be together.

In early May 1971 she went back for a week or so and then returned to LA. Knowing only what Buddy had told them about me, her parents, especially her mother, were adamantly opposed to her returning to Los Angeles to live with me. She defied them because she was committed to being with me and showing Buddy that he could not keep us apart. Before she left for Louisiana, we discussed the situation with Nell and she agreed that if Scottie returned, she would be welcome to live with us in her house. Her offer was sincere and generous, but this was an awkward situation since Scottie had quit her job at the telephone company and I had only a modest income from my UCLA graduate fellowship. But as Little Milton sang in a popular song of the early 1960s, we were determined that while "we may not have a home to call our own, we were gonna make it." We did, now for almost a half century.

Scottie returned in May, and after some hesitation on my part and with the prodding of my sisters we were married in August. All of my friends were opposed to our marriage. Dwight and his girlfriend Louisa and Larry and his girlfriend Linda rushed down from Berkeley to try to convince me it was a mistake to marry so early and to someone so young (Scottie was nineteen) and not college educated. Al thought it was a mistake, as did Margret who had brought us together. We married after services in a church where my niece Brenda was the pianist by her preacher. My sisters and Al were present but none of Scottie's family, whom we had not informed of the wedding. After the brief ceremony, we had a chitlin dinner at a soul food restaurant and drove to Tijuana, Mexico, for a one-evening honeymoon. Shortly thereafter Scottie got a job as a receptionist at a photography studio, and we were able to rent an apartment in Baldwin Hills.

Sometime shortly before or after our marriage, I began to call Scottie "Bird." I do not now recall why; perhaps it was from Chuck Jackson's "Any Day Now," where he sang of his "wild beautiful Bird" and his fear that one day she would fly away. Anyway, even if this was not the origins of the name, it is nice to think so because I have never wanted my beautiful bird to fly away. For all of my books I acknowledge Bird's assistance and indicate that without her they could not have been written. In a narrow sense this is true because she has edited and typed all of my manuscripts, beginning with the dissertation. Indeed, this is the first manuscript that I have typed (word processed) partly because I had nothing else to do and Bird was very busy.

Although a typing class was offered in high school, I did not take it because the teacher did not like me, and I was convinced she would not allow me to pass. In college my sister Cleo and Larry typed my papers and at UCLA I hired a typist. Bird began to type some of my papers in graduate school at Howard, but she really became my full-time typist when it came to the dissertation. I had planned to hire a typist but when Bird learned of the high cost of typing a five-hundred-page manuscript, she said that was too much for the family budget, so she developed the skills necessary to become a professional editor and typist. (At Howard when I was on the faculty, she occasionally edited and typed for other members of the faculty.)

But as I said this is only in the narrowest sense that Bird has been indispensable in my life. In the broad sense she has been my everything; lover, confident, best friend, and quasi-agent. Bird is one of the smartest, hardest working, clearest thinking persons that I have known. She aspired to be a lawyer; she would have been a good one, but she gave up her career ambition to help me with mine. She never hesitated or protested as she abandoned her education in order to support me.

When we moved to New York Bird attended Borough of Manhattan College evenings while working full-time at the city housing authority. She had to discontinue this schooling when we left for Washington for my study at Howard. In Washington she attended the University of the District of Columbia but again had to abandon her studies when we left Washington for the college at Purchase in New York. While we were at Purchase, she completed work for the associate degree at Westchester Community College and was accepted to Manhattanville College, the famous school for elite Catholic women, but she declined and instead went to Pace University, which was across the street from where we lived. But again, she had to drop out when I returned to Howard to teach. By this time, she probably had accumulated more than three and a half years of course credits, but she concluded that further pursuit of her education was fruitless because it was likely it would be again interrupted as I moved to yet another university.

Although I supported Bird attending college, I never gave any thought to not moving so she could complete her schooling. This was partly because I put my career ahead of hers, and partly because I still held to the tradition of not wishing my wife to work outside of the house. This was also for selfish reasons. If she worked full-time, she would of course have less time to help me with my work. My schedule allowed me to be home most of the time, and if she was not at work, we could be together and could make love whenever we felt like it.

While I was in graduate school at Howard and on the Purchase faculty Bird worked at a variety of jobs through temporary agencies, and for a year near full-time for the Coalition of Eastern Native Americans in Washington. My traditional view of having a nonworking wife was reinforced when we decided to have children. I insisted that when we had a child, she would become a full-time mother and our children would not be placed in day care. Our agreement was reinforced when Blanch, our first child, was born moderately retarded. We agreed that her first priority was taking care of Blanch, making sure she got the best mental health and educational opportunities available. Ironically, the focus on securing educational opportunities for Blanch eventually resulted in Bird carving out a career as an educational advocate, where she has in effect practiced a kind of law without a license. Partly because of her advocacy work she became an influential activist in local school politics and a prospective candidate for the school board.

In 1975 Congress enacted the Education for All Children Act, amended in 1990 as the Individuals with Disabilities Act. These laws prohibited discrimination against students with disabilities, provided federal funds to assist school districts in educating disabled students, and mandated specific requirements to assure a "free, appropriate, public education" to all disabled students. These requirements specified that an Individualized Education Program (IEP) be developed by each school in order to assure that each disabled student received an education to the best of her abilities. To implement these requirements federal, state, and local educational authorities developed a complex set of regulations. For many, these regulations constituted a maze that was difficult to comprehend. In order to make sure Blanch received what she needed as the law required, Bird mastered the regulations beginning in the White Plains School District while we were at Purchase and then in Montgomery County, Maryland, while we were at Howard. Once she mastered the law and regulations for Blanch, she began to help others through the IEP process.

In Maryland Bird's work was an avocation. When we moved to the Bay Area it became a vocation. In Richmond, the suburban city where we lived, Bird within several years of our arrival had established a reputation as an educational advocate initially for disabled students but eventually for all children whose parents needed help in navigating the educational bureaucracy or whose children faced disciplinary problems. Educational advocacy is now a course of study in universities, indicating a recognition that many parents need professional help in order for their children to get through elementary and secondary school. I think this is a sad commentary on the state of American education. But this appears to be the case throughout the United States.

In any event, Bird is a pioneer in this advocacy work and gained a reputation as the go-to person in Richmond if your child was having trouble with the school bureaucracy. She was so effective in this work that the school district offered her a job as its ombudswoman, which she declined. Although the work would have paid well, she declined the offer because it would have involved full-time work, and also because she wished to maintain her independence as an advocate and activist (typically she earned $15,000–$20,000 a year in fees paid by parents or the school district). She also knew I still objected to her having a full-time job.

In addition to her advocacy, she became an influential activist in school politics in Richmond, especially on issues concerning black students. This included organizing several parent groups and leading a fifty-mile march to Sacramento to secure more funding for the district when it was near bankruptcy. For years she was chair of the local NAACP's education committee and on the boards of the Richmond Education Trust and the Development Disabilities Council of Contra Costa County. She worked as a consultant in the San Francisco office of Parents Helping Parents, an advocacy group, and to Adams Esq., a law firm that specializes in representing students with disabilities.

She was implored to run for the school board, but I objected because it would have meant more disruption of our home, since the phone it seems was already constantly ringing and she seemed to be always at meetings, although I probably exaggerate. She said she did not wish to run but I suspect if I had not objected, she might have run and won. While not running herself, she worked in the successful campaigns of several progressive candidates.

Sometimes I feel guilty about always uprooting Bird from her schooling, not supporting her ambitions to become a lawyer, and always putting my career ahead of her aspirations. I am happy that she was able to turn an avocation into a vocation and become a pioneering educational advocate and an influential player in school politics. Even in this work I was not as supportive as I might have been, often complaining about the ringing phones and the constant meetings.

All and all I do not think Bird has major regrets about my patriarchal, paternalistic, selfish attitudes about her not having a career as a lawyer. Otherwise, I think I have been a good husband and father who treated her with love, loyalty, admiration, and respect. I have not had sex with another woman since our marriage and was never away from home for more than a few days, turning down opportunities for fellowships and visiting professorships that would have required being away from her and the children for months. Bird and I were married at a time when the traditional notion of marriage and family was under challenge by the feminist movement. If we had met a decade later, 1980 rather than 1970, she may have made different choices and my beautiful bird might have flown away.

Music after marriage began to matter less in my life. It was not that marriage changed my interest in music, although I did go to parties, dances, and clubs less frequently. But the more important reason was that the music changed. Rock, soul, and rhythm and blues declined, along with messages in the music. Prince and Michael Jackson, two of the most dominant figures of the time, in my view, ran away from blackness and displayed a disquieting androgyny. Disco, a dominant genre of the era, also seemed androgynous, which to an extent it was as it emerged out of the gay club scene in New York and Los Angeles. Finally rap emerged as the dominant genre of black popular music. I did not like rap; I did not consider it music but rather loud and often indecipherable talking.

When I was growing up and playing my music my mother would often say, "Boy, turn that noise off." To me rap was noise. As a teen I promised that as a parent I would listen to my children's music and not dismiss it as noise. But with rap I could not do it; I tried but I could not bear to listen. Each generation is shaped by its music and the times shape the music. As I contend the 1960s was the greatest generation, so was our music. So, I began to listen to the music of the past, Dylan, Motown, Curtis, the Beatles, and of course the blues.

By 1972 Bird and I were pleased we were going to leave LA and go someplace where we could begin anew, without the telephone calls of old girlfriends or the hostility of her family. It was therefore with anticipation that we looked forward to moving to Washington. Howard, however, lost my application and despite repeated queries did not respond in time for fall admission. Fortunately, I somehow learned of New York's New School for Social Research's new program in urban policy analysis, and the generous $4,500 RCA-NBC fellowship. While I had no particular interest in urban politics or policy analysis, the program was innovative and New York was a place we had read about and thought it would be a good place to live for a year while I straightened out the Howard application problem. Bird had a cousin who lived in Harlem, so we would not be completely alone in the big city. In August 1972 after a nice going-away party at Cleo's we were off to James Baldwin's Harlem.

CHAPTER 5

New York City, the New School, and Discovering Ethnicity

Scottie's cousin, Georgia Stokes, met us at LaGuardia and took us to her place in Harlem. This was very fortunate because without her assistance we would have been babes in the woods, having to take cabs and live in a hotel, which we could not afford, and we would have been nervous and a little afraid. We found Manhattan disconcerting, quite different from Los Angeles, which is really not a city but a series of relatively discrete places—Hollywood, downtown, Westwood, Century City—a series of cities within a city with no center or core. The thirty-four-square-mile island of Manhattan by contrast was a city, the towering skyline, the swarms of people all seemingly in a hurry, the noise, the endless cabs, the city underground—the complex subway system. All this was exciting but bewildering; we were lucky to have Georgia in the first weeks to introduce us to the complexity of the city.

Georgia, in her midfifties, had lived in the city for decades, with her mother—Sister Hunter (cousin sister to us)—in a building she owned in Central Harlem near 125th and Lennox Avenue. Georgia was a beautician, a numbers banker, and host of occasional weekend poker games. Her building included a small apartment, which was vacant when we arrived and in which she allowed us to stay until we could find a place uptown near the New School.

Living in Harlem for several weeks was a fascinating experience— Baldwin's Harlem coming alive—the stereotypical streetcorner men, people sitting on the stoops, the corner churches, the street orators, the junkies, the hustlers, and all the characters of Baldwin's novels and Claude Brown's *Manchild in the Promised Land*. We made the first of many visits to Adam

Powell's church, Michaux's famous bookstore, and to the Mosque of the Nation of Islam then led by Minister Louis Farrakhan. For the spectacle of it we went to a "service" conducted by the flamboyant Reverend Ike.

We became very close to Georgia, Cousin Sister, and Georgia's son Hillard, who lived in a small Greenwich Village apartment with the longest winding flight of stairs I had ever seen. When I returned to New York to teach at Purchase, we lived in suburban Westchester County but frequently visited Georgia and Cousin Sister in Harlem. While living in Georgia's place, Bird and I with the assistance of the New School staff were busy looking for a place of our own. The staff connected us with Andre Juneau, a French Canadian enrolled in the program, who was also looking for a place. We eventually found a place in Chelsea, a two-bedroom ground-floor apartment. Andre and his wife Luci and Bird and I shared the apartment for the year we spent in New York. Within walking distance of the New School as well as Greenwich Village and Times Square, Chelsea was a fascinating little village known for its large gay community. And the apartment building had a doorman!

After completing his master's in the New School program, Andre went on to have a noteworthy career in Canadian government, focusing on cities and rising to the position of first deputy minister of the federal department of infrastructure. In 2011 he was awarded the Queen Elizabeth Diamond Jubilee medal for service to Canada's cities. The last time I heard from Andre was a 2008 telephone call congratulating me on the election of the first African American president.

Through Georgia's daughter Frankie, Bird learned of a job as receptionist-clerk at the New York City Housing Authority and was employed within several weeks of our arrival. She also started night classes at Borough of Manhattan Community College. Shortly before we left New York for Howard she became pregnant with our first child, Blanch Elizabeth.

The "campus" of the New School was a large office building near Washington Square and New York University. During and after World War II the New School developed a reputation as haven for a distinguished group of émigré scholars from Europe who specialized in philosophy and studies in historical sociology. The program in urban affairs and policy analysis was near completely different from the New School's tradition of historical and philosophical studies, as it was founded on the idea of bringing knowledge to bear in the development of practical solutions to problems through professional policy analysis.

The Center for New York City Affairs was founded in 1968 by Henry Cohen, an urban planner and dean of the center, who was a former functionary in the Robert Wagner and John Lindsay mayoral administrations, rising to the position of deputy city administrator in Lindsay's administration. He left city government and established the center in order to train what he saw as a badly needed cadre of "urban professionals" in a curriculum of sophisticated urban research, planning, policy analysis, and evaluation. In teaching and research, the center worked in close collaboration with the departments and agencies of New York City government.

The core of the center was the Graduate Department of Urban Affairs and Policy Analysis, which awarded the MA as a terminal professional degree. The department was headed by Jacob Ukeles, a public administration scholar with experience in city government. What Cohen and Ukeles set out to do was what Daniel Patrick Moynihan in a 1965 article called "The Professionalization of Reform." This fatally flawed idea was based on the assumption that many of the seemingly intractable problems of domestic policy could, given the "econometric revolution" and the "exponential growth of knowledge," be rendered largely technical and administrative rather than political. This is how Moynihan put it in the article: "This is precisely the type of decision making that is suited to the techniques of modern organization, and which ends up in the hands of persons who make a profession of it. They are less and less political decisions and more and more administrative ones. They are decisions that can be made by consensus rather than conflict."

Although Ukeles as chair of the New School's policy analysis department was committed intellectually and programmatically to policy analysis and the professionalization of reform, he was aware of its inherent, possibly fatal flaws. In a 1977 article in *Public Administration Review*, reflecting in part on his New School experience, he wrote:

> Policy analysis is an activity faced with an essentially hostile environment in the classical policy-making process in the United States. The complex processes of negotiation and bargaining whereby policy is made have been well-documented in the literature. In such a fragmented rapidly moving process, it is not obvious what kind of analysis can be done and how it should bear on decision making. The political nature of data in policy making, very short time spans for research and relatively little staff resources, all place premium on "shooting from the hip," as opposed to careful thought and systematic weighing of options.

Nevertheless, Ukeles concluded that the way around these difficulties was the development of policy analysis as a "professional role with its own discipline" because "the activity is most likely to flourish, improve and become established if it is taught and practiced as a separate identifiable field." This was essentially the course of study we followed at the New School.

The core of the policy analysis process involved five relatively discrete although overlapping steps or procedures. First, identify and assess the relevant policymaking environment and decision makers. Second, identify the policy issue or problem to be solved. Third, identify the policy alternatives available appropriate to the policy environment and the decision makers. Fourth, identify criteria relevant to choosing among alternatives. Finally, on the basis of the best available information, assess the pros and cons of the alternatives in terms of relevant criteria and political feasibility. Each of these steps require the collection and analysis of a lot of data, often requiring the work of a team of analysts. We worked in teams of three to five, dividing the steps among team members. The innovative part of the New School's approach was that from the beginning to the end of the work the team worked in close collaboration with a relevant city agency. The final written report and an oral presentation were made to the staff of the agency, in addition to New School faculty and students.

In my year in the program, I was part of a team that attempted to deal with the real and perceived problem of growing drug addiction in the city, and its perceived connection to a rising crime rate. This was at the time of President Nixon's "war on drugs," and the draconian "Rockefeller drug laws," in which the governor persuaded the legislature to enact laws imposing long, mandatory prison sentences for the possession of even small amounts of any illegal drug. In our project we worked closely with the city's Addiction Services Agency, which provided data as well as making staff available for consultation. At the end we prepared a long, multi-authored report that we presented to the faculty and agency staff for critique and evaluation. Unfortunately, I did not keep a file on our work nor a copy of the final report, and I have only a vague memory of the report. I do recall that our major recommendation was to make it a crime not just to possess heroin but simply to be high on the drug. We envisioned, I think, arresting addicts but, rather than prison, forcing them into various treatment programs. This, I gather, we judged was an alternative to the Rockefeller policy because we treated addiction as a health problem rather than as a crime requiring punishment.

Looking back, I certainly wished I had kept a file on our work and a copy of the report because I cannot now see how we arrived at our recommendation. It was constitutionally dubious, and likely would have targeted the visible street addicts, who were disproportionately poor, black, and Hispanic. To put this in the best light for me now, I can recall that the team worked by consensus and I may have joined the consensus on this recommendation with reservations or I may have thought it was better than the Rockefeller approach, and thus supported it as a way to screen out worst alternatives. I cannot recall the response of the faculty or the agency staff to our report or the grade we received, but thankfully the agency ignored our recommendation.

Overall, I recall my year at the New School as pleasant, intellectually interesting, and worthwhile. The faculty was diverse including one woman and an African American, Robert Hearn, a political scientist, who after leaving the New School became a major policy advisor to Kurt Schmoke, Baltimore's first black mayor. The classes were heavily methodological, and in addition to the academics the faculty often included New York City government officials. The faculty attempted to foster collegiality with the students. Dean Cohen and Professor Ukeles, for example, each gave dinners for us at their residences. I recall Ukeles's dinner was completely kosher providing a bit of insight into that aspect of Jewish culture. There were also good and close relationships between the students in the program. The 1972 entering class of about fifteen was largely white and male although I recall several women in the class, including one black woman. Our teamwork required us to work closely, and the entire class socialized together. The New School was my first experience with collegial and friendship relations with white students, as the team often dined together and attended movies and plays.

Professional policy analysis was at its peak of influence in the 1970s, embraced by the Carter administration in its first years. Thereafter, it went into decline; I would say inevitable decline because in the end policy development in the United States is for the most part the product of ideological, partisan, and interest conflict rather than the systematic weighing of policy alternatives by policy professionals.

In addition to study and work, Bird and I explored the city, Harlem, Times Square, Greenwich Village, the United Nations. At a Village club we saw an intimate performance by the legendary blues master Big Mama Thornton. I do not recall attending any Broadway plays, but we attended multiple Off-Broadway shows and performances by Douglas Turner Ward's Negro Ensemble Company, which was then at its peak of influence.

I also experienced the nation's white ethnic diversity (and black in terms of West Indians) for the first time. Growing up in Benton white people were monolithic—all the same to me—although I recall one Italian

American (referred to almost universally as a Dago) and a Jewish resident, both storekeepers. I did not understand these ethnic differences—to me Italians were just white people and Jews were people in the Bible.

Los Angeles and the Bay Area were not much different; the major ethnic groups were blacks, Latinos, whites, and Asian Americans. Ethnic differences among whites while they likely existed (although California was more a melting pot than New York City) were not apparent in Los Angeles' cultural or political life. I was vaguely aware of a distinctive Jewish enclave in West Los Angeles, and Jews' role as a distinctive liberal voting bloc in city politics. But in general Jews in Los Angeles and the Bay Area remained people of the Bible more than a really existing ethnic group.

New York City was completely different. I had read Nathan Glazer and Daniel Patrick Moynihan's *Beyond the Melting Pot*, their 1963 detailed study of the Jews, Italians, Irish, Puerto Ricans, and blacks of New York City. But in my year in the city these groups became real people rather than chapters in a book. I was fascinated how whites and blacks in the city were able to make fine ethnic distinctions between whites, and how often both blacks and whites used Archie Bunker–type stereotypes to refer to the groups (an Italian American visiting the housing authority asked Scottie where we lived and when told we were sharing an apartment with a French Canadian, he used an ethnic slur and told her to be careful because the French could not be trusted). This was my introduction to the real world of ethnicity in American society.

By chance I had the good opportunity to reinforce my intuitive grasp of ethnicity in the city by becoming a part of a scholarly team that was conducting a major study of ethnicity in New York City politics. Dale Nelson and Michael Bucuvalas were PhD candidates in political science at Columbia. As part of a larger project to study New York City neighborhoods they received funds to conduct a detailed survey-based study of ethnicity in New York for their dissertations. Working as part of the staff of Columbia's renowned Bureau of Applied Social Research, Bucuvalas and Nelson decided that rather than do a citywide study they would focus on five ethnically distinct blocks in a single New York City neighborhood, which would allow for the use of observation as well as the survey as methodologies.

The neighborhood selected was Washington Heights–Inwood, a lower middle-class community in upper Manhattan. The focus on a single neigh- borhood rather than a citywide sample allowed for controls for sociode- mographic and contextual differences, and each ethnic group in the study would have similar contexts for their social, cultural, and political behavior.

Finally, rather than do a communitywide survey, we surveyed five relatively ethnically homogeneous blocks in Washington Heights–Inwood. The five blocks were selected with two basic criteria in mind: they should have a high concentration of each of the groups selected for study—Irish, Jews, Blacks, Cubans, and Dominicans—and the sociodemographic characteristics (such as gender and age) of their inhabitants should be as similar as possible. This procedure reinforced subcultural interaction between friends and neighbors of similar ethnic backgrounds.

In their design of the project, Nelson was responsible for the Hispanic blocks, Bucuvalas for the white blocks, but for the black block they and their advisors agreed that it would be useful to bring on an African American as a third coinvestigator. Somehow—I do not recall how—they learned of me at the New School and that I had a master's in political science from UCLA, where I had experience in teaching and researching black politics. So, they invited me to join the project. The five-block project was a great opportunity for me to learn the survey methodology and to study ethnic politics. When I joined the project, it was at the survey design stage. Thus, I had the opportunity to participate in the writing and pretesting of the questionnaire, its administration, and final analysis of the results. I also engaged in observation, hanging out on the black block and having occasional conversations with residents. In addition to this methodological expertise, I became thoroughly familiar with the literature on ethnic politics in the United States.

Ira Katznelson, then a young professor on the Columbia faculty, was an informal advisor to the project, and I used some of the data in his 1981 book *City Trenches*. Katznelson went on to become one of the leading political scientists of his generation. Nelson and Bucuvalas wrote dissertations based on the Five Block Project. Nelson pursued a career in the academy as a professor at Fordham University, while Bucuvalas pursued a career in the corporate sector. I wrote a long theoretical paper based on the project: "Sources of Urban Ethnicity: A Comparison of Alternative Explanations." The article argued that there were multiple theories of ethnic political behavior—class, ethclass, culture, interest—each with some explanatory power and that "there is little to be gained by the continuing debate between the advocates of class vs. culture vs. structural explanations of ethnic political behavior, especially if one perspective is presented at the expense of the other. Rather, each may play an explanatory role." I also concluded because blacks and Hispanics occupy subordinate positions in New York's social structure compared to the white ethnic groups, they tend to view their ethnicity as a strategic resource in their struggles for social, economic, and political advancement.

Dale and his wife Carol and Scottie and I became close friends after we moved back to New York in 1975. Ironically, he applied for the position at San Francisco State that I accepted in 1989. In 2000 he retired and moved to the Bay Area where we resumed our friendship, although by now he and Carol were divorced and he had remarried (I discuss in chapter 7 Dale's role in fighting a case of racism in Westchester's housing market that I had to deal with when I was on the Purchase faculty).

Meanwhile, while doing my studies at the New School, exploring New York City, and working on the Five Block Project, I renewed my application to Howard's PhD program. Inexplicably, there continued to be bureaucratic delays in processing my application. In February I wrote Andrew Billingsley, who had left Berkeley's Ethnic Studies program to become vice president of academic affairs at Howard, about the situation. He responded quickly, indicating he forwarded my letter to Walters. On November 28 Walters responded, apologizing for the delay and indicating his office had no record of my application or prior communications. But "certainly I welcome a brother who has training such as yours and who wants to make it his business to further his education as well as contribute to the process which we are building to serve the needs of black students and community."

Subsequently, I arranged a meeting with Ron when he visited New York. He brought with him my letter of admission to the program. Thus began nearly four decades of friendship and collaboration with a man I believe to be the most consequential black activist scholar of the last half century.

CHAPTER 6

Howard and the Black Experience

Howard University, founded after the Civil War and named for General Oliver O. Howard, the head of the Freedmen's Bureau, is the only comprehensive historically black university in the United States. Along with Gallaudet College for the Deaf and Hard of Hearing, it is one of two universities that receive a direct appropriation from the US Congress. Located in the nation's capital, it is the most prestigious of the historically black colleges and universities, the "capstone" of black education.

While black students at predominantly white universities in the late 1960s were protesting to establish black studies, students at Howard were protesting to transform Howard into a "black" university. In 1967 Charles Hamilton, the Black Power scholar, made the first systematic case for transforming traditional "Negro" colleges into "black" institutions. In the article "The Place of the Black College in the Human Rights Struggle" he listed criteria for creating or identifying a black college, which among other things include a rejection of white middle-class ethos and its replacement by a distinctive black ethos, assistance to the black community, and development of a curriculum grounded in African civilizations. More generally, he proposed a militant black liberation university as an adjunct to the Black Power movement—a black university "that would deliberately inoculate a sense of racial *pride* and *anger* in black students. . . . We need militant leadership . . . a black college which would use its accumulated knowledge and economic resources to bring about change and [dispense] with irrelevant PhDs . . . and recruit freedom fighters."

In 1966 students at Howard began lobbying and protesting to transform it into a black university. In 1968 the protests ended in a strike and a takeover of the administration building. Earlier in 1967 the students had formed a "Black Power Committee," which issued a manifesto calling for the "overthrow of the Negro college" and its replacement by a "militant black university which will counteract the white-washing black students receive in 'Negro' and white institutions." The faculty mentor of the student protesters was Nathan Hare, who became the first head of Black Studies at San Francisco State.

The Howard central administration and the Board of Trustees were initially opposed to the black university concept, but since student (and some faculty) pressures were considerable, the administration wished to respond but was concerned that doing so might jeopardize its congressional appropriations. The Ford Foundation solved the administration's problems when it awarded Howard (and Atlanta University) multiyear, million-dollar grants to become "centers of excellence" in higher education. These grants allowed the university to respond to the student demands with new faculty and courses.

The first step in the blackening process was the hiring of a new president, James Cheek, who was committed to the black university concept. Cheek appointed Andrew Billingsley from Berkeley's Ethnic Studies program as vice president for academic affairs. Billingsley then set about to recruit a large group of young Black Power–oriented scholars committed to the black university concept. One of his more audacious hires was the young Ronald Walters to chair the Political Science Department, although Walters had not formally been awarded the PhD.

After completing requirements for the PhD except the dissertation at American University, Walters, who specialized in international relations and African politics, was recruited as the founding chair of Black Studies at Brandeis. During his tenure as chair he wrote several epistemological, theoretical, and ideological papers on the parameters of the new discipline. In these papers Ron was clear on the ultimate purpose of black studies— to contribute to the liberation of black people. In this purpose he argued black studies was necessarily and unapologetically ideological in the broadest sense of the term, because "any time one moves from recitation of facts into the realm of meaning, one engages in value judgments, and in order for those judgments to explain phenomena they are set in one ideological framework or another."

I entered Howard during what Billingsley recalled as the "salad days" when the faculty had a cohort of young Black Power scholars in the arts, music (jazz), the humanities, and the social sciences that created for a time a synergy in scholarship and activism that rivaled Howard in the 1930s and 1940s, when Ralph Bunche, E. Franklin Frazier, Alain Locke, Merze Tate, and Rayford Logan were on campus. In addition to the ongoing blackening of the faculty and curriculum, Howard had the demography and culture for blackness. After seven years at predominantly white institutions, it was happiness to be in this black space. The demography and culture of blackness was more than that the administration, faculty, and staff were nearly all black. It was that, but it was more than that. There was the Pan-African composition of the faculty and students from Africa and the diaspora. This global diversity in blackness was complemented by diversity of domestic blackness, with students of all hues and colors from all parts of the country and diverse social and economic backgrounds. The culture of blackness provided a common existential framework for appreciation of the role of racial oppression in understanding the condition of African people, and our obligation as people of diverse backgrounds to develop common and unique theories and strategies of liberation for our people. There were cross-cultural continuities and differences in the expressions of blackness in speech, spirituality, dance, and dress, taking into account diasporic and regional differences within the US. At some point virtually everyone who was anyone in the black world—diplomats, politicians, preachers, athletes, artists, entertainers, scholars—came to Howard. The most memorable of these visits for me was when Robert Mugabe, the leader of the liberation struggle and newly installed president of Zimbabwe, gave an emotional speech to thousands in the campus quad, declaring that the success of Zimbabwe's liberation struggle demonstrated that "black could triumph over white."

The political science faculty was ethnically, ideologically, and intellectually diverse, but it had only one woman, a lawyer who taught classes on a part-time basis. Of the fifteen-member faculty six were white, and the blacks included a Haitian, three Nigerians, and a brother from Barbados. There were divisions between the old guard black faculty and the new, younger Black Power professors. The old guard, while not opposed to the black university concept, were ambivalent and skeptical. In general, the white faculty were opposed to the black university concept, but their opposition was expressed quietly and without rancor. There were also methodological divisions between those wedded to the traditional philosophical and institutional approaches to the study of politics, those enamored of the more quantitative scientific approach, and those committed to Marxist analysis. And although I was not aware of it at the time, virtually all of the faculty were angry and bitter about the way Billingsley and Cheek appointed Walters with little faculty consultation. The diversity of the faculty made for lively, sometimes passionate debates in the classrooms and hallways.

In addition to the traditional fields of study in political science—American politics, comparative politics, public administration, political philosophy, methodology, and international relations—under Walters's leadership Howard established the first black politics field in the discipline. This was a landmark development in political science, since the American Political Science Association did not list black politics as a valid field of study until 1990.

The black politics field was comprehensively defined as the "study of forms of behavior and thought which characterize the political activity of people of African descent in relationship to racial subordination and the ideology of white supremacy." Broadly comparative and Pan-African, the field was "particularly concerned" according to its brochure with "racial inequality and the political ideologies and behavior that can perpetuate or reduce racial subordination." Subfields or concentrations included Comparative Race Relations, History of Black Political Thought, Black Political Behavior, Electoral Politics, Race and Public Policy, Urban Black Politics, and Race and International Relations.

I took classes from each of the factions in the department—the blacks and the whites, the old guard and the Black Power scholars, the behavioralist and the traditionalists, and Hilbourne Watson's seminar on Marxism. I should say I took a couple of weeks of Watson's Marxism seminar. Watson, from Barbados, taught more than Marxism as philosophy and ideology, he taught Marx's methodology of historical and dialectical materialism. Probably one of the few scholars in the US who knew and used historical and dialectical materialism as methods, he insisted one could not understand Marxism unless you understood his methods and one could not understand his methods unless one read and understood *Capital*. Thus, in the first semester of his two-semester seminar the only assigned text was *Capital*. After a couple of weeks, the whole class rebelled, claiming we could not understand *Capital*. We petitioned the chair to get Watson to assign more readable Marxist texts. He refused, insisting that to know Marxism you had to know *Capital*. The seminar was reassigned to Professor William Ellis, who assigned more understandable Marxist writings, such as *The Communist Manifesto*, *Anti-Dühring*, *The German Ideology*, and *The Origins of the Family, Private Property, and the State*.

In addition to classes, I was a teaching assistant for old guard professor Vincent Browne in his introduction to American government class and a research assistant for Walters. The research work with Walters came about in an unorthodox way. The department awarded nine-month fellowships to doctoral students. I mistakenly assumed that the stipend was for a year. So, for the summer I had no income and no prospect for employment. Bird was busy taking care of newborn Blanch and could not work. Thus, we faced the prospect of no income during the summer. I explained the situation to Ron, who in an extraordinary act of generosity used his own resources to provide enough money for the summer. In exchange he asked me to do some research on a project he was working on dealing with black access to higher education. After I completed the research, in another generous act, he asked me to coauthor the article he was working on based on the research. This resulted in my first article in a peer-reviewed journal, "The Black Education Strategy in the 1970s."

At the time the Howard doctoral program in political science required examinations in four fields (subsequently reduced to two). This was an almost impossible task, to master the literature of four fields. I took exams in American politics, public administration, black politics, and methodology. I received a pass with honors in black politics, pass on American politics, low pass in public administration, and a no pass in methodology. Having taken nine classes in methodology between Berkeley, UCLA, and Howard and a methods course at the New School, I thought I had enough knowledge to pass a methodology exam in the field. But the committee voted 2 to 1 to award a no pass. I appealed the decision and on the basis of a technicality the committee decision was reversed. One of the members of the committee who voted to fail me did not have the PhD, and department rules required faculty evaluating doctoral exams to also have the doctorate. Professor Victor Ferraos, a Filipino, only had a master's so he was replaced on the committee and I was given a low pass.

In my first year with the approval of Professor Charles Harris, my advisor, I selected a dissertation topic and begin research and writing. Although I had come to Howard to study with Walters, I only took one class from him, and because he was frequently away traveling, I decided to ask Harris to be my advisor. Harris, a part of the old guard, was nevertheless enthusiastic about the new black politics field. Although his major field was public administration, he quickly retooled and became an integral part of the new field. I took my first black politics class with him and given Walters's schedule I thought it prudent to select Harris as my advisor and dissertation chair. For the dissertation I decided to study the incorporation of blacks into the political system, focusing on the federal level. This process of systemic incorporation, sometimes referred to as a transformation from protest to politics, involved the transformation of the civil rights protest groups into routine interest groups, the creation of new black interest organizations, the election of larger numbers of blacks to Congress, the formation of the Congressional Black Caucus, and the appointment of larger numbers of blacks to positions in the executive branch.

I relied on documentary and statistical sources and the Joint Center's newspaper clipping files, but the major source of data was a series of focused interviews with black elites in Washington. I interviewed scholars and journalists knowledgeable about national black politics, and then representatives of black interest groups, members of Congress and their staffs, and black appointees in the Nixon administration. A total of seventy-seven persons were interviewed, including two scholars, twelve journalists, three persons on the staff of the Congressional Black Caucus, nine other congressional staff persons, twenty black presidential appointees, twenty representatives of black interest groups, and six black members of Congress. (As an aside, Texas congresswoman Barbara Jordan consented to an interview, telling me to meet her in a House hallway—this was at a time when the public had easy access to Capitol hallways and corridors—and we could talk as she walked from the House floor to her office. However, when I saw her, I was so intimidated by her presence that I was afraid to approach her. I was chagrined afterward, and Bird found my behavior inexplicable.) Conducting these interviews literally required a lot of leg work. I did not have a car, no money for cabs, and Washington's public transportation was expensive and unreliable. So, I spent many days walking from our apartment on Sixteenth and R to the federal complex downtown and to Capitol Hill. Bird spent many hours preparing the correspondence and follow-up telephone calls to arrange the interviews.

When I left Washington for the college at Purchase, I had completed the research and written several chapters as seminar papers. I completed the remaining chapters in my first year at Purchase and returned for an uneventful oral defense, and a delightful celebratory party arranged by my classmate Paula McClain. The members of the dissertation committee in addition to Harris as chair included Walters; Morris Levitt, a specialist in interest groups and the only white on the committee; William Ellis; and Augustus Adair, a professor at Morgan State and former staff director of the Congressional Black Caucus.

I revised the dissertation for possible publication as a book and sent queries to several publishers. Princeton was the only press to ask to see the manuscript and its editors rejected it as too descriptive. I also revised parts of it for journal publication, eventually publishing three chapters in journals: "The Black Congressional Delegation," "Black Appointed Officials: A Neglected Category of Political Participation Research," and "The Political Behavior of Black Presidential Appointees, 1960–1980."

Bird worked off and on at temp jobs and typed my papers and correspondence while waiting for the birth of our first child. Blanch was born at Howard's hospital. Apparently, as a result of neglect by the hospital staff, she was born with a mental disability. Her disability was due to damage to the brain caused by deprivation of oxygen during a long, unattended labor (the hospital at that time did not allow spouses in the delivery room). We were told of the long unattended labor by Shelly, an old friend from Cal State, LA, whose boyfriend worked at the hospital and by a Dr. Cohen of the hospital staff, who urged us to sue. Bird was inclined to do so; I was not. First, I did not think there was anything wrong with Blanch (she was three or four before I recognized her disability). Second, my affection for the university made me hesitant. Failure to pursue the litigation is a major regret of my life. I thoroughly enjoyed my two years at Howard. The political science faculty was excellent and their teaching and the culture and demography of blackness I think made me appreciate in a way Berkeley or UCLA could not the importance of trying to do black liberation scholarship.

An interesting aside; at the time I arrived in Washington Bird's cousin Emma Jean McCloud arrived to begin work as a foreign service officer at the State Department. As we arrived at the same time, some of her superiors apparently worried this might not be coincidental, informed her of my "radical" past, and told her to be warned and wary. This is further evidence the government maintained some kind of file on me. Emma Jean ignored the warnings and established close relations with us until she was posted to Kenya. She married a Kenyan, Omar, while posted there. Her and Bird's family objected because Omar was her "houseboy." When I returned to Washington to teach at Howard, Emma Jean had again been posted to Washington. She and Omar reestablished a close relationship with us, and we often dined with them with plenty of drink and delicious Kenyan cuisine prepared by Omar. Sadly, Emma Jean died several years later of leukemia. Omar moved to El Paso; we tried to stay in touch with him and their young son but eventually lost contact.

I also frequently had Saturday dinners with "Saleem" (this is a bastardization of his name, which I do not know the spelling of) and his wife and young daughter. Saleem was a Palestinian doctoral student who was passionately committed to the liberation of his people and their land. During the dinners, he and his wife prepared traditional Palestinian dishes, and Bird and I reciprocated with soul food dinners, and we discussed the Israeli occupation of their homeland (on a wall they had a huge map of Palestine where he pointed to his family's ancestral land that was now a part of Israel). In 1973 or 1974 he arranged for me to attend as an observer the meeting of the Palestine National Council in Jordan. I planned to attend but delayed getting my passport until it was too late. After I left for Purchase, I lost track of Saleem and do not know if he finished the PhD and returned to Palestine as he had planned. Saleem and I did not agree on the ultimate solution of the Israel-Palestine conflict. I favored withdrawal of Israel from the lands it occupied after the 1967 war and the preservation of the Jewish state within its 1967 boundaries, while he favored the abolition of the Zionist "entity" and the establishment of a secular state as a homeland for both peoples. Despite our differences, it was partly I think a result of those Saturday afternoon dinners that I became a passionate advocate of the Palestine liberation struggle (see chapter 8 where I discuss my leadership role in getting the National Conference of Black Political Scientists to join a handful of other academic organizations in the "BDS" movement—Boycott, Disinvest, and Sanction Israel until it withdraws from the occupied territories and helps to facilitate the creation of a Palestinian state).

Several members of my Howard class went on to have distinguished careers. Paula McClain, the only woman in the class, became a leading scholar of Black-Latino politics, vice president and provost at Duke University, and the second black woman elected president of the American Political Science Association. William Lightfoot, after completing the MA in political science, earned a law degree from Washington University, St. Louis. Returning to Washington, DC, he became a prominent attorney, chairman of the District of Columbia's cable commission, a frequently mentioned candidate for mayor, a member of the City Council, and strategist in the successful mayoral campaigns of Adrian Fenty and Muriel Bowser. Alvin Thornton, after earning the PhD, taught at Morgan State and returned to Howard where he became department chair, associate provost, and senior advisor to the university president. Appointed by Maryland's governor to chair the Commission on Educational Equity, Thornton was instrumental in the "Thornton Plan," credited with making significant contributions to equity in educational funding in the state. Alvin was president of the Prince Georges County, Maryland, Board of Education and a candidate for Congress. James Tinney, the first openly gay person I knew, after earning the PhD, became an authority on the black press and the black Pentecostal church, and a speech writer for Congressman John Conyers and Samuel Jackson, an assistant secretary of Housing and Urban Development in the Nixon administration. Excommunicated from his Pentecostal church for his advocacy of gay rights, Tinney, who was also a preacher, founded Faith Temple as a congregation for black gays and lesbians. At his death by AIDS at age forty-six he was professor of journalism at Howard.

After becoming a PhD candidate in 1975, I applied for positions throughout the country, including the Riverside campus of the University of California. Although I did not like Riverside, which is on the edge of the desert, it was the only position in California. In any event, I was not offered the position, nor was I offered a position at Atlanta University where I also applied. I was offered a position at Portland State University in Oregon, but then came John Howard, the newly appointed African American dean of the social sciences at the State University of New York's college at Purchase.

In order to identify possible black faculty recruits, John decided to personally visit Howard and Atlanta, the two black PhD-granting historically black universities. Although I cannot recall the circumstances, ultimately John invited me to Purchase and I was appointed as a lecturer in political science, pending completion of the dissertation, at a salary of $12,750. This was a fortunate appointment since the college at Purchase was an ideal place to begin teaching. But it was more than that, it was where John became a mentor, friend, and the person most responsible for my initial socialization into the academic world. We have been friends and collaborators for the last forty years and, with the possible exception of Ron Walters, he is the most important person in the making of me as a scholar.

After nine years of higher education, I ended with $7,000 in student debt, most of which was used to purchase cars. My attendance at each of the California colleges and universities was tuition free (tuition was first imposed by Ronald Reagan several years after he was elected governor in 1966), and my five years of graduate study were supported by fellowships and Bird's work.

CHAPTER 7

The College at Purchase and the Conservation of Human Resources

John R. Howard, a sociologist and attorney, is a scholar of eclectic interests. His first book, *The Cutting Edge: Social Movements and Social Change in America*, is a study of the conditions and consequences of social change movements in the United States. His coauthored *Life Styles in the Black Ghetto* in its insights and sensitivity calls to mind Kenneth Clark's *Dark Ghetto*. Both of these books demonstrate the use of sociology to study problems of relevance and significance in contemporary society. After years of teaching and research and community service (which included publishing a weekly newsletter, *Black Life in Westchester County*), John earned a law degree from Pace University. His interest in the law was less its practice and more about bringing sociological insights into the development of law. *The Shifting Wind: The Supreme Court and Civil Rights from Reconstruction to Brown* is an engagingly written, sweeping overview of the court's civil rights jurisprudence focusing on the court sociologically in terms of the dynamics of small group decision-making. *Poor Joshua: The DeShaney Case and Child Abuse in America* is a sociological and jurisprudential indictment of the Supreme Court's failure to provide adequate constitutional protections to children abused by their parents and who are not protected by the responsible government child welfare and protective agencies. To show further the catholic nature of his interests, John in 2010 published *Faces in the Mirror: Oscar Micheaux and Spike Lee*, a comparative analysis of the works of the two legendary black filmmakers. Over the years John's scholarship was a model and inspiration for me, beginning at the college at Purchase and continuing to this day.

111

Watching John at Purchase in my beginning years as a professor gave me a sense of how the work was done, of how to do the work of scholarship. It is almost certain that he was black, and the dean of the social sciences was important as well to me as a young black scholar. It was more than John's scholarship and leadership that were influential. He and his wife Mary, a professor at Brooklyn College, brought Scottie and I into their circle of colleagues and friends by inviting us to a series of salon-like dinner and cocktail parties they hosted. This too was important for a young black scholar's socialization process in a largely white academic world. But John' contribution to my development has been more specific and direct. In 1977 he secured a contract with the prestigious Academy of Political and Social Sciences to edit a special issue of its *Annals* on urban black politics, which was the first collection of scholarly papers on the transition in US urban politics from white dominance to the era of black incorporation and mayoral leadership. He asked me not only to contribute a paper but to join him as coeditor. This was important to a young scholar's vita and allowed me to make contacts with some of the top scholars in the field and learn something of the process of writing and editing for journal publication.

More important than coediting the *Annals* special issue in my work as a black scholar was John's decision in 1980 after I had left Purchase for Howard to ask me to coedit with him State University of New York Press's African American Studies series. After a term on the Press's editorial board, he secured a contract to start the series, which was the first book series in African American studies in the nation. This was a landmark development for the new black studies field. Coediting the series brought me into contact with senior and beginning scholars in the field while learning the process of reviewing, editing, and publishing scholarly books. John and I coedited for more than forty years, publishing more than fifty books. The series is recognized as a premier outlet for publishing work in black studies.

Finally, John has been a close reader of virtually all of my books. Always willing to take the time to render both substantive and editorial comments on my drafts, his has been a steady hand in my development in scholarly writing from my days at Purchase to the writing of this book. In any profession one succeeds in part because of the luck of good mentors who help to show the way. I was lucky that in 1974 John decided to come to Howard to search for promising young black scholars. I do not know what course my career would have taken without him, but I do know what course it has taken with his presence, guidance, and assistance.

I assume my appointment to the Purchase faculty was at least partly on the basis of affirmative action. That is, John and the college deliberately set about to hire more blacks to create a more ethnically diverse faculty. John played the leadership role in this affirmative action recruitment. As a strong supporter of affirmative action and a beneficiary since my days at Berkeley, I was not bothered by being hired in part because I was black. I recall my pre-appointment interview with Abbott Kaplan, the Purchase president. He said something to the effect, "Bob, wouldn't you feel bad if you got this job or any job because you were black." "No," I replied as I have to all such queries since, "if the money is good, I have no problem whatsoever. It makes up a bit for all the jobs my daddy did not get because he was black."

The college at Purchase, established in 1971 as one of the fourteen campuses of the state university system, has been described as "Rockefeller's dream college." Located in Westchester County near Governor Nelson Rockefeller's estate, the college was an effort to introduce the elite, private school model of education into a public university system. Adding to its elite character, the college was essentially a series of conservatory programs in the arts, dance, design, theater, and music. The divisions of natural and social sciences were basically complementary to the conservatory programs.

The design and organization of the curriculum was nontraditional and innovative. There were no required courses and professors were encouraged to develop new, experimental classes. Classes were small, usually less than a dozen students. There were no letter grades. Instead, each student received a written evaluation and a "grade" of pass, no pass, and honors. In the first year, students were required to take an interdisciplinary "Freshman Cluster," an experimental class team taught by three professors from different disciplines on a subject of broad interest. In the junior year students took a comprehensive examination in their major and wrote a senior thesis in the final year. Because the college was located in the isolated hamlet of Purchase with little public transportation, students were almost required to live on campus, which facilitated close interaction between students and to an extent faculty. The faculty was drawn disproportionately from Ivy League or prestige state universities and the nearby arts community in New York City.

In many ways Purchase College was a noble experiment by wealthy persons to bring the best of an elite liberal and arts education to middle- and working-class families. It, however, was not without its critics, foremost among them Henry Etzkowitz and Joseph Fashing, sociologists on the Purchase faculty, who wrote a scathing critique in *Liberal Education*. Etzkowitz and Fashing contended that the creation of the college and its location reflected more a concern with status and "the privatization of education, than with a full-scale consideration of the needs and concerns of those who generally compose a state university's primary constituency. Although the larger cultural ambitions of the college do not constitute an absolute barrier to meeting the more general needs of the community, the elitist ethos that prevails is one that makes such larger goals a more formidable task than it need be." Furthermore, "the character of the educational program and the virtual necessity of campus residence tend to restrict access severely. In this sense Purchase fits neatly into a growing state and national pattern of privatization of public education." They concluded that rather than the elitist Purchase model, the state should look to the open university model of the City University of New York: "Rather than serve an exclusive clientele of constituents whose class advantages are already formidable, the public university should serve all the people. Anything short of this, we think, is a default in the public university's historic mission."

Etzkowitz and Fashing were especially critical of the college's Educational Opportunity Program (EOP). These programs in general offered special admissions, counseling, tutoring, and financial aid to disadvantaged students, mainly black and Hispanic, to enable them to successfully complete college work. Unlike most EOPs that are located on campus, the Purchase program, headed by Major Thomas, an African American community activist, was located in Mount Vernon, a largely black city fifteen miles from the campus. The program in Mount Vernon operated more like a junior college than a traditional EOP. Students who completed the two-year program could transfer to Purchase or any other campus in the SUNY system. Etzkowitz and Fashing noted that aspects of the "take the college to the people" approach were "worthy," but they concluded that many saw the Mount Vernon program as a "plantation that allowed the College to maintain its elite status while not having to deal with the problem of students from different backgrounds who might not fit into its program." Further, "with no EOP program at the main campus, and the co-op college open only to those in Mount Vernon or commuting distance of it, potential EOP students from other parts of the state are automatically excluded from attending Purchase."

While there is merit to their critique of the Mount Vernon program, I taught classes in the program and served for two years on the college liaison committee to the program. I concluded that it was a unique and useful attempt at bringing college to the community, which on balance outweighed the deficiencies identified by Etzkowitz and Fashing. Their overall critique of the college also raised critical concerns, but in my view the Purchase experiment was a worthy endeavor to bring the best of an expensive liberal and arts curriculum to one campus in a multicampus state system. I thoroughly enjoyed my five years at the college; in some ways it was the best teaching experience of my career. As I was preparing to leave Purchase, plans were being discussed to close the Mount Vernon program and establish a traditional EOP on campus. And under financial and student pressures some of the more innovative features of the Purchase model—the freshman cluster, no letter grades—were abandoned, but nearly fifty years later it still offers a distinctive and innovative undergraduate education.

The social science faculty was relatively young and included a number of persons who had or would have noteworthy scholarly careers. Political scientist and influential feminist theorist Jo Freeman's 1975 book *The Politics of Women's Liberation* was the first major study of the politics of the modern feminist movement. Jo also wrote a number of influential articles on feminist politics and a textbook, *Women: A Feminist Perspective.* A volunteer in the civil rights movement in the South in the early 1960s and a participant in the Berkeley Free Speech movement, she wrote a memoir of her Berkeley experience, *At Berkeley in the Sixties: The Making of an Activist.* She was also a key organizer of the Women's Caucus of the American Political Science Association. Jo, for reasons I could not discern, was not well liked at Purchase and left a couple of years after I arrived, never to hold an academic appointment again. I regret I did not get to know her well, but I appreciated her activism, her pioneering scholarship and its contribution to understanding how social movements are incorporated into the political system, which paralleled my work on the black movement.

As I mentioned in a previous chapter the black feminist scholar Linda La Rue was on the Purchase faculty, as was Nancy Foner, anthropologist and a part of the famous Foner family of scholars. Foner became a leading authority on migration and immigration. Alfred Eichner, the post-Keynes specialist, was a senior member of the faculty. In addition to his writings on the imperatives of government intervention to maintain full employment and price stability, he coauthored with Eli Ginzberg *The Troublesome Presence: American Democracy and the Negro.* I discuss below Eichner's relationship to my work at Columbia University's Conservation of Human Resources Project. Peter Schwab, an Africanist and later a human rights specialist, was on the faculty. Peter became a good friend. And then there was Mary Edwards, a delightful person and friend, who was a founding member of the political science faculty and the organizer of its women's studies component. Mary and I did an evaluation for Westchester County of its youth street theater program. Although the fee for our work was modest, we loved working together and with the young people, and were pleased to recommend the program's continued funding to the county. Sadly, Mary died of cancer a couple of years after I left the college.

As the Americanist on the political science faculty, I taught classes on Congress, the presidency, urban politics, black politics, ethnic politics, and political repression. I cannot recall exactly but I think the teaching load was three classes a semester, plus work on junior exams and senior theses. In addition to the Purchase classes, as I indicated, I also taught in the Mount Vernon program.

Most of the students were white. Of the small number of black students, three, all about my age, became very close friends. Yusuf and his Iranian girlfriend and later wife Sudabeh were the first of these student friends. I cannot recall Yusuf's last name, but he was a visual artist and I have several of his wood carvings in my home today. Yusuf's close friend was Larry Carson, an ex-convict, who majored in political science. Larry and Yusuf were friends, and they spent many hours at my house dining, drinking, smoking weed, and talking. Larry was an excellent student; his senior thesis on the war on poverty's community action programs is one of only two student papers I have cited in my work. However, his inclinations toward petty crimes got the best of him. The last time I heard from Larry was a letter requesting support for his application for parole.

By far the most enduring friendship with a Purchase student was with John Hipps and his wife Carol, and later with his mother Mary Roberts. John was a mature student, somewhat older than me, with three children. A political science major, John was a Republican, active in the local party organization in Peekskill, New York, where he operated a cleaning service. He was active in the civic life of Peekskill, a member of its Republican Committee, and twice a candidate for local office. He was a Republican not because he was committed to the party's conservative ideology, but because he saw party membership as the best way to advance his business and political interests in Peekskill. John and Carol, Bird and I became the best of friends, dining and picnicking together frequently and sharing holidays with his mother and sister. After I left for Washington the friendship continued as we talked frequently on the phone and they came to visit. In 1983 his wife Carol died suddenly of a heart attack and Bird and I returned for the funeral. The last time I saw John was in 1997 when he picked me up from a conference I attended at Vassar College and took me to John Howard's house for dinner. He was killed in a traffic accident shortly thereafter. We stayed in touch with his mother Mary, and I tried, after John's death, to be a mentor to his young son Courtney. We spoke on the phone and he visited once, and I took him to a baseball game at Baltimore's Camden Yards.

In addition to teaching I was busy trying to get the dissertation published and preparing articles for journal publication. I also started to attend professional meetings. My first was the Southern Political Science Association in the picturesque Smokey Mountain village of Gatlinburg, Tennessee. Holding the southern meeting in Gatlinburg was something of a tradition of the southern association because for a long time it was one of a few places in the South that had integrated accommodations. I attended my first meeting of the National Conference of Black Political Scientists (NCOBPS) in Washington in 1977, where I made my first acquaintance with Eddie Williams, president of the Joint Center for Political Studies, who was a fellow panelist. NCOBPS, the professional association of black political scientists, was founded in 1969. Yet almost inexplicably in my years at Howard as a doctoral student I did not hear about it, although it had an active graduate student association. Again, I find this inexplicable. NCOBPS was indispensable in my development as a black liberation scholar because it was a gathering place for the most creative and committed of my generation of black politics scholars. After graduate school, I became a member of the American Political Science Association (APSA), the leading professional organization of the discipline, but I rarely attended meetings. After several years, I allowed my membership to lapse because with NCOBPS the APSA became irrelevant.

Meanwhile, Scottie was attending Westchester Community College and working occasionally at a variety of temporary jobs. But her main job was rearing Blanch, typing my manuscripts, and coming to grips with Blanch's disability. As probably is the case for most parents with developmentally disabled children, we—I more so than Bird—resisted the idea that there was anything wrong with Blanch. Finally, she was given a complete neurological examination with the equivalent of CAT scans of her brain, which showed beyond doubt that during Bird's prolonged labor Blanch had suffered oxygen deprivation, which damaged her brain. The damage was permanent and as a result she would always be intellectually impaired. This devastating news confirmed that Howard Hospital had been negligent in its care of Bird and Blanch, as Dr. Cohen had told us at the time of her birth. There was now nothing we could do in terms of seeking damages for the harm done to her since the time for filing a suit had long since passed. We then resolved to make sure that Blanch got the best care and education possible, which as I said earlier was the beginning of Bird's educational advocacy career.

In a previous chapter, I indicated during my year at the New School I got my first experience with ethnic diversity among whites, eventually doing a study of ethnicity in New York City. When we returned to New York the force of white ethnic diversity there became a fact of existence. We lived in an apartment complex in White Plains, the largest city in Westchester County. The apartment complex displayed New York's ethnic diversity in miniature—Irish, Italians, Jews, and others. Our next-door neighbors, Gerald and Kathy O'Connor, were Irish. Kathy, who later became a close friend of Scottie's, told us when she saw that her next-door neighbor was black, she cried, but her father told her she was wrong and had no right to make assumptions about people simply because of their color. When we placed a black Santa Claus on our door, her young son cried, insisting that Santa Claus could not be black. But Kathy did not just have animosity toward blacks but Jews and Italians as well. And the Italians and Jews reciprocated. Angus and Jane, a black-Jewish couple, were often the target of negative stereotypes. What was fascinating about this were these ethnic slurs were sometimes openly expressed in conversations with us and we presumed they used similar negative stereotypes about blacks when we weren't around. Everybody used garish stereotypes about Joe Decento, the Italian American building caretaker who lived in the basement of the building, and he reciprocated. The building had a dumbwaiter in which tenants placed their garbage for disposal by Joe. On one occasion he remarked, "What has the world come to when a white man has to haul a colored man's garbage."

This ethnic rivalry was all new to Bird and me since to us all white folks were the same, and prior to New York we heard the words "Dago," "Mick," "Spic," and "Heb" only when we watched the Archie Bunker television program. I came away from these ethnic encounters with the sense that they were relatively harmless—inheritances from past that had no future. Over the five years in the building, we had numerous gatherings where people came together as people, without consciousness of ethnic identity, but as neighbors and friends to share fun, food, talk, and drink. Kathy and Bird became lasting friends, staying in touch long after we left White Plains.

In the building were an elderly white couple—Mr. and Mrs. Young—and a middle-aged white woman—Ms. Smith—who showed Bird and I the utmost kindness, almost as surrogate uncles and aunts. I did not know their ethnicity or recall them engaging in ethnic stereotyping. The Youngs often inquired of and encouraged my career and expressed genuine regret and best wishes when we left for Washington. In addition to expressing regret and wishing us well, Mrs. Smith gave us expensive lamps, a dropleaf table, and an antique piece of furniture.

Overall, then, as I said, the ethnic differences and stereotypes were in their consequences inconsequential. In the apartment building and at the college I perceived or experienced no racism at all. Not so in the larger communities of White Plains and Westchester County where I experienced racism, which I wrote about in my 1995 book, *Racism in the Post–Civil Rights Era: Now You See It, Now You Don't*.

Westchester County was segregated along race and class lines, which gave rise to three encounters with racism—one was individual and two were an interplay between individual and institutional racism. The individual racism occurred while I was shopping with Blanch at the neighborhood supermarket. An elderly white woman called the police and said I had snatched her purse in the store the week before. The officers took the charge seriously and if I had not had the good fortune to be on the faculty of the local university I might have been arrested, tried, convicted, and imprisoned like many other black men wrongly accused by racist whites. As it turned out, the university president called the police chief and in effect told him, "You got the wrong nigger, he is one of us." I was released with profuse apologies to "Dr. Smith."

The second incident involved my search for a better to place to live. My friend Dale Nelson from the Five Block Project at Columbia, now on the faculty at Fordham, lived in a nicer apartment complex. I asked him to let me know when a vacancy occurred. At the next vacancy Dale called me, and Bird and I rushed over to make a deposit, only to be told there were no vacancies, and none anticipated. The building manager later angrily told Dale, "Never send another nigger to me again." We sought the assistance of the local Urban League (its executive director was an acquaintance) in filing a complaint; nothing came of this until a year or so later when we heard on the radio that the US Attorney had filed a racial discrimination suit against the apartment's rental agency. We contacted the US Attorney's Office and we and the Nelsons became witnesses for the government. On the opening day of the trial the rental agency entered into agreement that required it to establish an affirmative action program of rentals to minorities in all of its buildings in the metropolitan area, and to pay modest damages to us and the Nelsons because they had been denied their right to live in a racially integrated building. This was a case of individual racism, buttressed, according to the government, by an institutional pattern of racism.

Westchester consisted of many small towns and villages segregated along race and class lines. We lived in White Plains, a relatively large city also segregated by race and class but also with some racially integrated neighborhoods. The nearby town of Harrison was an upper-class town, possibly all white, with very expensive houses. The town operated a beautiful park that was nominally open to residents only, but was used by White Plains residents, at least its white residents. Our neighbors the O'Connors frequently used the park without hinderances, and one day Bird, Blanch, and I accompanied them. Immediately the park attendant asked for our residence card; our neighbors had never been asked for cards. Yet immediately when a black family is involved residency becomes an issue—race serving as an indirect indicator that we were not residents either because there were no black residents in the town, or the attendant knew all two or three of them. Thus, we were deprived of the right to use a public park on the basis of race as surely as when I was in Louisiana during the days of Jim Crow segregation, and yet it was legal.

At Purchase I chaired two committees, the social science division's lecture committee and the collegewide affirmative action committee. In the several years I chaired the lecture committee, in addition to the local congressman Richard Ottinger (who also lectured in my Congress class), we invited the distinguished Yale economist Paul Samuelson; Frances Fox Piven, the well-known scholar of protest and poor peoples' movements; and as I mentioned in chapter 4, my old UCLA professor Harry Scoble. We also invited Mack Jones, the founding chair of Atlanta University's doctoral program in political science, as well as the founding president of NCOBPS. Jones is a seminal contributor to the development of the black politics field. And as I discuss in chapter 9 his writings are an important influence in my work. It was kind of a personal honor to host his lecture. This was our first meeting, which started decades of friendship, scholarly correspondence, and cooperation between Mack and me including a year teaching at Prairie View University when he was head of its social science division. In 2015 I was pleased to publish in the SUNY series in African American Studies a collection of his work, *Knowledge, Power, and Black Politics: The Collected Essays.*

I was appointed to the Purchase affirmative action committee in 1976, my second year on the faculty. I served three years, two as chair. I have written in this and earlier chapters on the importance of affirmative action to me personally. Clearly, it has been advantageous to me, and I believe it has been advantageous to many blacks in getting access to higher education and employment. I also believe it has been advantageous to the collective black community, while doing no damage to the collective white community. Yet when it is defined in term of explicit preferences affirmative action is opposed by overwhelming majorities of all categories of whites—men and women, old and young, educated and uneducated, southerners and northerners, liberals and conservatives, and Democrats and Republicans. In the more than forty years of polling on the issue, never more than 25 percent of Americans have supported the use of racial preferences as a means to implement affirmative action.

The term "affirmative action" has been traced to the Wagner Act of 1935, where it was used to require employers found by the National Labor Relations Board to have engaged in unfair labor practices to take "affirmative action" to remedy and compensate for the violation. It was first used in a racial context by President Kennedy in Executive Order 10925 requiring companies with government contracts to take affirmative action to ensure persons were employed without regard to race. In 1965 President Johnson issued Executive Order 11246, which required government contractors to engage in affirmative action with respect to the employment of blacks. The Kennedy and Johnson orders were largely broad, symbolic proclamations of intent without an effective implementation mechanism. It was President Nixon's 1971 revision of Johnson's Order requiring employers to establish "goals and timetables for the employment and promotion of specific numbers of blacks in specific job categories" that put teeth in the enforcement of the executive orders.

Historians continue to debate why Nixon issued such a robust order. Many think it was for a cynical reason—to drive a wedge between blacks and organized labor—which were two key constituents in the Democratic Party coalition. Most labor unions initially opposed affirmative action, while it was supported by most black interest groups. So, there was early conflict that Nixon might have anticipated. However, Arthur Fletcher, the African American assistant secretary of labor in the Nixon administration, claims he was the author of the goals and timetables standards in Nixon's revised order in his "Philadelphia Plan," which required for the first time construction companies in that city to use goals and timetables as measurable means to assess their progress in hiring and promoting blacks. In an interview for my dissertation research Fletcher told me, "Affirmative action was my baby. When I came in there were no specific standards for equal employment opportunity. It was viewed as social engineering and not as a labor standard enforceable at law. So, one of my conditions for accepting the job was that I could make equal employment a labor standard. When [George] Shultz [the labor secretary] asked me to take the job, this was what I told him." Fletcher's Philadelphia Plan did become the basis for Nixon's revision of Johnson's order, and this became the model or template for affirmative action programs in both the private and public sectors.

Purchase as a recipient of federal funds in the form of loans and grants to students was a federal contractor required to comply with Nixon's order to develop an affirmative action plan with goals and timetables for hiring and promotion. When I joined the committee and especially after I became the chair, I had two objectives: (1) to hire a competent full-time affirmative action officer, and (2) to work with that officer to write an effective, implementable affirmative action plan for the college. In the end I was successful at neither. But before the committee could get to work on these matters with the administration, we waited anxiously in anticipation of the Supreme Court's decision in the *Bakke* case, which threatened the constitutional viability of Nixon's revised order and our work at Purchase.

In the 1978 case *Regents of the University of California v. Bakke*, Allan Bakke, a white applicant who was denied admission to the medical school at the Davis campus, sued claiming the university's affirmative action plan violated his rights under the Civil Rights Act of 1964 and the equal protection clause of the Fourteenth Amendment. The members of the affirmative action committee at Purchase worried about the possible consequences of the court's decision for the work we were doing. The case involved two issues: first, whether it was legally and constitutionally permissible for a state to take race into account in the allocation of a material benefit—in this case a seat in medical school—and second, if the use of race was permissible, whether the state could use a numerical quota to allocate the benefit (in this case the setting aside of sixteen of one hundred seats in the class for minorities only). In deciding the case the court was deeply divided. The four conservative justices led by Chief Justice William Rehnquist ruled the university's program violated both the Civil Rights Act and the Fourteenth Amendment, both of which they argued categorically prohibited the use of race to allocate material benefits. The four liberal justices led by William Brennan and Thurgood Marshall held that a state university in order to remedy past racism or to create diversity could take race into consideration in allocating material benefits, and if it wished it could use a fixed quota. The moderate Justice Louis Powell split the difference between his colleagues, holding that a state university could for purposes of diversity use race in its allocative decisions but not a rigid or fixed quota.

Although I was disappointed by the narrowness of the decision and preferred the more unambiguous opinions of Justices Brennan and Marshall, I was nevertheless elated that affirmative action was held to be permissible. After I studied the opinions and the commentary, I drafted a memorandum for committee transmittal to the deans and heads of other administrative units indicating the *Bakke* decision was a legal and constitutional greenlight to move forward with the development of an effective affirmative action plan with numerical goals and timetables for hiring and promotion of minorities and women. I drafted the memorandum and distributed it without consulting the president of the college. If he was annoyed that I did so, he never said anything to me.

In my three years on the committee, especially the two as chair, I found myself doing more work on Section 504 of the Rehabilitation Act of 1973 dealing with equal access and opportunities for the handicapped, and the Title IX Education Amendments dealing with sex or equal opportunity for women than with affirmative action hiring and promotions. While discrimination against women and the disabled were important issues for an affirmative action committee to address, they were not my reasons for wishing to be on the committee. My main objectives for the committee was to hire an affirmative action officer and develop and implement an affirmative action plan. To some extent the development of the plan and its implementation were the major duties of the officer; his or her hiring therefore became the committee priority. While the college did eventually hire an affirmative action officer, he was marginally competent and turned out to be an alcoholic.

We advertised for an affirmative action officer/assistant to the president at a salary range of $16,000 to $20,000, preferably with a master's or law degree, although a bachelor's was acceptable if the candidate had experience in affirmative action or personnel administration. I thought the officer should have been full-time rather than serving also as assistant to the president performing other duties as assigned by him or her, but the committee was unable to persuade the president—Michael Hammond—on this point. The committee also thought the officer should have a full-time secretary/administrative assistant, but the president also rejected this proposal. The search for the officer was characterized by misfortunes. First, our preferred, first choice candidate died of a heart attack as we were about to offer him the job. Our second choice demanded compensation higher than the advertised salary, and college regulations apparently prohibited this kind of adjustment. We then hired our third choice. Unfortunately, and inexplicably, I have little in my files on this person, who was an African American, and he and his girlfriend became friends of Bird and me. Having little in the file about him, I only recall that in his year or so in the position he was not very competent and did little to develop an affirmative action plan, perhaps because he was an alcoholic.

Overall, I enjoyed my work on the committee; I learned a lot about the law, regulations, and policy process of affirmative action. The work was tedious, time-consuming, and in terms of my major objectives as chair, unsuccessful. As I wrote in my final report as chair:

> This is the final report I will submit as chair of the committee. I have served on the committee for three years, the last two as chair. During this period, despite the diligence and hard work of a number of persons on the committee, no discernible progress has been made in the development and implementation of an effective affirmative action program at Purchase. The racial, ethnic, and sex composition of the faculty is sad evidence of our failure. While a number of reasons may be essayed in explanation, the clearest and most remediable is the absence of a competent affirmative action officer. While the presence of an officer will not assure progress, the absence assures we will continue to drift. And this drift represents not only a failure of the College to live up to its moral and legal obligations but also is likely to increase the sense of frustration and cynicism in the community of persons affected by affirmative action at Purchase.

Through John I became acquainted with Ernie Prince, the head of the Westchester County Urban League. Ernie hired me as consultant with a modest honorarium to prepare the report "Enhancing Citizen Participation in Westchester County"; in the civic life of the county, including voting, community organizing, telephone, and letters to government officials and the media; and protest. Under league sponsorship, I did three lectures at the Westchester County prison.

In 1973 Professor Eichner told me he had recommended me to his friend and colleague Eli Ginzberg, professor of business and head of the Conservation of Human Resources Project (CHRP) at Columbia University, that I be brought on as coinvestigator to the project to investigate employment discrimination against blacks and women. I was surprised by the recommendation. Eichner and I had not discussed this before, and while we had cordial relations and occasional conversations about race and the need for full employment if blacks were to make economic progress, we were not close. Thus, I saw this unexpected recommendation for this research position at Columbia's prestigious manpower research center as evidence of Eichner's confidence in me as a promising young scholar.

CHRP was founded at Columbia in 1939 as a place for research on manpower planning, with a particular focus on the employment of blacks and women. By the 1970s it was recognized as the leading university-based place for research on these issues. For a long time it had been headed by Ginzberg, perhaps the nation's leading manpower scholar. Ginzberg's career went back to the New Deal, where as an economist he advised FDR on manpower policy. Later he wrote extensively about the integration of blacks and women into the workforce and of blacks into the military. The author of scores of books, Ginzberg advised every president on manpower issues from FDR to Carter. I considered it an honor to have the good opportunity to work on a project under his supervision.

The project, an exploratory study, investigated the employment of women and blacks in two large industries—health and electronics—in Boston and Houston. It was originally conceived as a collaborative study with me and Katherine Lewis, a young assistant professor on the Columbia Business School faculty. But in the midst of the study, without explanation to me or anyone on the CHRP staff, she abruptly quit the study and resigned from the Columbia faculty. It was left to me to complete the study alone, which I did with the assistance of the project staff, especially Charles Brecher and Dale Heistand. It became my first book, *Equal Employment Opportunity: A Comparative Micro-Analysis of Boston and Houston* published in 1982 with a foreword by Ginzberg.

The study's theoretical framework, which I inherited, was based on the work of economists who viewed the "neoclassical" formulation of the problem of employment discrimination as too limited and proposed what they called a "behavioral model," which looked at the behavioral attributes of employers, unions, governments, interest groups, and individuals in their interactions with each other and the local labor markets in which they operated (an important advocate of the behavioral model was University of Texas economist Ray Marshall, who was then serving as labor secretary in the Carter administration). Theoretically, the study sought to explain black and female employment opportunities as a function of four factors: time, place, industry, and group. Empirically, we addressed the penetration and mobility of blacks and women in the two industries—electronics and health—in Boston and Houston for the years 1965, 1970, and 1975. By "penetration" was meant the share of jobs held by women and blacks, and "mobility" was understood as the degree to which blacks and women progressed through the higher wage structures and job hierarchies of the industries.

Admittedly a modest study, it contributed to the body of literature that contends economic growth per se is not the key determinant of equal employment opportunity, but rather structural differences between cities in terms of economic base, political culture, and patterns of institutional racism are also important variables. For example, I concluded that it may well be the case that black employment opportunities are a function of black political power in a city; to increase the latter is to increase the former. Overall, I argued, "national policy makers should be sensitive to these kinds of variations and relationships in the design of effective national manpower and equal opportunity policies."

Altogether, I was pleased with my work at the college at Purchase and life in suburban Westchester County, a half-hour train ride from all the allures and attractions of the big city including visiting Georgia and Cousin Sister in Harlem. I had no plans to leave, except I received at almost the same time queries from Louisiana State University (LSU) and Howard asking me to join their faculties. I do not recall now how the LSU inquiry came about, but for a couple of years Bill Ellis and Ron Walters had talked to me about coming back to Howard as a faculty member.

The LSU query was alluring because it was our home state, and Bird and I would be close to our parents. The interview at LSU went well, although I admit it was a bit off-putting to be picked up by a professor wearing a cowboy hat and speaking in a slow southern drawl. It also was a bit concerning that what I initially thought was Baton Rouge's nighttime skyline was actually multiple oil refineries. But nevertheless, I might have taken the job except for my mother. I thought she would have been pleased I was returning home to work at the state's most prestigious university. She was not. Rather, her response was stay where you are or go to Howard, "I don't trust these white folks down here," she said. That was it; I decided to accept the position at Howard.

As word circulated around campus that I was contemplating leaving Purchase, I received nice notes from Nathaniel Siegel, the vice president for academic affairs, and Michael Hammond, the college president. Siegel wrote, "While we have never had a chance to really talk together, I have been impressed by your honesty, commitment, and desire for truth. I've always been more impressed by behavior than rhetoric, and possibly, that is why I value you and your counsel. I guess what I am trying to say is that you're not unnoticed by 'the administration' and I hope that someday soon you'll want to sit down with Michael and myself, as friends, and just chat." Hammond wrote, ". . . your leaving is a serious loss to Purchase. I have always been impressed with your clear sense of scholarly purpose, your personal dignity and thoughtful restraint in all discussions, even where the subjects were of importance to you: you have been a valuable colleague to me personally."

The college at Purchase was a good place to begin my teaching career. The small, intimate, innovative design of the college, and the collegiality of the faculty, likely made it a better place to begin the work of scholarship than, for example, a large research university. And, as I indicated at the outset of this chapter, having John Howard as my dean, mentor, and friend was serendipitous. Purchase, however, could not provide the kind of grounding in blackness and liberation scholarship available at Howard, which has as its mission teaching, research, and service unapologetically committed to the liberation of black people.

CHAPTER 8

Howard Redux and Prairie View

At the time of my appointment to the Howard faculty, Marguerite Ross Barnett was chair of the Political Science Department. Widely recognized as a "rising star" among young black political scientists, she subsequently went on to become president of the University of Houston, the first black woman to head a major US university. At the time of the discussion of my appointment, Barnett was planning to leave Howard for an appointment at the City University of New York. In her letter offering the job, it was agreed I would be appointed at the rank of associate professor, with tenure possible in two years, at a salary of $21,000. Two months later, however, she informed me the Liberal Arts College Committee on Appointments and Promotions had refused to approve the associate rank, and I would be appointed as a lecturer. I wrote Barnett a long letter protesting the reneging on the agreement. She could not respond because, she replied, "It was my last day as chair." Although I was promoted to associate a year after my appointment and granted tenure a couple of years later, this bureaucratic snafu in my initial appointment was replicated in my appointment as full professor, which was a factor in my eventual decision to leave the university.

The teaching experience at Howard was unique and rewarding at both the graduate and undergraduate levels because I taught only in the black politics field, an opportunity available at no other university. This allowed for a deepening of my understanding of the field and facilitated my research. Among the classes I taught were introductory undergraduate and graduate courses, and seminars on black leadership, black ideologies, electoral politics, urban black politics, and race and public policy.

Although the salad days of the 1970s were gone, Howard's Political Science Department faculty was still noteworthy, with the addition of young scholars such as the white feminist theorist Jane Flax, the public policy and housing specialist Joseph McCormick, Middle East specialist and Egyptian Mervat Hatem, the Africanist James Sulton, and the renowned public administration scholar Jean-Claude García-Zamor.

The students, especially the undergraduates, were from diverse parts of the black world and in general were quite good. I do not recall having any white students during the eight years at Howard. A humorous incident involved my thinking there was a white student in the class. When I referred to him as white, the class almost in unison shouted: "Do you know who he is?" He was Adam Clayton Powell III, the grandson of the legendary Harlem congressman.

Kwame Ture's (Stokely Carmichael) All African People's Revolutionary Party (the small cadre organization he formed to advance his Pan-Africanist ideology) met in the basement of Douglass Hall where I conducted my evening seminars. Occasionally, he would stop in and ask us if we were "ready for revolution," and on one occasion spent a half hour or so with us discussing the beginnings of Black Power.

Three members of the faculty became lifelong friends. I first met Joe McCormick at a political science conference and immediately established what would become a strong, lasting bond. A native of Washington, Joe and his wife Janet became our best friends while in Washington. He, Jim Sulton, and I spent countless hours in his basement drinking, smoking grass, discussing the multifaceted problems of black people, and the ways of white folk. Joe and I team taught the race and public policy course and wrote a couple of articles on the Jesse Jackson presidential campaigns.

Rick Seltzer was one of two whites added to the faculty since my graduate studies (the other was Jane Flax). Rick was one of two department methodologists. I often joked, "Rick is someone who knows little about anything but knows how to know about everything." A specialist in surveys and quantitative analysis, Rick often teamed with colleagues on a substantive issue that he knew little about and joined them to do an original survey or analyze existing surveys on it. Many of his scores of articles were coauthored in this way.

Rick and I wrote multiple papers and journal articles in this kind of collaboration, including on race and ideology, race and civil liberties, race and alienation, and "Color Differences in the Afro-American Community and the Differences They Make." We wrote the skin color article as kind of a lark, but it turned out to be one of our most widely cited articles. In 1981 the National Opinion Research Center rated black respondents on the basis of their color—dark, medium, and light skin. We analyzed these color differences in relationship to socioeconomic status and political attitudes. We found lighter skin blacks had higher socioeconomic status but, controlling for class, there were few skin-color differences in political attitudes. Again, we thought this was a rather trivial article, but it attracted a large audience.

At the outset of the AIDS crisis, the Urban League asked me to review the available polling data on black attitudes toward the disease, looking toward publication in their annual *State of Black America* report. Rick assisted me in the collection and analysis of the data, and I traveled to New York to present the preliminary findings. Although the findings were not surprising—see further discussion later in this chapter—it was clear to me that many on the league staff (including John Jacobs, the president) were uncomfortable with the league being identified with AIDS, because it was viewed as a disease associated with illegal or immoral behavior. In the end, the league declined to publish the study but released the rights to us to publish elsewhere. We published the paper in the new *AIDS and Public Policy Journal* as "Racial Differences and Interracial Racial Differences Among Blacks in America in Attitudes Toward AIDS." We found racial differences in knowledge and attitudes toward the disease, with blacks being somewhat more likely to be misinformed about its modes of transmission, more fearful of contracting it, more likely to indicate that AIDS affected them personally, and that they engaged in high-risk (multiple sex partners) heterosexual behavior. The findings, we suggested, required more education and outreach in areas of intravenous drug use, risks of multiple sex partners, and the advisability of condom use by persons with many sex partners.

Rick and I wrote three books. The first, *Race, Class, and Culture: A Study in Afro-American Mass Opinion* (1992), was the first book on black-white opinion differences since the end of the of the civil rights movement. We found that compared to white Americans blacks were culturally distinct in terms of religiosity and alienation, and politically distinctive in their near-monolithic adherence to the liberal ideology, except on social issues such as gay rights and abortion. The next was *Contemporary Controversies and the American Racial Divide* (2000), which was also kind of a lark. During the highly publicized O. J. Simpson trial Rick called and said, "Everybody else is making some money on O. J., we should too. Let's write a book." The book thus started as a study of the deep racial divisions on the Simpson case, but we expanded it to include other contemporary cases of deep racial cleavages in opinion (the young white woman editor at the press that published the book insisted that Simpson's name not appear in the title; otherwise we had planned to title it *The O. J. Simpson Case and Other Controversies Across the Color Line*). The other cases included in the book were the Rodney King police beating and the subsequent Los Angeles riot; the Tawana Brawley case in Wappingers Falls, New York; the reelection of Marion Barry as Washington mayor after his arrest, trial, conviction, and imprisonment for crack cocaine possession; race differences in opinion on whether AIDS and the presence of illicit drugs in the black community were part of a conspiracy against blacks; and opinions on selected black leaders, Colin Powell, Louis Farrakhan, and Jesse Jackson.

Our last book, *Polarization and the Presidency: From FDR to Barack Obama* (2015), was initially to be a study of why Obama was such a polarizing president in terms of race, ideology, and party. But we expanded it to a broad historical inquiry, using survey data, into the origins and consequences of the contemporary polarization of American politics. We found that FDR's presidency was highly polarized, as it broke with the tradition of limited government and created the American welfare state. It was followed by a series of depolarized presidencies from Truman to Carter. These presidencies were depolarized because until Ronald Reagan, the Republican presidents (Eisenhower and Nixon) accepted FDR's welfare state. Reagan was the first Republican president since FDR who rejected the New Deal premises on the welfare state and taxes (Reagan here was the heir of Barry Goldwater, the defeated 1964 Republican nominee, who opposed the New Deal as well as the *Brown* decision and the Civil Rights Act of 1964, both of which Reagan also opposed). Reagan's election immediately repolarized American politics along fundamental liberal-conservative ideological lines and, with the exception of the depolarized George H. W. Bush, every presidency since Reagan has been polarized.

Rick and I were more than collaborators, we were close friends. We talked, visited, and dined frequently. I recall his wedding with humor. Rick is Jewish and his wife Grace is Italian. Attending the wedding and reception recalled some of the ethnic tensions from my New York days, and the 1970s comedy *Bridget Loves Bernie*, about the marriage of a Jewish and Irish couple.

Another lasting friend I made at Howard was Raymond Boone, the legendary African American journalist. Boone, then on Howard's journalism faculty, took one of my classes as part of his work for the master's in political science. A former White House correspondent for the Afro-American news chain, he later edited the *Richmond Afro* and in 1992 he returned to Richmond where he was founder, publisher, and editor of the weekly

Richmond Free Press. It was a pleasure to have a person of Boone's broad experience and knowledge in the seminar; he almost became a coinstructor.

After the class we became friends, having dinner at my house and at his Baltimore residence or later at his Virginia estate and subsequently conversing on the phone when I moved to California. He mailed the weekly *Free Press* to me, and we often argued about its editorials, especially during the Clinton impeachment, which he editorially opposed and which I and Samuel Yette, the former *Newsweek* correspondent and author of the widely read 1980s book *The Choice: The Issue of Black Survival in America* and the *Free Press*'s columnist, strongly supported.

The always dapper Boone was a great raconteur, hosting glittering gatherings at his home. A memorable one was a party in Baltimore where a who's who of Maryland politics were present, including the governor and Senator Paul Sarbanes, who embarrassed the brothers by being the best dancer at the party, doing a mean version of the Twist that would have put Chubby Checker to shame. Boone died in 2014 of cancer. He was seventy-six.

In my years at Howard I tried to avoid administrative and committee work, although like all tenured faculty members, I served on the hiring and promotion committee. I also throughout my time served as chair of the black politics field committee, and in my last year as director of graduate studies. I tried to avoid administrative and committee work so I could devote most of my time to research and writing. I developed a particular interest in the study of African American leadership, historical and contemporary. I taught the graduate seminar on black leadership and did extensive research and writing. In 1985 I coedited with Walters a special issue of the *Urban League Review, Reflections on Black Leadership.* The purpose of the volume was to "let black leaders speak for themselves." So, after historical and theoretical papers by Ron and I, the volume included essays by Louis Farrakhan; Jesse Jackson; John Jacobs, head of the Urban League; Benjamin Chavis, former NAACP head; the president of Howard; the president of Delta Sigma Theta; John Johnson, the publisher; Marc Stepp, the labor leader; Eleanor Holmes Norton, chair of the Equal Employment Opportunity Commission; Ambassador Elliott Skinner; and Congressmen John Conyers and William Gray.

The Joint Center for Political Studies, the Washington-based think tank on African American politics and policy, commissioned a monograph on black leadership, but as was typical of my work with the center (discussed later) after multiple reviews the center declined to publish "On Black Leadership," claiming it was "too academic." I did publish a monograph comprehensively reviewing the social science literature on "Negro" and "black" leadership from the 1930s to the 1980s. Published in 1987 by Howard's Institute of Urban Affairs and Research, it was later slightly revised and included as part 1 in *African American Leadership* (1999), coauthored with Walters and published in the SUNY series in African American Studies. My most important and influential book is *We Have No Leaders: African Americans in the Post–Civil Rights Era* (1996), also published in the SUNY series.

Off-campus, I was involved in several quasi-academic activist formations and organizations. The first was the so-called Hampshire Group, after Hampshire College where the group first met. Although the group did little beyond holding its organizing meeting, it did provide the good opportunity to meet James Baldwin. The group included Alex Willingham, Jerry Watts, William Darity, Adolph Reed, Willie Legette, and Robert Starks. I cannot recall whose idea it was to form the group (probably Reed's), but its purpose was to organize a small group of left black scholars who would think through the black predicament and come up with concrete strategies and policy ideas. At the first meeting we agreed to examine industrial policy, which was then the subject of extensive discussion in Congress and the media, in terms of its likely impact on economic development and employment in the black community. Although we exchanged correspondence and suggested readings on the subject, nothing else came of the group's work and it soon faded away. My files indicate a second meeting was scheduled at Howard (I reserved rooms), but the meeting did not occur.

At the time of our meeting Baldwin was writer in residence at Hampshire and other area colleges. He stopped by and spent some time exchanging small talk with us. I cannot recall any of what he said; what was most memorable was how obviously and flamboyantly gay he was. This was somewhat off-putting to us. We shared dorm-like accommodations at the conference and that night there was much off-color humor about who would share a room in terms of who showed the most homosexual proclivities.

Wilbur Rich, editor of *African American Perspectives in Political Science* (2007), five years after Hanes Walton's death in 2013 wrote that "arguably he was one of the greatest political scientists of his generation. He was more than just a pioneer scholar. For years Walton set the research agenda for scholars of black politics. His research and insights into black politics have influenced scholars of American politics and electoral politics in general. Scholars of black politics still rely heavily on his work."

Like most budding students of black politics in the early 1970s, I first encountered Hanes through his pioneering, first in the field, textbook *Black Politics: A Theoretical and Structural Analysis*. For a young beginning graduate student aspiring to be a scholar of black politics, the book demonstrated the potentials of the emergent field to contribute to a more scientific approach to understanding black liberation politics and was a crucial reference work in my early years of graduate study.

I first met Hanes in 1980 when he came to Howard as a visiting scholar at Howard's Institute of Urban Affairs and Research, the same year I joined the political science faculty. He had just completed the manuscript for *Invisible Politics*, his groundbreaking critique of the behavioral approach to the study of black politics. I had just become coeditor of the SUNY series in African American Studies. Hanes graciously consented to allow us to publish the manuscript as the first volume in the series (after thirty years and fifty books in the series, *Invisible Politics* remains the best-selling volume). Thereafter we became close friends and colleagues, reading and critiquing each other's work, exchanging ideas in correspondence and phone conversations, and writing jointly several articles. In 1991 he conceived a new textbook in black politics and asked me to join as coauthor. Until his death in 2013 we worked on multiple editions of this text, *American Politics and the African American Quest for Universal Freedom.*

Hanes wished the text to appeal to multiple political science constituencies. It followed the format of the standard American government text, integrating the presence and influence of African Americans throughout. Thus, it could serve as the principal text in American government classes for instructors who wished to teach from a black perspective. Hanes thought this might be especially appealing to professors at HBCUs. Second, the text could serve as a companion or supplement in the traditional American government course. And finally, he thought, it could be used as the basic text in black politics courses in black studies. In other words, he wanted a book that would integrate, systemically, the black experience into the American experience. "Race," we argued in the preface of the text, "is the most important cleavage in American life, with enormous impacts on the nation's society, culture and politics. Indeed, as we show throughout this book, race has always been the enduring fault-line in American politics, thus the need for a volume that treats this important topic with the seriousness it deserves."

Herbert Aptheker, editor of the indispensable two-volume *Documentary History of the Negro People in the United States*, writes, "The Negro people have fought like tigers for their freedom, and in doing so have enhanced the freedom struggles of all other people." This epigram at the beginning of the book highlights the two interrelated themes of the text: the concept of universal freedom and the idea of minority-majority coalitions. Hanes originated both themes. In the first he argued that in their quest for their freedom blacks universalized the idea of freedom. In their attack on slavery and racial subordination blacks and their leaders embraced doctrines of universal freedom for all peoples. In doing so they had important influences on shaping democratic and constitutional government and expanding the idea of freedom not just for themselves but for all Americans.

But Hanes contended that because of their status as a subordinate, relatively powerless minority racial group, blacks could not act alone. Rather, in their quest for freedom, they had to form coalitions with whites. Thus, *minority-majority coalitions* are defining features of black politics. Historically, however, these coalitions because of the nation's ambivalence about race and racism have tended to be unstable and temporary, requiring that they constantly be rebuilt in a Sisyphean struggle. This too is a defining feature of black politics, and the two themes constitute the organizing framework of the text.

Published in 2000 by Longman and since 2017 by Routledge the book is now in its ninth edition. After Hanes's death, I asked Sherri Wallace, a young political scientist on the faculty of the University of Louisville who had written detailed, nuanced peer reviews for several editions, to join me as coauthor. Sherri brought a much-needed black feminist perspective to the text, as well as expertise in preparing online teaching guides and auxiliaries.

Hanes was the first person (in 1967) to receive the PhD in political science from Howard, which in 1993 awarded him its Distinguished PhD alumni award. Hanes taught from 1967 to 1992 at historically black Savannah State University where he was Fuller E. Callaway professor. From 1992 until his death he taught at the University of Michigan. The American Political Science Association after his death established the Hanes Walton Jr. Award to recognize political scientists whose lifetime of scholarship makes a significant contribution to understanding racial and ethnic politics, and the University of Michigan established the Walton Endowment for Graduate Study in Racial and Ethnic Politics and a chair in his honor in the Political Science Department.

In my *Hanes Walton Jr.: The Architect of the Black Science of Politics* I credit Hanes with codifying the field of black politics, and as the person principally responsible for its institutionalization in the discipline of political science. In the making of me as a black liberation scholar, I am so glad to have had the opportunity to work with this grand scholar of black politics.

During the summer of 1985 I was guest scholar in residence at the Joint Center. Established in 1970, by the 1980s under the leadership of Eddie

Williams the center was recognized as an authoritative source on black politics and race policies. I proposed to the center's director of research, Milton Morris, to conduct a study of the five majority-black congressional districts—New Orleans, Queens, New York, Newark, New Jersey, Atlanta, and the Mississippi Delta—that elected white representatives. Given the poor representation of blacks in Congress and the perceived need to maximize representation, the study's underlying premise was that black districts that elected whites should elect blacks, given the reluctance of whites to vote for blacks.

This would enhance black descriptive, symbolic, and substantive representation. This premise was rejected by some members of the center staff. Ed Dorn, the deputy director of research, wrote:

> While I believe the research will yield some useful case study material, I do not understand why it is being undertaken, that is, the "so what" that motivates the effort. The study appears to be informed by the unstated belief that there is something wrong with the fact that majority or near majority black CDs are represented by whites. There may be some normative basis for that belief. But if there is, then, the converse may be true: There may be something wrong with the fact that some majority white CDs are represented by blacks.

Given the history of white racist voting behavior compared to blacks, I thought Dorn's observation was rather obtuse, but the normative basis of the study was that whites were proportionately overrepresented in Congress and blacks were proportionately underrepresented and therefore could not afford to "waste" seats, and that blacks were more likely to understand and advance black interests than even the most sympathetic of liberal whites.

After I completed the study—"When Majority Black Districts Elect White Representatives: Case Studies in Race and Representation"—and after it went through multiple reviews by the center staff and external experts, and multiple revisions, the center declined to publish it, I guess because it disagreed with its basic normative premise, which was made explicit in the study's introduction. Although I was disappointed that the study was not published (its principal findings were that the advantages of incumbency, factionalism in the black community, and low black voter turnout were the major explanations for the failure of the districts to elect blacks), I did publish two journal articles based on the research and the $10,000 honorarium for the project provided the down payment on my first house.

In 1987 Myrna Adams, the assistant vice provost at SUNY Stony Brook, invited me to an invitational conference to address ways to increase the number of minority faculty. The other invitees were mainly minorities—blacks, Latinos, Native and Asian Americans. I was invited, presumably, because at the time I was director of graduate studies in political science at Howard. Myrna, African American, was passionately committed to getting professional academic organizations to commit to working for diversity in faculty and curriculum, as well as the development of appropriate state and federal policies. The Stony Brook conference included more than eighty faculty and administrators, and similar numbers attended subsequent meetings in Albuquerque, Denver, and Ann Arbor. At the 1989 Ann Arbor meeting we established Open Mind, an organization devoted to enhancing "excellence and diversity through the fullest participation of people of color in the faculty and administrative ranks of institutions of higher education." In its several years of operation Open Mind used publications and lobbying at professional associations to increase minority faculty and broaden the canons of knowledge, scholarship, and pedagogy. Our major publication was the 1989 report, *Meeting the National Need for Minority Scholars and Scholarship: Policies and Actions*, which was distributed to professional disciplinary associations, associations of university administrators, and state and federal higher education officials. Members from each of the social science and humanities disciplines were asked to write articles for their disciplines' journals explaining our concerns, with disciplinary specific recommendations. John Garcia of the University of Arizona and I prepared an article for political science: "Meeting the National Need for Minority Scholars and Scholarship: What Professional Associations Might Do." Working with the Open Mind group was a good learning experience. I especially learned from our Native American colleagues from across the country who brought unique indigenous epistemological perspectives to broaden the basis of research and teaching.

Because of Ron Walters, I became involved as activist and voluntary staff in the 1984 Jesse Jackson presidential campaign. I initially dismissed the idea of a black running for president in 1984 as a waste of time and resources that would inevitably help Reagan get reelected. But as a result of listening to and reading Ron's papers I was persuaded that a black presidential campaign inside the Democratic Party might have some advantages in enhancing black power in the Democratic Party and the party system generally. (Walters's thinking on strategies of black presidential campaigns is developed comprehensively in *Black Presidential Politics: A Strategic Approach* published in the SUNY series in African American Studies in 1988.)

Although I did not hold the opportunistic, flamboyant Jackson in high regard, during the 1984 campaign I came to see him, flaws taken into account, as the most significant black leader of the post–civil rights era. In 2000 I conducted a poll of a sample of NCOBPS members asking them to select in rank order the five greatest black leaders of all time. To my surprise Jackson came in number seven in a list of ten (actually twelve, since two were tied). The only living person on the list, he came in ahead of Ida Wells-Barnett, Fannie Lou Hamer, and Adam Clayton Powell.

The main reason I became a supporter and worker in the 1984 Jackson campaign was that Ron was named deputy campaign manager. I had great respect for his political sagacity; how could I turn down a call to action from my mentor and friend in what he believed to be a historic moment in the liberation struggle? I did minor staff work, assisting Ron in recruiting other black political scientists to the campaign; writing invited op-eds in *USA Today* (explaining Jackson's "Hymie Town" remarks and trying to defend Louis Farrakhan's role in the campaign); writing a couple of position papers (on the Second Primary and patronage appointments in Democratic administrations); and an extended critique, circulated privately to selected black political scientists and journalists, of Adolph Reed's *The Jesse Jackson Phenomenon*, the most critical attack on the campaign by a black scholar. Ron got a staff pass for me for the Democratic Convention in San Francisco, but I did little work and rarely attended the convention, spending most of the time visiting Larry and other Berkeley friends.

Reed's book was a scathing critique of the Jackson campaign and it received equally scathing responses from the black intellectual community. Shirley Washington in *The Black Scholar* (November/December 1986) described the book as cynical, sarcastic, and mean-spirited. In the *American Political Science Review*, Dianne Pinderhughes wrote, "Reed must be faulted for his consistent lack of restraint. A *sine qua non* for serious work is rational discourse, but Reed too often succumbs to the cutting comment or witty thrust instead of analysis, which suggests a basic lack of respect for his subject matter." And Kenneth Clark wrote, "Reed's emotionality renders him unable to deal seriously with the phenomenon of Jesse Jackson. The repeated diatribes left this reader wondering about the purpose of the book and the motivation of the publisher."

The Jackson campaigns of 1984 and 1988 did not achieve their major strategic objective of halting the Democratic Party's drift to the right and moving it in a more progressive direction on race and related issues such as welfare and crime. To the contrary, that drift was accelerated by the campaign and presidency of the next Democratic president, Bill Clinton. But the campaigns were symbolically and historically important as the first really serious and credible black presidential campaigns: they mobilized a significant black vote (for the first time the black vote in the Democratic primaries may have exceeded that of whites), they established the parameters of the rainbow coalition that nominated and elected Obama twenty years later, and the Jackson campaigns inspired changes in the delegate allocation rules that were indispensable to Obama winning the nomination in 2008.

Given the failures of the Democratic Party and its nominees to respond to Jackson's policy demands, Ron favored Jackson running as an independent in the general election in order to end the "captive status" of the black vote and show it could not be taken for granted by the Democratic Party. I was skeptical about the strategic efficacy of an independent campaign because it would result in the certain election of the Republican candidate. Ron was willing to pay this price in a couple of elections in order to teach the Democratic Party a lesson and establish the "independent leverage" of the black vote. I was not as convinced of this as a strategy but if Ron and Jackson had mounted an independent campaign, I probably would have joined them.

Jackson's esteem as a black leader was diminished when the *National Enquirer* reported he had fathered a child with a young member of his staff. I feel I was a bit responsible in a way since I had an indirect role in bringing Jackson and Karin Stanford, the young staff member, together. Karin was a graduate student at the University of Southern California (USC). On the advice of my old UCLA friend Gerald Bender, who was then on the USC faculty, she got in touch with me about doing doctoral work at Howard. She called and I facilitated her admission and then left the university before she arrived. However, I advised her on the dissertation, which was on Jackson's foreign policy ventures. I also assisted in revising the dissertation, which was published in 1997 in the SUNY series in African American Studies as *Beyond the Boundaries: Jesse Jackson in International Affairs.*

This is in a roundabout way my bit of responsibility for the two of them coming together. Karin interviewed Jackson for the dissertation, and she subsequently joined his Washington staff. On a visit to Washington in the 1990s Bird and I had lunch with her and Jack White, the *Time* magazine columnist and television commentator. When we saw Ron later that evening, he told us he sensed something untoward was going on between Karin and Jackson, and exclaimed, "Bob, we got to get her out of there" (Karin out of Jackson's office). When we learned Karin was pregnant, we thought Jackson was likely the father. Nevertheless, I was angry and yelled at the reporter from the *New York Daily News* who first called and asked me about the *National Enquirer* story. Reporters called me presumably because I was an editor of Karin's book on Jackson. I was disappointed and angry about Karin and Jackson's behavior. When I was interviewed by the *Washington Post* I expressed this disappointment and anger: "I am very disappointed with him. I don't think his behavior is defensible in any way. This conduct, it seems to me, undermines one of the principal bases of his leadership which is moral authority." Later in an interview with BET News I was even harsher in my condemnation of their immoral behavior, and their betrayal of family and community. After the interview I thought it too harsh and called the reporter and asked her not to use the interview; she did not. Karin and I remained friends. I contributed an article on Ron to the two-volume *Encyclopedia of Black Power*, which she coedited, and a chapter on the NAACP to *Black Political Organizations in the Post–Civil Rights Era*, which she also coedited.

I consider myself an "ebony tower" intellectual. Since my undergraduate days of activism at Cal State and Berkeley, I avoided activism to concentrate on scholarship. Ron, the scholar-activist extraordinaire, occasionally pulled me into his activist orbit, as was the case with the Jackson campaign. It was also the case when he led protests of the National Research Council's study of the status of blacks, and his efforts to create a national organization of black faculty. In November 1985 Bernadette Chachere, a friend and an economist on the faculty of Hampton University, told me that at a meeting of Ford Foundation minority postdoctoral fellows she learned of an in-progress study of the status of blacks in America sponsored by the National Research Council (NRC). Bernadette said the black fellows objected to the study because it was headed by a white scholar and the panels of scholars conducting the research appeared to be dominated by whites. In a phone conversation sometime later I casually mentioned this to Ron. He did not take it casually. To the contrary, he said something to the effect of "Bob, this is outrageous; we can't let this stand." After speaking with Bernadette, Ron argued black scholars should organize to protest the study. Bernadette and I agreed and joined him as co-organizers. Ron's immediate call for protest was based on his belief, subsequently proven correct, that the study was undertaken without input from the organized black scholarly community and consequently would lack black perspectives. Paraphrasing Du Bois Ron said that a study of the status of blacks organized by whites should have as much legitimacy as a study of the status of Catholics organized by Protestants.

Ron's strategy of protest was to inform the heads of the black social science associations and the heads of the social science departments at the major black universities to learn if they had been consulted by NRC about the study—they had not—and seek their assistance in a national protest whose aim would be to insert more black scholars and perspectives into the study. If that failed then its cancellation would be sought, and if that failed, delegitimization of the study in the eyes of the black academic community and the public would be sought. Over several months we visited black scholarly conferences to discuss the protest, issued press releases, held press conferences, and contributed to a special issue of *Transaction/Society*, which focused on the controversy our protest had generated (vol. 24, 1987). Overall, our protest did not result in cancellation of the study, but a few more black scholars were added to the project probably as result of the protest, the protest likely heightened sensitivity of the panelists to black perspectives, and the protest probably contributed to the poor reception the study received when it was published. Subsequently, the study *A Common Destiny: Blacks and American Society* edited by Robin Williams and Gerald Jaynes was published in 1987. After a couple of newspaper articles, the study was forgotten, and it is rarely cited in the literature.

In the course of the protest Ron concluded that the arrogance of the NRC in attempting to impose on black people its study of us without consulting us was a display of white imperial intellectual power that could best be combated by more effectively organized black intellectual power. Therefore, he called for the establishment of a National Congress of Black Faculty. To create a national organization of black faculty from different disciplines, backgrounds, and campuses was a herculean undertaking. At Howard on October 23, 1987, with 175 persons in attendance the National Congress of Black Faculty was formally established, with Ron elected president. The first meeting was the most successful. At the second meeting in 1988 only fifty persons were present, dues were not forthcoming, and efforts to attract philanthropic support were unsuccessful. A couple of years later we formally disbanded the congress.

By the late 1980s Bird and I were having constant California dreams. We were tired of the cold weather, the snow, shoveling snow, of snow tires; I never really learned how to drive in the snow. My salary at Howard was not sufficient for our growing family (Jessica Juanita was born in 1981 and Scottus Charles in 1985). In 1988 I filed bankruptcy mainly to discharge my student loan and credit debt, and yet ends were barely meeting (Congress subsequently passed laws making it impossible to discharge student loan debt and virtually impossible to discharge credit card debt). It also became clear that even after promotion to professor the salary would be inadequate (when I told Ron how much I expected when promoted, he laughed and exclaimed, "Bob, you won't get that; you would be making more than I am"). I therefore decided to look for a new job, with the basic criteria being: (1) no snow and (2) more money. Although I clearly preferred California, preferably the Bay Area, I was willing to consider any place that met the criteria. There were no job postings in California, but in 1986 I got a letter from Charles Nixon, one of my old UCLA professors (I took my first class, a methods course, from him) inviting me to apply for a position in American/African American politics. I was delighted and immediately sent my vita, but I was not called for an interview. The position went to Reginald Gilliam, who went on to have a long career in teaching and administration.

My interest in leaving Howard was reinforced when there was an unexpected delay in my promotion, which I thought should have been easily approved. The delay angered and to some extent depressed me because I thought I had clearly earned promotion. The department committee recommended promotion 11 to 1 but the college committee rejected it, claiming I had "insufficient articles in peer reviewed journals" and "the marginal quality of some of the work." (This may have been, in part, because on instructions of the department I submitted publications only since my promotion to full professor rather than the full file.) I was outraged by the decision and filed a long letter of protest with the college. After much delay the college committee reversed itself and approved the promotion.

Ron's observation that the promotion would not mean much of a salary increase was confirmed. I was appointed in 1980 at a salary of $21,000; by 1987 I was earning $38,155 (the maximum for an associate was $38,398). The maximum for a full professor was $51,098, which I was told would take several years to reach. This salary was not acceptable. Therefore, I intensified my efforts to find a place with no snow and more money. My salary was the sole source of income since Bird worked only occasionally, partly because I still did not wish her to work full-time, and the cost of good child care probably would have been prohibitive.

While I was eager to leave Howard and Washington, there was one thing I knew I would miss—the Saturday afternoon blues show hosted by Jerry "the Bama" Washington. As I indicated, by the time I left California I had stopped listening to contemporary music and turned to the music of the past. Since Berkeley my favorite music of the past was the blues, and *The Bama Hour* on Saturday afternoons on WPFW, the local Pacifica station, was the best blues show in the world. In addition to playing the classic blues of the Robert Johnson era, he also played the best of Bobby, B. B. and Sonny Boy, and all the rest, mixed in with downhome wisdom and humor delivered in a slow southern drawl. Sometimes called the black Garrison Keillor, the Bama had a "Delta chic" that was unique; he was the philosopher for the blues people. Knowing I would soon leave Washington I began recording the show and I have today a wonderful collection that I listen to nearly all the time while driving. On my return to the Bay Area, on Saturday afternoons, I listened on the local Pacifica station, KPFA, to Tom Mazzolini's *Blues by the Bay*. While not the Bama's Delta chic, Mazzolini's through knowledge of the roots of the music and its classic and contemporary artists was evident.

I sent a letter to Duke University's Political Science Department about the possibility of an appointment, although it had not advertised a vacancy. I was invited for an interview. Like my interviews at Yale and MIT while at Purchase, I found the Duke faculty arrogant and condescending. For example, I was told as soon as I sat down with one Yale faculty member that I would never get tenure because Yale tenured only the best scholars in the world. Presumably just by looking at me he could tell I could not be among the world's best (a subsequent examination of his vita indicated that neither was he). At Duke there was a young African American assistant professor with a couple of years on the Duke faculty with few, if any, publications, yet the chair of the department had the gall to suggest that Howard hire him as a full professor!

I was invited to Texas A&M for an interview. The faculty was pleasant enough, but once I arrived on the campus, I immediately knew it was not for the place for me. Texas A&M was a military school and once I saw the young cadets marching in formation on campus, I knew this was not a politically congenial place, the weather and the money notwithstanding. If an appointment had been offered, I may have accepted, knowing it was a mistake. My friend from Howard graduate school days, Paula McClain, asked me to join her at Arizona State. Knowing of my wish to return to sunny California, she quipped Arizona was California without the beaches. The visit went well, and Arizona State made a good offer in terms of salary, but I declined; the desert was a bit too much sun.

Meanwhile, Mack Jones had left his position as the longtime chair of Atlanta University's Political Science Department and had joined Howard's faculty as senior professor. We became good friends. When he later became head of the social science division at Prairie View A&M University, he asked me to join him as part of a cohort of new faculty he was attempting to recruit. I enjoyed teaching at a black college, and I respected Mack, so I was inclined to accept the appointment at the rank of professor at a salary of $45,000. Another reason Bird and I were inclined to accept was that Prairie View was less than a day's drive to our parents' homes. Many of my colleagues thought it foolhardy to leave the capstone of black education to go a small black college in rural Texas (Paula found it inexplicable I would turn down Arizona State in favor of Prairie View).

In the midst of discussions with Mack I got a call from Rufus Browning, chair of the Political Science Department at San Francisco State. He told me the department was conducting an affirmative action search to hire its first black faculty member in the near hundred-year history of the university. I was surprised and delighted for it appeared our California dreaming was about to become a reality. A reality not just in California but in my favorite city and at the university that was the birthplace of black studies and one of the most self-consciously radical universities in the nation. Rufus was another reason I found San Francisco State alluring, for he and his San Francisco State colleague David Tabb were students of black and minority group politics and coauthors of one of the most influential and often-cited books in the field, *Protest Is Not Enough: The Struggle of Blacks and Hispanics in Urban Politics.* Their book did at the local level—tracing the incorporation of blacks into urban political systems—what I was researching at the national level. Thus, I knew I would have at least two colleagues of parallel research interests.

The interview went well, and I found the faculty in the department eager to have me come. In his letter offering the position the president of the university, Chia Wei Woo, was also eager, writing in a handwritten postscript, "I sincerely hope that you would accept and join our team at San Francisco State University. We need you!" Although alluring, I found the specifics of the offer unsatisfactory. The appointment was at the associate rank with tenure at a salary of $48,017. Given the high cost of housing in the Bay Area, I thought the salary inadequate. I also thought I merited appointment at the full professor rank. So, I reluctantly declined my dream job, writing the president, "The offer was generous, and I really believe I would have enjoyed San Francisco State. Yet, given the high cost of housing in the Bay Area my wife and I judge that acceptance of the offer would not be prudent at this time." I wrote letters to Rufus, David, and Kay Lawson explaining my decision, and was encouraged when they responded that they would try to seek changes in rank and salary so as to make it possible for me to join them. In the meantime, it was off to Prairie View.

Prairie View A&M University is one of the oldest historically black universities in the nation, founded in 1876 during Reconstruction. A part of the Texas A&M system, the campus is located in rural Waller County about fifty miles from downtown Houston. The university offers undergraduate and master's degrees. When I arrived, the social science faculty included the venerable "mother" of black political science, Jewel Prestage, the longtime former chair of the Political Science Department at Southern University and now dean of Prairie View's honors college. The second African American woman to earn the PhD in political science (after Howard's Merze Tate), as chair of political science at Southern she was probably responsible for training more black political scientists than any other person. Coming from Louisiana, Jewel sometimes seemed to take it as a personal affront that I went to California rather than to Southern to study with her, but it was a good opportunity to have the chance to be "mothered" by her for the year I was at Prairie View.

Also, on the faculty was the indomitable Imari Obadele, the provisional president of the Republic of New Africa (RNA). The RNA favored the division of the United States into separate white and black nations. A man of principle and courage, Obadele put his liberty and life on the line in pursuit of the goal of a separate black nation to be carved out of several Deep South states. In 1973 he and several of his RNA associates were victims of a predawn raid by the FBI and state police at the group's Jackson, Mississippi, headquarters. He and his associates spent several years in prison. After his release Obadele earned a PhD and became a professor of political science, writing largely on the philosophical, ideological, and legal basis for a separate black nation-state. I did not think the idea of a separate black nation either possible or desirable. Nevertheless, I enjoyed the spirited debates with Imari, which always ended in a stalemate with his ultimate rejoinder: "Bob, the idea of a separate black nation is as realistic as your idea of a racially integrated nation where blacks live in freedom and equality with whites." I always had to admit that both ideas were probably utopian.

Obadele was also principally responsible for keeping the idea of reparations—which I did and do support—alive in black politics. The founder of the National Coalition of Blacks for Reparations in America, which through writings, conferences, petitions to Congress, and litigation worked to advance the idea of reparations for slavery and Jim Crow segregation, Imari argued that reparations were a just and equitable solution to the two centuries of African oppression by Europeans. He argued also that reparations were the only possible means to an integrated and racially equitable and just

America. A courageous man of indomitable spirit, I consider it an honor to have worked with him and one of the great pleasures of my time at Prairie View. In 2000 I wrote an essay about him which included a rare interview: "Imari Obadele: The Father of the Modern Reparations Movement," which was published in Henry Louis Gates's short-lived online journal, *Africana*.

Overall, however, my year at Prairie View was a difficult one—without doubt the most difficult teaching experience of my career. The first difficulty was the teaching load of four classes a semester. In my schedule this required teaching three introduction to American politics classes of about fifty students each, and a black politics class. This required teaching five days a week instead of the usual academic schedule of two or three days a week. I found this a silly waste of faculty time, since the three American government classes I taught could easily have been combined into one or two large sections, saving both faculty and student time. I was told this rather commonsense idea was prohibited by Texas A&M regulations.

The second difficulty of Prairie View was that, like many small black colleges, it operated essentially as an open admissions institution, consciously admitting a large number of students marginally qualified for college work. This is a worthwhile, even noble, endeavor for a college, especially one serving oppressed people. As Hulan Davis, the senior member of the political science faculty, told me, he had seen countless students come to the university woefully unprepared but then go on to become good—sometimes outstanding—students and to have good careers and make good contributions to the community.

Nevertheless, this created difficulties because it required failing a large part of each class. I found this distressing and depressing, and along with the heavy, daily teaching load, it made me know I could not stay at Prairie View for long. I admire my colleagues who work under these difficult circumstances. They make an unheralded contribution to the liberation of black people. (While at Prairie View, I received letters from Michael Giles at Emory and Colin Palmer at Chapel Hill asking that I apply for joint appointments in political science and black studies. I declined both, still California dreaming.) While the work was stressful, it was mitigated by our frequent visits with our parents. On one memorable visit my mother accompanied us to Bird's parents where her father slaughtered a hog for us. A whole hog just for us—we indeed lived high on the hog and had parts of the pig to share with friends for a year.

I cannot leave Prairie View without discussing Harold Cruse and his visit to the campus. I read Cruse's monumental classic *The Crisis of the Negro*

Intellectual when it came out in 1967, and it has influenced my thinking and work as a black intellectual ever since, and I turn to it frequently for insights and inspiration. I read his other books and his articles on black politics that appeared in *Black World* during the 1970s. An iconoclastic scholar and writer, Cruse had the distinction of being one of the few persons to receive a tenured faculty appointment at a major research university—the University of Michigan—with only a high school diploma. In 1988 Mack invited Cruse to campus for a two-day visit. It was at one of his campus lectures that I got the title for my book *We Have No Leaders*. At the lecture a student asked Cruse to evaluate black leaders. He responded, "What leaders; we have no leaders," because he said none of the persons recognized as leaders individually or collectively had any kind of program, organization, strategy, or plan to mobilize or lead blacks in directions that would address their communal problems.

In addition to his public lectures, we had long illuminating conversations over dinner and drinks at Mack's house. After the visit, we began to exchange correspondence, and he provided a long, thorough handwritten assessment of parts of *We Have No Leaders*. In 1992 I had the good opportunity and honor to be invited to deliver the keynote address at the University of Michigan's celebration of the twenty-fifth anniversary of the publication of *The Crisis*. There was even some talk of my collaborating with him in the writing of his memoirs, but the distance between Ann Arbor and San Francisco and the cost of travel and accommodations made that impossible. I would have liked the opportunity to work with this "ardent black nationalist," as the *New York Times* titled its obituary. Cruse's two-day visit and getting to know Obadele were the highlights of my year at Prairie View.

CHAPTER 9

San Francisco State

Controversies, Contradictions, and Black Liberation Scholarship

In 1988 Robert Corrigan became president of San Francisco State University. Without his bold leadership and wholehearted commitment to affirmative action and diversity, the offer that allowed me to join the faculty the following year probably would not have been made. Corrigan, who served as president for twenty-four years (1988–2012), near three times the tenure of the typical university president, came to San Francisco after serving as chancellor of the University of Massachusetts. Earlier at the University of Iowa, he created one of the first Black Studies programs in the United States, one of the few white scholars to organize a Black Studies program. Married to an African American, Corrigan arrived in 1988 with a vision to enhance faculty research, recruit top-quality faculty, and enhance faculty and student diversity. Toward enhancing faculty research, he reduced the teaching load from four to three classes and indicated that future promotions and salary increases would be tilted more toward research than teaching and service. With respect to minority and gender diversity of the faculty, Corrigan inaugurated "two for one," which allowed departments and programs to hire two faculty instead of one if both were minorities or women. When he arrived, the faculty was 84 percent white and 71 percent male; when he retired it was 37 percent minorities and 48 percent female.

The scholarly output of the faculty increased during Corrigan's tenure. As part of the middle-level California State University system, San Francisco State, like the other twenty-two campuses, was designated as primarily a teaching institution. As a result, in tenure and promotion decisions a good assessment in teaching was often considered as important as research and publications. Many faculty members as a consequence concentrated on teaching, with some abandoning research and publications altogether after earning tenure and promotion. Amid some faculty grumbling Corrigan over the years changed this, giving priority to publishing. He also sought to recruit "top rate" faculty, citing my appointment in 1989 as an example of the university's success in this effort. My appointment, a year after having rejected the final offer of his predecessor the year before, is an example of Corrigan's bold commitment to affirmative action and to recruiting faculty that, if not top-ranked, were at least of considerable scholarly productivity. When I was appointed, I had published twenty-two articles in political science, black studies, and other social science journals; the Conservation of Human Resources book on equal employment opportunity; the Howard University monograph on black leadership; and coedited and contributed to special issues of the *Annals of the American Academy of Political and Social Science* and the *Urban League Review*. Again, if not the record of a top-ranked scholar, at least one of an accomplished and productive one.

The offer I declined the year before was appointment at associate professor rank with tenure at a salary of $48,000. In rejecting the offer, I suggested appointment at the professor rank with a minimum salary of $60,000. Both were unprecedented; the department had never made an appointment at full professor with tenure and the maximum salary for full professor was then $52,000. Nevertheless, the department chair, the dean of the School of Behavioral and Social Sciences (BSS), the provost, and most of the political science faculty, with the approval of Corrigan, agreed to supplement my salary from "special contingency funds." This generous out-of-the-box offer was evidence that my colleagues in the department and at top levels of the administration were anxious to have me join the faculty. Rufus Browning, as an example, wrote a nice handwritten letter: "I don't think I've ever looked forward to a new faculty member with as much enthusiasm." I accepted the appointment with alacrity, and despite alluring queries from more prestigious universities, I remained at San Francisco State for the next three decades.

Not only were my colleagues welcoming, many, like Rufus, were enthusiastic and generous. Kay Lawson and her husband Toby welcomed Bird to stay at their house while she searched for a place (the university provided reimbursement for moving expenses), and multiple colleagues drove her around the Bay Area until she found a satisfactory house. Over the years, I developed lasting friendships with some of them, Rufus and his wife Sandra Luft, who was on the humanities faculty, Kay and Toby, Amita Shastri, Gerald Heather, and David and Judith Tabb. David was like a "brother"; that is, he treated me like he was black without any of the inhibitions of the kind Gerald Bender wrote me about when I was at UCLA (see chapter 4). David, who is Jewish, was a scholar of race politics, and sometimes in his frankness about black-Jewish foibles he reminded me of the Jewish comedian Jackie Mason (we were both fans of Mason). His candor and camaraderie in discussing all things from presidential politics to family, from black-Jewish relations to reparations, from religion to drinking and drugs, to our health and finances, made him one of the best friends I have ever had.

While making new friends at San Francisco State, my best friends from the Berkeley days died. The fixation on the Kennedy assassination, which I discussed in chapter 3, ultimately destroyed my friend Dwight. He began to use hard drugs heavily, lived off disability payments, and eventually became homeless on the streets of Berkeley. I saw him once when I returned to the Bay Area in 1989, but there was little basis for communication. Years later he was found near beaten to death on the streets of Berkeley. With his brother, who came up from LA, I literally watched him take his last breath in the hospital. This was the first and only time I watched a person die. Dwight's brother, Larry, and I scattered his ashes over the hills of Berkeley overlooking the campus.

Larry was the best friend I have ever had, my personal and intellectual soulmate. He had a keen intellect and like me he majored in political science, and eventually earned a law degree from Berkeley's law school. But his real interest was philosophy. He read Hegel, Heidegger, the existentialists, as well as Indian and Japanese philosophy (the only course at Berkeley that I got a C in was Non-Western philosophy, which he talked me into taking). A favorite of his was Herman Hesse. I found these philosophical writings boring and near impenetrable but with wine and weed we spent many nights in Berkeley poring over these texts with Dwight, his girlfriend Louisa, and a few other hearty souls whose names I have forgotten. Larry remained in Berkeley after his law degree, but we continued our philosophical dialogues in long telephone conversations until I returned to the Bay Area and resumed them face to face. Larry also became a close critic of my writings, rendering detailed critiques of *Racism in the Post–Civil Rights Era: Now You See It, Now You Don't* and *We Have No Leaders: African Americans in the Post–Civil Rights Era*.

Unfortunately, shortly after graduation from law school Larry was diagnosed with kidney failure, which was genetically transmitted from his father to him and his brother. From 1973 until his death in 2004 he underwent multiple surgeries, transplants, was on multiple drugs, and in the last decade of his life twice-weekly dialysis. My wife, his longtime girlfriend Linda, and I were at his bedside on the day he died. The last things he told me were that he would miss our conversations and that I should abandon God for spirituality. At his request, there was no funeral or memorial service; instead we commemorated his death by going out to dinner and a movie. A group of us the day of his cremation went to see Michael Moore's *Fahrenheit 9/11* and had Chinese.

Larry was more than a best and dearest friend, he was a family friend (he was especially fond of my daughter Jessica, leaving her a modest sum of money—he had only a modest sum), he was my alter ego and confidant, and the only person (including my wife) with whom I shared my deepest thoughts and anxieties. I miss him as I write this memoir because he is the only person whose shared recollections could have meaningfully contributed. Indeed, a year or so before he died, we contemplated writing together a memoir of Berkeley in the 1960s.

At Berkeley, as indicated in chapter 3, I essentially ignored the political science faculty. However, on my return to the Bay Area I did get to know Aaron Wildavsky, one of the more distinguished members of the Berkeley faculty. This came about as a result of an article I wrote in a political science journal in 1989 in which I lamented that for blacks to win office in majority white constituencies it seemed necessary for them to abandon black interests and policy preferences. I wrote that if this became the pattern in America, it would represent the death of black politics. In the article I used as a frame Nelson George's 1989 critical study, *The Death of Rhythm and Blues*, in which he argued that the development of crossover music and artists, and their effective marketing to whites, had resulted in the death of the music as an authentic cultural expression. I contended that the new crossover black politicians seeking to market themselves to whites could have the same result: "Like the transformation of black music," I wrote, "it will be a hollow victory if in order to achieve equitable descriptive-symbolic representation blacks are required to sacrifice their substantive policy agenda. The new black politician would then become a shell of himself, more like a Prince or Michael Jackson than a B. B. King or a Bobby Bland."

Reading the article, Wildavsky called and said, "Let's talk." At lunch he tried to convince me that there was no necessary contradiction between a black politician representing the interests of whites as well as blacks, since their interests in many areas—in education, housing, employment, and health—converged. I took the point but pointed out that on some core issues—full employment, antipoverty policies, affirmative action—there were some basic black-white differences. Thereafter we had lunch regularly, and dinner at our homes. I had the impression he might have been looking me over to see if I might be suitable to become the first black appointed to Berkeley's political science faculty. If that were the case, I did not pass the test and it would be years before Berkeley's Political Science Department employed its first African American. At our dinners and lunches, I had assumed that Wildavsky was a typical white liberal, although I had heard that he was among the professors who had defended the war on Vietnam in the early campus teach-ins. But Wildavsky was not your typical white liberal; he was a leading neoconservative intellectual writing several articles decrying Great Society—like government programs to address the problem of racialized poverty because, he argued, poverty among blacks was largely caused by their cultural deficiencies and thus was not amenable to public policy solutions. I did not know this at the time, only discovering it after his death when I was doing research for my 2010 book *Conservatism and Racism, and Why in America They Are the Same.* If I had known of his conservative writings on race, it certainly would have made for more spirited debates and perhaps even ended the friendship. He died of lung cancer in 1993. I joined family and friends after his death in sitting shivah, and appreciated the opportunity to have gotten to know him.

When I retired in 2017, I was the most senior member of the faculty. In my near-thirty years there was a near-complete generational turnover in the department. I played a role in recruiting the new faculty and along the way established more enduring friendships. Throughout my time at the university I was an active member of the department faculty, although because of my disdain for administration I declined to serve as chair. I did serve for twenty years as chair of the department's committee on hiring, promotions, and tenure, which gave me the good opportunity to oversee the recruitment, appointment, and promotion of the new faculty. Among the many outstanding young scholars we hired were Sujian Guo, the prolific scholar of Chinese politics; James Martel, the political theorist and postmodernist scholar who was the first openly gay person hired by the department; and Tiffany Willoughby-Herard, the feminist and Africanist scholar who unfortunately remained with us for only two years before leaving to join the political science/African American studies faculty at the University of California, Irvine.

Given San Francisco's international reputation for gay and lesbian politics, Martel in 2000 was the first openly gay person hired in the department.

When I retired there were three LGBTQ faculty members (Tiffany, who served briefly, was a lesbian). Committed to ethnic and gender diversity, Corrigan did not evince a similar concern about the hiring of gay and lesbian faculty notwithstanding his leadership of a university in a city where gays and lesbians were an important cultural and political force. While my sensibilities about homosexuality continued to be influenced by my southern religious and cultural background, I was enthusiastic about the recruiting of gays and lesbians in the department so it could reflect the city's people and the university's students.

I became close colleagues and friends with Tiffany, James, and Sujian. James was the best department chair during my time at San Francisco State, bringing a laid-back, postmodern sensibility to administration. He also brought his insights as a theorist to two of my manuscripts, the introductory political science textbook, and to *Conservatism and Racism, and Why in America They Are the Same*. Tiffany and I became friends, working together after she left for Irvine on several projects in NCOBPS where we, among other things, coauthored the resolution adopted by NCOBPS supporting the (BDS) movement to boycott Israel and support the Palestine liberation struggle (discussed later in the chapter). Sujian and his wife Yuan became close friends with Bird and me. This was partly because of my longtime interest in Mao's revolution and Chinese politics generally. I enjoyed the delicious Chinese dinners Sujian prepared, and he and Yuan the soul food dinners Bird prepared. Although we could not critique each other's work, I did assist Sujian in the mechanics of textbook writing and publishing for the text he wrote on Chinese politics. As chair of the promotions committee, I made sure he got early tenure and promotions based on his prolific scholarship.

In 2006 Sujian arranged for me to be a part of a San Francisco social science delegation on a week-long visit to several leading Chinese universities. During the thoroughly informative and gastronomically delightful visit, I found Chinese scholars and students uneasy and wary trying to reconcile China's turn toward "market socialism" and the growing and glaring inequality with the equalitarian ethos of the still-venerated Mao (really giant statues of Mao were ubiquitous in Beijing). Sujian, who maintained close ties to the Communist Party and lectured frequently at the top Chinese universities, viewed the party's new economic policy as a means for China to reclaim its status as one of the world's great, if not preeminent, powers. The resulting economic dislocations and inequalities were part of the price to become a global power.

Amita Shastri joined the faculty at about the same time as I did. An immigrant from India, Amita was a scholar of East Asian politics. Perhaps because we were the only "people of color" in the department, and perhaps because I admired Nehru and Indira Gandhi, we became friends, lunching together at the end of each semester. We also had spirited debates about whether Western liberal democracy was universal, or culturally specific (I thought the latter). On a visit to Philadelphia for a political science conference, we spent a memorable afternoon at Independence Hall debating the issue. It was always interesting to compare her views on this issue with those of Sujian; it was like a tutorial on comparative paths to economic development—the Indian liberal democratic model compared to the Chinese communist model. I should have had them over together for dinner; it would have made for a spirited conversation.

After I returned to the Bay Area in 1989, I regularly attended church and continued to enjoy the rituals of the services. Indeed, I would often sing old one hundreds and preach to my children in make-believe worship services. However, sometime in the 1990s I abandoned faith, and became an atheist. Several things caused my decisive break with religion and the church. First, when I returned to the Bay Area, I briefly attended a prominent black Baptist church in Richmond, the suburb of San Francisco where I lived. However, in rapid order two pastors of the church were forced to resign because of corruption involving adultery or misappropriation of church funds. This kind of corruption to an extent has always been associated with the church and its popes, priests, rabbis, and preachers. But I guess I had just had enough. Another reason was that the churches I attended had increasingly abandoned the traditional rituals I grew up with—no fervent prayers by deacons, no old one hundreds, no traditional hymns. In other words, the modern urban black church was increasingly losing its Africanisms. Finally, as I said, I was influenced by the last words of my best friend, a lifelong atheist, Larry Mason. As he lay on his bed dying, he said, "Smitty, more and more people are leaving the church and becoming spiritual." When I told family and friends about my becoming an atheist, my sisters lamented and my largely atheist friends and colleagues celebrated. My sisters worried less about my "salvation" than about the bad influence this would have on my children. Most of my San Francisco State colleagues said, as Rufus Browning put it, "An ethic or morality based on reason is better than one based on superstitions and illusions."

Given my work on black studies in the 1960s at Cal State, LA, and Berkeley, I looked forward to coming to San Francisco and sharing close working relationships and friendships with my black studies comrades. I anticipated cross-listing my black politics class, perhaps teaching a special topics class in black studies and working on some joint projects. Given my writings in multiple areas of black politics, publishing in the leading black studies journals, and my history in creation of the discipline, I thought I would be welcomed and the department would become a kind of second home. I was assured of this likely good relationship and synergy when I met with the dean of Ethnic Studies on my visit to the campus for the interview. The dean, Philip McGee, an African American, reviewed my vita and expressed appreciation for my work in black studies during the 1960s. Yet, to my astonishment, rather than synergy there was protracted, bitter conflict with the black studies faculty. For my near-thirty years at the university, I was barely on speaking terms with my would-be black studies comrades.

Shortly after I arrived on campus, I arranged to meet with Oba T'Shaka, the longtime (1984–1996) chair of the Black Studies Department. T'Shaka was something of a hero in the San Francisco black community. In the 1960s he, then Bill Bradley, as head of the local CORE (Congress on Racial Equality) chapter, was a leader of the local civil rights movement. He led boycotts of Safeway and Lucky supermarkets that resulted in an affirmative action (this was before the term was used in civil rights policy-making) agreement to hire blacks and other minorities. After the boycott, influenced by Malcolm and the Black Power movement, Bradley changed his name and embraced Pan-Africanism and Afrocentrism. He earned a PhD from the nonaccredited Institute of Research in Berkeley, joined San Francisco State's Black Studies Department, and became chair in 1984. His several books include a study of Malcolm, and works on "the art of leadership" and African and African American cultures. Among Afrocentric black studies scholars, T'Shaka was well regarded.

At the time of our meeting, which took several weeks to arrange, I sensed something might be amiss because I believe he deliberately kept me waiting for a long time (probably an hour or more) before he came out of his office to begin the meeting. As I recall, the meeting was cordial; he certainly gave no indication that he planned to object to my teaching black politics in political science. Months passed and I did not hear from T'Shaka, although I repeatedly called and wrote two letters inquiring as to when Black Studies would sign off on the course. Meanwhile the Political Science Department formally submitted my course, PS 464, for approval. While I was not in contact with T'Shaka, Joseph Julian, dean of BSS, was meeting with Ethnic Studies School dean McGee and was assured that neither the Black Studies Department nor the school objected to my class. And then without notice to me, the department and BSS, the School of Ethnic Studies filed a formal objection to my teaching black politics in political science on the grounds that it "duplicated" a course T'Shaka was teaching, "encroached" on two other black studies courses, and would result in a "proliferation" of similar classes, all allegedly in violation of university regulations. Associate vice president for academic affairs Richard Giardina, after reviewing the syllabuses for my class and T'Shaka's, ruled that my class could not be offered because it duplicated T'Shaka's and encroached on two other black studies classes. The BSS School appealed this decision to Marilyn Boxer, the academic affairs vice president, and she reversed Giardina's decision and approved the course for offering in the upcoming fall semester.

In her memorandum of reversal, Boxer acknowledged she was breaking with university precedents. She argued this was imperative for two reasons:

> First, at the time of the establishment of the Department of Black Studies and the School of Ethnic Studies, few if any faculty with appropriate expertise were employed in existing, traditional departments. This continued to be the case for many years, during which period substantial new scholarship in ethnic studies areas was developed by researchers across the nation as well as locally. . . . Partly in response to the development of the new scholarship and partly owing to concerns for equity and diversity, each year brings to SFSU additional faculty whose interests and expertise includes subject areas falling, at least partially, within disciplines housed, on this campus, in the School of Ethnic Studies. To deprive these faculty of the right to teach material central to their academic expertise and, similarly, to deny students the opportunity to study and to enroll for credit in courses in their major fields that incorporate the spectrum of ethnically diverse peoples, would be to hinder achievement of at least one of the original—and ultimate—goals for which ethnic studies programs were established; that is, to make university courses and curricula (as well as administration, staff, faculty, and student bodies) ethnically diverse and inclusive of the total human experience.

And second:

> revision of the existing practice flows from the nature of recent and contemporary explorations in knowledge; that is, the increasing prominence across the natural and social sciences as well as the humanities and creative arts of interdisciplinary research and

teaching. As is often noted SFSU has a long and rich tradition
of fostering cross- and interdisciplinary studies. . . . Therefore,
I believe it is time for a review of our current Guidelines for
Course Review and Approval, with the goal of articulating new
guidelines that permit greater flexibility in allowing relevant
departments to offer courses in subject areas that clearly cut
across established discipline, department, and school lines.

Pleased with Boxer's decision and its reasoning, I looked forward to the fall,
and, after teaching the class for near a decade to classes that were all black,
to teaching in a multi-ethnic setting. Black studies faculty and students were
also looking forward to the fall, planning a major attack on me personally,
and to disrupt the class and force its cancellation.

    When I arrived on campus the first day of class, I was greeted by
political science faculty and students with news that a rally by black students
had just concluded where I was denounced as an "uncle tom" and "white
Negro," and where the speakers pledged to use "any means necessary" to
force cancellation of my class. When I arrived at the classroom, the hallway was filled with placard-carrying student protesters, uniformed campus
police, and (unbeknownst to me) plainclothes officers as well. As students
shouted and hung signs, they were recorded by television news cameras
and interviewed by reporters from the campus paper, the *San Francisco
Chronicle*, and the *San Francisco Examiner* who had been alerted about the
protests by the students. Also present were several political science faculty
members, including the department chair and the dean of the BSS School.
The protests went on for a couple of weeks (the class met on Tuesdays and
Thursdays). I remained calm throughout, debating the merits of the class with
the protesting students, reviewing my history in the black studies movement
in California in the 1960s, my teaching at black colleges, and explaining
my views on black culture. It was necessary to discuss my views on black
culture because someone had taken an obscure footnote from my Howard
monograph, *Black Leadership: A Survey of Theory and Research* in order to
claim I had written black people in America had no culture, when I had
actually written that while the evidence was ambiguous, I was persuaded
blacks did not have a culture distinct from the general American culture.
This also gave me the good opportunity to discuss some of the findings
on black culture from my forthcoming book, *Race, Class, and Culture: A
Study in Afro-American Mass Opinion*, which impressed my political science
colleagues, if not the students.

When the class started, it had an enrollment of about forty students. When the protest ended only five white female students remained. Of the forty students initially enrolled, I guess half enrolled to protest and disrupt the class and dropped after that work was done. Another half I guess were genuine students who dropped because of the disruption and fear and intimidation. There was no violence during the protests and none of the students were arrested. This was partly because we (the political science faculty) insisted on no use of force by the police and no arrests, and eventually that the uniform officers be withdrawn. University regulations required that a class with less than eight students be canceled, but the dean of BSS on the first day of class said that as long as one student was enrolled, the class would remain open.

In addition to the student protests, some black studies faculty led by Jimmy Garrett, a student leader during the 1960s black studies protest at the university and briefly a faculty member at Howard, engaged in personal attacks and vilifications of me. My political science colleague, Sandra Powell, nicely summed up what happen: "The Black Studies faculty moved from 'operation shut down' to 'operation slander'; engaging in a disinformation campaign worthy of the KGB." Among the lies, it was said I was married to a white woman; that Corrigan had bought me a house and gave me "instant tenure" in order to get me to do his bidding; that I was a former CIA agent; that I had worked for the racist, colonial Ian Smith regime in Rhodesia; and that I was a plagiarist. Except for the plagiarism allegations— the most serious allegation that can be made against a scholar—I ignored the calumnies. The plagiarism lie was spread by Garrett after I arranged reprinting in the campus paper of my 1968 Cal State, LA, campus paper op-ed "Black Studies: Its Need and Substance." Garrett told people on campus and around the country that I plagiarized the op-ed from something he had written. This was ridiculous. I had never read anything written by Garrett. But this particular lie I thought was defamatory so I sent certified letters to Garrett and Dean McGee (because he had transmitted the lie to Corrigan) warning that the allegation was knowingly false and defamatory, and if they did not immediately "cease and desist" I would sue both of them for slander. As far as I know, they stopped this egregious lie.

As to the substance of the controversy—whether my class duplicated T'Shaka's—this was a smokescreen masking the real, substantive basis for Ethnic and Black Studies' objection to the class. My class clearly did not duplicate T'Shaka's. First, his class had an Afrocentric perspective, beginning with a comparison of African and American conceptions of democracy.

Second, it was a sociological social movement class (its title was Black Politics: Social Movements and Liberation Themes), focusing on black nationalist movements from Garvey to Malcolm and comparing Malcolm and Martin Luther King's philosophies and strategies during the 1960s. My class had a political science focus on power and power relations between blacks and whites; second, it focused on racism and white supremacy as theoretical frameworks; and finally, it was institutional, focusing on the incorporation of blacks into US systemic institutions, mainly Congress and the presidency. Rather than duplicative, the classes were complementary; students could take both courses and learn almost wholly different theories, approaches, and substantive material about the politics of black people in the United States—the classes were as different, if I may use the phrase, as white and black.

The real, substantive reasons for Black Studies' objections were articulated by black studies professor Laura Head, perhaps my most fierce antagonist during the controversy, in a position paper she circulated to all faculty. She raised two interrelated objections. First, she contended, "The present administration has begun a plan which *will* result in the destruction of the School of Ethnic Studies. In 1988 President Corrigan said faculty of color should be able to teach in their area of expertise in their home departments. This in conjunction with actions to hire faculty of color in traditional departments could lead to the duplication of most if not all courses in the School of Ethnic Studies. Once this happens, the next logical step would be to question the need for a separate ethnic studies school." Second, she wrote, "once it is agreed to let faculty of color teach black courses, then it follows it must be granted to whites with expertise in ethnic areas. Note, once a class is approved it can be taught by whoever the department assigns." She concluded that my class was the first step in the administration's long run plan to eliminate not just black studies but the entire School of Ethnic Studies.

I doubted that Corrigan had a nefarious, grand plan to dismantle ethnic studies, partly because the university was nationally recognized for its ethnic studies school. Also, Corrigan had a long personal and professional engagement with black studies and frequently and strongly spoke in favor of it on and off campus. Further, black studies, especially San Francisco State's department, claimed to be a separate, distinct discipline with unique, nonduplicative approaches to the study of black people. To the extent this was the case—and at San Francisco State this was to some extent the case—then faculty, black or white, in the traditional departments could not duplicate black studies classes. Further, Head's arguments appeared to undermine affirmative action by implying that blacks and other people of color should not be recruited by traditional departments if their areas of specialization were ethnic, or if they were recruited they should only be allowed to teach their specialized courses in ethnic studies departments (presumably, this principle would also apply to women and women's studies and gays and lesbians and their departments as well). These are manifestly untenable propositions, almost Orwellian when advanced by ethnic studies faculty founded on principles of faculty and curriculum diversity.

The controversy about the class was extensively covered in the *Golden Gater*, the campus paper, and the Bay Area print and electronic media. Thinking that the controversy might have national significance for black studies and multiculturalism, I sent clips from the campus paper and the San Francisco dailies to the education reporter for the *New York Times* and to the *Chronicle of Higher Education*. Partly perhaps as a result of those clips both did stories on the conflict. The *Chronicle* story by Denise Magner was a straightforward overview of the controversy. The *Times* ran two stories. On Wednesday, January 2, 1991, it ran a long half-page story with a photo of me teaching the five white students on the last day of class: "Hard Won Acceptance Spawns New Controversies around Ethnic Studies" and a brief account in the Sunday edition, "Learning While Doing," on January 6, 1991. As I pointed out, I thought the *Chronicle of Higher Education* account was a straightforward presentation of what happen; the January 2 *Times* account I thought was a bit tilted toward the black studies perspective. It quoted the associate director of the National Council of Black Studies, "All our programs are under siege and threatened with being neutralized, destabilized or eliminated altogether." T'Shaka on my class was quoted, "There was no control over the quality. It might, we feared, have too much of the traditional perspective and not represent the Afro-American perspective." I was quoted but the quotes did not reflect my major point that the teaching of courses like mine in traditional departments enhanced rather than endangered black studies, or my rebuttal to T'Shaka's arrogant assertion that he had the right to monitor another professor's class for "quality control." But that's journalism; I don't know, T'Shaka might have thought the story was biased the other way. In any event, I was pleased the *Times* and the *Chronicle* had brought the controversy to the attention of national audiences. The *Los Angeles Times* and *Black Issues in Higher Education* also did stories that I also thought were a bit tilted toward the black studies perspective on the controversy.

One of the most disturbing aspects of the controversy was that in the media coverage I found myself among the strange bedfellows of conservative, reactionary opponents of affirmative action, black studies, feminism, and multiculturalism in the university. Using the then-popular "PC" (political correctness) moniker these opponents had organized the National Association of Scholars, which focused on exposing the alleged radical forces undermining academic freedom and degrading the Western canon. Their reactionary views were summarized and popularized in Dinesh D'Souza's *Illiberal Education: The Politics of Race and Sex on Campus.* In order to confront this reactionary response to long overdue changes in faculty and curriculum at American universities, Duke University's Stanley Fish and Harvard's Henry Louis Gates organized Teachers for a Democratic Culture to defend liberal values, affirmative action, and multiculturalism on campus. Since it was somewhat akin to the Open Mind group I was a part of (see chapter 8), I immediately sent queries as to how I could join this new group. The media used the controversy about my class—especially its disruption by students—as a poster child for PC gone amok, and for all that was wrong with the liberal academic culture. *Newsweek*, for example, in its April 1, 1991, cover story on the issue, "Upside Down in the Groves of Academia," cited the controversy as an example of the "corrosion of American values and a new intolerance on college campuses." The conservative columnist Mona Charen cited the class disruption as an example of the "dreary, tyrannical politicization of the campuses." I was booked on the local NPR station (KQED) with John Bunzel, of Stanford's Hoover Institution, a founder of the National Scholars Association, and a vociferous opponent of black studies at San Francisco State when he was on its political science faculty, and Vincent Sarich, a Berkeley anthropology professor, whose class was disrupted by students protesting his teaching that blacks and women were in intelligence genetically inferior to white men. The host of the hour long program ("Forum," October 28, 1990) assumed the three of us were comrades in the struggle against PC, but I spent most of my time defending black studies, defending the right of students to protest, even disrupt classes (noting I had disrupted a few in my student days) and upbraiding Sarich for teaching discredited ideas about race, gender, and IQ.

While President Corrigan, my colleagues in the Political Science Department, and the dean and I gathered most of the BSS faculty were supportive of me and the class, the campus faculty in general and the academic senate in particular supported black studies. The academic senate refused to condemn the student disruption of the class, and after much delay it voted to oppose Boxer's decision to approve the class and later, partly because of that decision, it voted no confidence in her. Meanwhile, T'Shaka used his influence to mobilize opposition to me and the class among San Francisco's black leadership. At a meeting in Corrigan's conference room shortly after the protest began, a delegation of a dozen or so of the city's black leaders including the heads of the NAACP, the Urban League, the black ministers' association, and the black trade unionists asked me to stop teaching the class. When I refused, they asked Corrigan to cancel the class, and when he refused, they threatened to bring people from the community to join the students in protest. This gathering of some of the city's top black leaders I thought was unseemly, particular since none of the local worthies had bothered to contact me before the meeting. I sent letters to some of them protesting their heavy-handed interference when they did not have all the facts. Partly I guess to make recompense, the NAACP sponsored a community forum where T'Shaka and I debated the issues before a large audience.

In the course of the calumnies directed against me, colleagues from across the country came to my defense. Ron Walters said, "You don't have someone here that's out to do black folks harm—not the Bob Smith we know. You have someone as black conscious as most other people." And Mack Jones told the campus paper, "Bob is a good brother even though we disagree adamantly about some things. He is unconventional in many ways in the causes of black people. I understand the turf war problem, but I never would have expected the claim Bob is a negative character to the race. He has always used his knowledge to help liberate black people."

The specific conflict regarding the class was resolved in April 1991 in an agreement worked out between BSS, ethnic studies, political science, and me. The course was renamed and renumbered; PS 464, Black Politics, became PS 466, Racial Politics and American Democracy.

The agreement was a capitulation to Black Studies' demand that all courses with black or African American in the title be taught only in their department. I acquiesced in the agreement because Vice President Boxer and Dean Julian thought it was a reasonable compromise to end the controversy and "move on." I did not agree with giving Black Studies a monopoly on black or African American, but in another surprise the agreement ignited conflict over the meaning of race or racial. Colleagues in Asian American Studies objected to the use of racial in the new course's name unless material on all races was included. The Asian American Studies chair in a letter to me said, "Racial politics has to be construed to include Latinos, Asian Americans, and American Indians." I responded, "The notion of race or racial employed in the course title refers not to biological or anthropological attributes but to the notion as a historical and socio-political phenomenon in the United States." Rufus Browning wrote, "Race in the American historical context is often taken to refer to the history of relations between persons of European (white) origin and African Americans, and numerous books published even within the last ten years use race in that sense. . . . There is precedent for the use of the term 'race' in courses and published works that focus on the politics of African Americans." The Asian American studies faculty and students did not decide to protest or disrupt the class, and the issue was soon forgotten.

The resolution of the conflict about my class, however, did not resolve the broader issue of whether ethnic minority faculty hired in traditional departments who were expert in some aspect of black, American Indian, Latino, or Asian American studies could teach classes in their home departments. I sensed Corrigan was reluctant to pursue the matter, and as far as I know no other ethnic-labeled class was approved for a traditional department during my near-thirty years at the university. In a bit of irony, the accrediting association in a 1992 report cited San Francisco State's record of recruitment of minority faculty, the high graduation rate of minority students, and its large number of multicultural classes as exemplary, putting the university "on the cutting edge in the nation of institutions dealing fundamentally with issues of diversity."

Overall, in the final analysis putting the conflict over the course in the perspective of time I guess I am more sad than angry—sad about the lack of collegiality with Black Studies, and the national spectacle of blacks fighting among themselves, leaving our white overlords to settle something that never should have been a conflict, or that we should have worked out among ourselves. Near thirty years later I found a bit of solace in a July 2016 email from Heather Ziemer, who took the black politics—racial politics—class the second time I taught it:

> I took your class after the huge blow-up with the Black Studies Department. I was looking at the department page today after a conversation with someone and saw you were still there and thought I'd drop you a line. Specifically, I wanted to thank you for teaching me a perspective on race that I never understood until you taught me. What you taught me (back in 1990 or 1991) I carry with me today. . . . I am so glad you stood your ground with the Black Studies Department. If you had moved

to their department, I would never have taken your class. But you stayed—and being the curious person that I am—I wanted to see what this "uncle tom" professor was all about. I think I can say you made this true-blue liberal white woman a better person who is more aware of the racial politics and history of this country and how they impact the black community. I wanted you to know you made a difference.

Making a difference is what any teacher, whether kindergarten or graduate school, will tell you is what is most fulfilling about the work.

As I said, I had anticipated a collaborative relationship with my black studies colleagues at San Francisco State, because I considered myself a black studies scholar working in political science. I was not a member of the black studies professional association and I did not attend its meetings, but I read the journals and tried to stay abreast of the epistemological and theoretical developments defining the parameters of the discipline. In my view black studies is an interdisciplinary discipline like American studies, where faculty from the humanities and the social sciences come together using their discipline-specific theories and methods to study the black experience from black perspectives, focusing on the criticality of racism and the ideology of white supremacy, and developing theories and strategies of liberation. The discipline was centered on the African American experience, but with a comparative, Pan-African approach focusing on Africa and the diaspora. This black-centered, Pan-African approach to research and teaching is what made the discipline Afrocentric, and an unquestionable break with the Eurocentrism of the traditional disciplines.

This understanding of the epistemological and theoretical parameters of black studies put me at odds with the Afrocentrism of T'Shaka, Maulana Karenga, and Molefi Asante, which focused on the discovery and propagation of African culture and traditions as epistemological and theoretical foundations of black studies. I rejected this narrow approach to Afrocentrism for two reasons. First, the notion of a discoverable, all-encompassing African culture is nonsense. Rather, there are many African cultures, often in conflict and often existing uneasily in a single nation-state. Second, T'Shaka and Karenga's notions of African culture appeared rather superficial to me, based more on myths manufactured in America than extant historical and anthropological research. Overall, in my view, this version of Afrocentric scholarship was not relevant to black liberation scholarship, nor the lived experience of blacks in the United States.

Although I had held these views since my work in black studies at Cal State, LA, I did not articulate them until 1994. During the course controversy at San Francisco State, I decided not to raise these epistemological and theoretical differences with T'Shaka, because I judged they would have only exacerbated the situation. In 1993 I did publicly engage the issue for the first and only time when I was asked by Paula McClain, the book review editor of the *National Political Science Review (NPSR)*, to review Asante's *Kemet, Afrocentricity and Knowledge*. Asante, the longtime editor of the *Journal of Black Studies* and chair of African American Studies at Temple University (Temple under Asante's leadership was the first to offer the PhD), perhaps more than any other scholar devoted his career to the development of a distinctive Africa-centered or "Africologist" perspective in black studies. *Kemet, Afrocentricity and Knowledge* was his definitive work on the subject (my review appears in volume 4, 1994, of the *National Political Science Review*).

The point of departure for Asante is that black studies is not just an interdisciplinary collection of courses, as I contend, but rather it has, or should have, a distinctive "Africology" rooted in the classical civilization of Egypt (Kemet). Epistemologically this means that accurate knowledge of the experience of African peoples cannot occur without a foundation in this classical African culture. Asante claims that ancient Egypt is the fundamental source of classical Greek civilization and therefore of Western culture, and that the ancient Egyptians were black. Many historians and anthropologists (including African Americans) dispute these claims. It is beyond my competence to adjudicate this dispute, but if Asante's claims are not sustainable then the epistemological foundations of his Africology are substantially undermined, because for him the classical history of a people is indispensable in the development of the concepts and methods that structure research on their experience.

Asante postulated several Kemetic concepts and methods that should structure research and analysis of the black experience, from literary movements to urban black politics. But those concepts were so amorphous as to be near useless in scientific research. For example, he introduced the concept "soul of method." What is the soul of method? Asante writes:

> There is nothing mysterious. . . . Soul, a creative force, activates research by engaging the researcher in an effort to explain human functioning by relating it to concrete human conditions and cultural factors. . . . Soul represents a specific intervention in

the methodological process. . . . It breaks the structural, lineal monotony by investing research with soul, the rhythm of assessing and synthesizing in order to create understanding and meaning.

Throughout the book when Asante attempted to give operational content to his Kemet-based Afrocentrism, he resorted to abstractions of this sort. Whatever one's view of the Kemet controversy in terms of its historical accuracy or as a philosophical posture, as a conceptual and methodological framework for scientific research it was near useless. The concepts are so vague that there is no way in which they may be rendered operational for purposes of empirical research. Asante's interchangeable use of Afrocentric, Afrocentricity, and Africology is also confusing. The latter two may be properly understood as an attempt to use Kemetic or other African-derived epistemologies to study African phenomena, while Afrocentric may be simply an effort to give centrality to the experience of Africans as opposed to Europeans in teaching and research. For example, an Afrocentric may hold, as I do, that in the United States race and racism is central—more so than class, more so than the Anglo-Saxon ethos, more so than the liberal tradition—in explaining the past, present, and future of the African American. This approach to an Afrocentric perspective is likely to be more productive of historical and social science scholarship on the African American experience than Kemet and the soul of method.

Asante, along with James Turner, Ronald Walters, and Nathan Hare, are among the architects of black studies. Although I disagree with Asante's Africology, such disagreements are likely an inevitable part of the construction of a new discipline, and in no way diminished my appreciation and admiration of Asante's contribution to the architecture of black studies (I found inspiration in his engaging memoir *As I Run Toward Africa*). Nor, I should add, do these differences constitute a basis for the kind of rancorous conflict that marked my relationship with T'Shaka and the black studies faculty at San Francisco State.

A year after the black studies course controversy I was involved in another that also generated local and national news coverage. This time it involved debates about family, marriage, feminism, and the black community. More so than the course controversy I found this controversy contrived, counterproductive, and annoying. I viewed it then and now as a phony news story manufactured by Bay Area newspapers for almost purely commercial reasons.

A reporter from the campus paper was monitoring the start of my teaching the black politics course for the second time to see how things were going. In the course of discussion of female-headed households in the context of the so-called black underclass and the problem of bias in social science research, I remarked young African American women should be more concerned about finding a good husband than a good job: "I would urge my daughters to make the choice of having a good man rather than a career." I went on to say I would give the same advice if I had sons, although they would less likely have to make that choice. The campus paper ran a story on its front page with my comments. I was only mildly annoyed when the story appeared in the campus paper, but I was really upset when reporters from the city's two dailies called and said they were doing stories.

I had good relations with Perry Lang of the *San Francisco Chronicle* and Greg Lewis of the *San Francisco Examiner*, African American reporters who covered race for the papers. Both had interviewed me several times about local and national issues. When they contacted me about the story in the campus paper and indicated their wish to do a story, I urged them not to, arguing that story was trivia, campus news perhaps, but not of interest or significance to the broader Bay Area community. I am not sure if they agreed, but both said they had no choice because their editors insisted they do the story because it was a nice companion to stories on the Clarence Thomas Supreme Court confirmation hearings then going on in Washington, where the would-be justice was accused of sexual harassment of Anita Hill, a lawyer, formerly in his employ. This, Lang and Lewis said, their editors saw as the "hook" for the story. The *Chronicle* ran the story on the front page below the fold with a photo of me; above the fold was a photo of Thomas at his confirmation hearing. The *Examiner* the same day ran a story by Carl Irving and Greg Lewis headlined "Black Women Told to Seek Husbands Not Jobs, SF State Professor Draws Criticisms over Classroom Lecture." The *Oakland Tribune, USA Today*, and the *Chronicle of Higher Education* later picked up the story and the Associated Press distributed it nationwide. It was in the news on Bay Area television and radio for a couple of days (when I told reporters that I thought the story was trivia and I did not wish to talk about it, they said they would report I was unwilling to defend my views on air). In addition to Bay Area media, I received queries from news outlets or talk shows from all over the country, which I declined, and an invitation to appear on the *Sally Jesse Raphael Show*, which I also declined after what I thought was a sensationalized appearance on *People Are Talking*, a local equivalent.

From the beginning I was critical of the media's coverage, the hype, what I called its "preoccupation with sensationalism," and I described the

San Francisco Chronicle story as "much ado about little. . . . It was uncalled for the way they put that on the front page as the second most important story of the day. Above the fold was Clarence Thomas as this black man who did this terrible thing to a black woman at work, and then they ran my face underneath, branding me as among the ranks of black male chauvinist."

As I recall, most of the anger and rejection of what I said came from the white women in the class while the several black women said nothing or were supportive of my position. One mature black woman whose name I cannot recall spoke in defense of my position during the class. We later became friends partly because of that but more because she hosted a radio blues show and shared with me blues lore and recordings (she was a huge Ma Rainey fan). I did an hour-and-a-half call-in talk program on KDIA, the most popular Bay Area black radio station, and every caller—mostly black women—supported my position. Many of the supportive calls were along the lines of this letter I received from Bev Allard: "I agree with you and your wife's life-style as mine is somewhat similar. I saw you on 'People Are Talking' and wanted to let you know you are doing the right thing. . . . it's not a popular position today as there are so many two-income families. However, my husband and I felt that the children are important, and their welfare should supersede all else. . . . I have never regretted it." But by far the most interesting words of support came in a two-sentence telegram from Nathan Hare: "Congratulations. Although you are a quarter century late, you're still light years ahead of your colleagues."

Julianne Malveaux, the economist formerly on the faculty of San Francisco State and then a columnist for the *San Francisco Examiner*, wrote a rather balanced critique: "Giving Brother Smith the benefit of the doubt (and he did say he would advise his sons as well as his daughters to choose family over work), I'd say he is advocating family values over materialism. . . . But even giving him the benefit of the doubt, he is using black women as the hook in his argument, suggesting that our careerism is the problem with black families." Julianne and I debated the issue at a forum sponsored by Berkeley's Delta Sigma Theta, the African American sorority.

Again, it is my recollection that the most vocal opposition came from white women. As soon as the story broke Kay Lawson rushed to the house to comfort Scottie (she did not need comforting, she supported my stance, writing a letter to the editor at the *Chronicle* that it did not print) and "straighten me out." Sandra Powell wrote a long letter to the campus editor: "What Smith suggested is a horror for all women, white or black, who have wanted to do something with their intellectual lives. I would not like a professor saying that students had a choice whether to love or work. There is no reason why a woman cannot fulfill herself intellectually as well as being a lover, mother and wife." Lee Heller, a former San Francisco State student, in a letter to the *Chronicle* wrote: "Professor Smith should be fired. His scapegoating of women in his classroom for this society's economic problems were unprofessional and demonstrates a complete lack of understanding of his alleged subject, political science, which was my minor. . . . We have just seen the President attempt to railroad a judge onto the Supreme Court with a written record of anti-women positions. We have a Professor Robert Smith at San Francisco State promoting anti-women views, with no objections from the administration of the university."

Discussing media coverage of the black studies and black women's controversies, David Kirp, a public policy professor at Berkeley, wrote: "While these renditions make news, they shrink an academic with provocative ideas into a stick figure. Amidst all the ruckus, no one's noticed that these tempers are really the contours of academic freedom—about a professor's right to speak his mind. . . . As intellectual provocateur—whether from a black perspective in the traditional halls of ivy or new ideas on old social issues—Robert Smith deserves cheers, not jeers."

Putting aside the trivia, the media, and the jeers and the cheers, I believed then and I believe now that critical to the liberation of black people are strong families, which are the base for strong communities with the capacities to struggle. When Daniel Moynihan wrote his famous (some say infamous) report on the black family, about a quarter were headed by women; when I made my remarks, near three-quarters were headed by females. The routine oppression of black men in the labor market, in schools, in the drug trade, and in the criminal justice system renders many black men ineligible mates, which leaves many black women alone, poor, and without the material and psychological benefits of a good husband and father. This is a systemic crisis that cannot be resolved by individual black men and women choosing spouses over careers. Nor is this to suggest that women cannot successfully rear children without a man; my mother did as countless thousands and thousands in the past and in the present. If the United States followed the model of the European social democracies and provided income adequate for all families and children, even more could, making the choice between spouses and careers less materially necessary.

Meanwhile, my daughters made their choices. Jessica chose career, adamantly insisting she would never have children and might never marry. Meanwhile Scottus has a good husband and is a stay-at-home mother and full-time online student working on a degree in social work at Arizona State University. Both were free to choose (our disabled daughter Blanch was not; she has neither children nor husband), but from when I was forty-four and involved in the controversy about black women and family at the university to my early seventies, enjoying the pleasures of the company of my two grandchildren, I think Scottus made the best choice.

Living on the East Coast for near two decades, I paid little attention to immigration and its possible harmful effects on the black community. In his review of *We Have No Leaders*, Hugh Davis Graham, the noted historian of civil rights policymaking (his 1990 book *The Civil Rights Era: The Origins and Development of National Policy* is still the definitive work on the subject), wrote, "Smith largely ignores other state policies, such as US immigration policies, which arguably have been enormously damaging to the black underclass." Initially, I found Graham's observation a rather minor criticism given my advocacy of polices such as full employment and national health insurance, polices that would clearly be disproportionately helpful to the so-called black underclass. However, the force of his observation about immigration policies hit me when I returned to California and experienced the impact of immigration on black Los Angeles.

I lived in Los Angeles from 1965 to 1969, and from 1970 to 1972. At those times there were distinct ethnic enclaves—Jewish, Asian, Black, and Latino. When I returned in 1989 black Los Angeles as a distinct ethnic place had almost disappeared, having been transformed into a Black-Latino space. While blacks in the city remained largely segregated from whites, they saw their probability of having a Hispanic neighbor increase from about 10 percent when I left in 1972 to more than 40 percent when I returned in 1989. Many of the traditional black economic, recreational, and cultural institutions had disappeared, and relatives and friends spoke bitterly of the intense competition between blacks and the new immigrants for space, jobs, housing, and education. Witnessing this impact of immigration on black Los Angeles led me to pay more attention to immigration and its impact on African Americans than when I was researching and writing *We Have No Leaders*.

My first writing on the problem was with my friend Kwasi Cobie Harris, then on the political science and African American studies faculty at nearby San Jose State University. A native Californian, Kwasi earned the PhD from UCLA, with specialties in comparative politics and African studies. I first met him at an NCOBPS conference when he was on the faculty at LSU. When he joined the San Jose State faculty, he and his wife Carla quickly became among our best friends in the Bay Area. I wrote letters of recommendation for Carla and assisted Kwasi in putting the final touches on his dissertation. A decade or so younger than I, Kwasi was a militant Pan-Africanist and Black Power man. In 1996 he asked me to join him in writing an article on immigration's impact on the black community in California for the *Newsletter of the California Black Faculty and Staff Association*. The article "No Way In" was a critique of the paper "No Way Out: Immigrants and the New California," which was widely circulated among California progressive scholars and activists. The paper was written by Jeff Lustig, a radical Berkeley activist in the 1960s and later professor of political science at Sacramento State, and Richard Walker, a Berkeley geography professor and a founder of the California Studies Association. "No Way Out" was a fulsome defense of illegal immigrants from Latin America, especially Mexico. It suggested that those blacks and whites who opposed the flow of immigrants into California were largely "racist, irrational, xenophobic immigrant bashers."

Kwasi and I took exception to this perspective and argued Lustig and Walker and white progressives generally needed to take account of the legitimate black concerns about immigration, concerns not rooted in irrationality, racism, or xenophobia. We wrote, "To fold the African American position into the position of whites is an example of white supremacist thinking because it renders blacks and their interests invisible." We argued, using Los Angeles as a case study, that it was clear that illegal immigrant labor from Mexico had a negative impact on the black low-income labor force, depressing wages and facilitating union busting. As our principal example, we cited a 1988 study by Congress's General Accounting Office (GAO) of the impact of undocumented workers on wages, working conditions, and union organizing in Los Angeles. The study found that until the early 1980s half of the janitors working in the high-rise districts of Los Angeles were black. Under the leadership of the Service Employees International Union (SEIU) they had won excellent wages and working conditions. But in the early 1980s a group of aggressive nonunion firms were able to wrest the best building contracts from the SEIU.

The competition between the large unionized firms (staffed by US-born labor at wages of more than twelve dollars an hour) and the smaller nonunion firms (largely staffed by undocumented Hispanic workers from Latin America at wages of less than four dollars an hour) eventually eliminated the unionized contracts and the African American workers. According to the GAO in 1977 about twenty-five hundred black janitors were working under union protection in Los Angeles, but by 1985 this number declined to six hundred, of which only one hundred were still protected by high-wage union contracts. We pointed out that Lustig and Walker nowhere in their paper mentioned these negative effects of immigration on black workers. We argued this was unacceptable and that white progressives should consider the interests of blacks as well as the new immigrants and how the "conflicting interests of the two exploited groups—low wage immigrants and displaced black workers might be reconciled." Instead of this coalition building they simply dismissed African American opponents of widespread illegal immigration as "xenophobia racists." We concluded, "This hegemonic position of white progressive intellectuals is unacceptable to us, and we believe the broad masses of the African American people. We therefore cannot remain silent and nor will African Americans long suffer a coalition animated by such arrogance and self-righteousness."

The newsletter of the black faculty was not widely circulated, but several of my white progressive colleagues at San Francisco State heard about the article and came to me with concerns that while blacks *may*—I emphasize they said may—have concerns about immigration, I should be careful not to get in bed with the likes of xenophobic immigrant bashers like California governor Pete Wilson and conservative columnist and presidential candidate Patrick Buchanan. I must say I was mildly offended by this paternalistic attitude of my white colleagues.

My next foray into immigration politics came about in an unusual way. John Whitehead, a professor at the City College of San Francisco, was editing a collection of papers and planning a conference at the college on the impact of globalization on African Americans. For the conference and the edited volume, he solicited a paper from Steven Shulman, a white economist on the faculty of Colorado State University who specialized in the study of the impact of racial discrimination on African American well-being. Shulman prepared a paper on immigration and blacks for delivery at the conference and inclusion in the volume dealing with the harmful effects of illegal immigration on black well-being. Because there were no blacks scheduled for the conference at the City College, Whitehead asked me to edit Shulman's paper and sign on as a coauthor and presenter at the conference. I thought this was an unusual arrangement and it bothered me, but after talking with Shulman I accepted. But in addition to editing, I inserted new material on the failure of black leadership, because of its perhaps myopic focus on building a coalition with Latinos, to deal with the harmful effects of immigration on the black community honestly and forthrightly, especially its large strata of low-income workers.

In the paper we first reviewed the literature, ethnographic and quantitative, on the impact of illegal immigration on the black community. At the outset we conceded that much of the research was not unambiguous and there was not a consensus about the impact of immigration on the black community. We concluded that the following propositions, however, could be accepted "with a reasonable degree of confidence": (1) the net impact of illegal immigration is negative, reducing public resources available for native-born persons in general and blacks in particular; (2) there was "educational crowding out" as expenditures for the education of immigrants (especially bilingualism or English-as-a-second-language classes) took away funds that could be used for special programs to assist low-income black students; and (3) immigration depressed the wages of low-income black workers and eventually led to their large-scale displacement. We acknowledged that low-wage immigrant labor had positive effects on the overall economy, and that while it was harmful to low-wage black workers, it was helpful to the immigrants and their home countries. Thus, there was conflict between the black community and the immigrant communities. Finally, we argued black leaders in pursuit of the establishment and maintenance of a "rainbow coalition" of peoples of color and progressive whites were deliberately neglecting the interests of blacks. We contended this was a mistake, and that black leaders should embrace policies such as those advocated by Texas congresswoman Barbara Jordan and the commission she chaired in 1994.

When we presented at the City College conference, most of the white and Latino participants predictably disagreed with our interpretation of the data, and just as predictably called us racist. Agreeing to disagree about the research findings, I asked, if it could be conclusively shown that immigration had the harmful effects on blacks we suggested, would they favor restrictive policies? All said they had not thought about it, but most said they would continue to oppose restrictive policies and consider those who supported them racist. In 2003 I presented a revised version of the paper at Michigan State's occasional Race in the 21st Century Conferences. Angela Davis was in attendance and she commented that if the paper was not racist, it at a minimum gave aid and comfort to racist opponents of immigration. In 2004 Manuel Pastor, a professor of Latin American studies at the University of California, Santa Cruz, and a participant in the City College conference, presented a thoughtful critique of our paper entitled "Somewhere Over the Rainbow: African Americans, Unauthorized Mexican Immigrants and Coalition Building." He contended that even if immigration harmed blacks it would be a mistake for blacks to support restrictive policies because it would antagonize Latinos—the fastest growing segment of the American population—and "memory matters." Thus, blacks should subordinate their concerns in order not to make enemies of a potentially powerful Latino community that would not forget. Curtis Stokes, the organizer of the Michigan conference, wrote of my paper, "You raise issues that most mainstream black leaders and many left intellectuals aren't willing to address; doing so makes a powerful contribution to the immigration conversation as it impacts blacks."

If there was the slightest chance that black leaders would embrace policies to restrict immigration in the interest of their low-income constituents, it ended with the election of the openly racist, xenophobic Donald Trump to the presidency. His rantings about "shit-hole" countries and his inhumane policies at the Mexican border made supporters of restrictive policies recoil from association with anything resembling what Trump favored regarding immigration. But even before Trump, I had reached the conclusion that the time for effective restrictive policies had passed. As I told the *Nation* in 2006, "The damage to African Americans has been done. There is no way to undo it. I would support the US exercising its right to secure its borders and to remove people who have no right to be here, but it cannot be done in a rational and humane way. The only solution is to support legalization."

It has been clear since immigration became a perennial national issue that black leaders are not going to support policies to control immigration, notwithstanding its harmful effects on black people. In the long run this may be the best strategic decision, but in the long run it may also result in the further isolation, stigmatization, and exclusion of the so-called black underclass as Latinos become "white." History suggests there is little reason for blacks to be sanguine about the future in their relationships with Latinos.

In October 1995, I attended the Million Man March called by the Nation of Islam's Louis Farrakhan. I respected Farrakhan for his work in revitalizing the Nation after Mr. Muhammad's death, and for keeping the spirit of militant black nationalism vibrant. At a time when accommodationism was the dominant impulse in black politics I thought his brand of militant nationalism was a useful antidote, despite my reservations about Minster Farrakhan's tendencies toward demagoguery and his all-too-frequent lapses into anti-Semitic rhetoric. I did not take part in the march because I supported its stated mission of black male atonement on the national mall—which I thought was a silly idea. Rather, I joined the march in order to help show the powers-that-be that blacks had the organizational wherewithal to bring a million black men to the Capitol. That is, I thought the march was a valuable demonstration, notwithstanding its dubious leader and mission.

In 1996 I initiated in NCOBPS a project to study local NAACP chapters. This was an effort to shift part of our work from routine academic studies to action research that could more directly contribute to the liberation struggle. The focus on the NAACP's chapters derived from a paper I prepared for Ron Walters's African American Leadership Institute at the University of Maryland. Walters created the institute, on whose advisory board I served, shortly after he left Howard to join the political science and black studies departments at Maryland A center or institute to study black leaders and black leadership had long been a Walters's goal, and he made a commitment by the university to establish one a condition of his coming to the university. One of the first projects of the institute was to commission papers to study the major black civil rights and political organizations, including the NAACP, CORE, SCLC (the Southern Christian Leadership Conference), the National Council of Negro Women, the Rainbow/Push Coalition, black churches, and the Nation of Islam. I was asked to do the paper on the NAACP.

In the paper, I concluded the NAACP in the late twentieth century was, as Gunnar Myrdal described it at midcentury, "without question" the most important organization in the black freedom struggle, but that it faced a number of problems that raised questions about its continuing influence in the twenty-first century. Among those problems were a declining membership, a shrinking budget, a conservative judiciary, an unsympathetic Congress, indifferent presidents, a somewhat hostile public opinion, and an uncertain agenda as to how to address the problems of the so-called black underclass. In this situation I suggested that perhaps the NAACP's greatest resource was its near quarter million membership and its more than a thousand local chapters.

Former House Speaker Thomas O'Neil's refrain that "all politics is local" might be applied to the NAACP. Black scholars and activists constantly call for "grassroots" community leadership and organization, while ignoring the NAACP, which in its local chapters has one of the largest grassroots organizations in the nation. Generally, local chapters in cities and towns across the country are recognized as a leading voice on black community interests and usually have at least nominal access to local political authorities. They are therefore potentially important for leadership development and democratic, grassroots deliberation.

Yet, we know hardly anything about these local chapters. To remedy this gap in our knowledge I proposed that NCOBPS members conduct studies of their local, hometown chapters, using a common research design. I envisioned a multiyear project involving at least fifty chapters in all parts of the country to include urban, rural, and suburban areas. The papers were to be initially presented at NCOBPS meetings and then assembled, evaluated, and edited in a volume for presentation to the NAACP national office. The national office then might be able to develop models for best practices based on the research, and this could be shared with chapters throughout the country via the *Crisis* and the internet.

When I presented the paper at an African American Leadership Institute symposium held at the Smithsonian in Washington, Julian Bond, NAACP board member and soon to be its chair, was one of the commentators/discussants. Bond was enthusiastic about the project, subsequently writing me: "I am vitally interested in your project, both as board member and as board chair of the *Crisis* magazine. I hope that some of your researchers will want to share some of their findings with *Crisis* readers in the future." Unfortunately, the project was stillborn. While many NCOBPS members expressed interest in doing the papers, over a three-year period only seven were written (including one by my wife on our local chapter, and one by Sekou Franklin, a San Francisco State graduate student, whose paper on the San Jose chapter derived from his MA thesis). After three years, recognizing there was insufficient interest I reluctantly abandoned the project.

Bond was disappointed with the failure of the local chapter project, but in later discussions he and I agreed it would be useful to do a study of the NAACP's sixty-one-member national board. He supplied me with the names and addresses of board members from 1989 to 1996. Based on this information, I was able to do a limited social background analysis of the board in terms of gender, region, and occupation. I wished to do a more in-depth analysis based on interviews, but Bond suggested that was not a good prospect because of the privacy concerns of board members, telling me he had shared the information about the board on a confidential basis without board authorization.

In 1991 I had the good opportunity to cochair with JoNina Abron, the last editor of the Black Panther Party newspaper, and Kwame Somburu (aka Paul Boutelle), a Malcolm confidant and former socialist party vice presidential candidate, the Bay Area committee to commemorate the twenty-fifth anniversary of the death of Malcolm X. The committee, like others around the country, sponsored lectures, symposia, films, and did radio and television appearances.

As our twenty-fifth wedding anniversary approached, Bird and I decided to celebrate in Cuba. We selected Cuba first because we are long-time admirers of Fidel and his revolution. Second, Cuba has a substantial African presence, and finally we wanted to do our little bit to protest the US travel ban and embargo. This would be our first trip abroad, not counting our afternoon honeymoon in Tijuana. In Havana we stayed at the Hotel Seville, a centuries-old building recently restored as part of the government's effort to attract tourists, in the heart of old Havana right across the street from the Museum of the Revolution. Living in and touring old Havana was educational and fun. In addition to the Moorish-style architecture, it was also striking to see the cars and the traffic; it was like a time warp or a scene from *The Twilight Zone* since the streets were filled with 1950s-era Chevys, Buicks, Fords—even an Edsel or two.

Tourism in 1996 was the major means for Cuba to earn foreign currency—the American dollar—since even European tourists were required to convert their currency into the dollar. Indeed, we found the US dollar was virtually the only acceptable currency since the Cuban peso was all but worthless. Employment in tourism as a result of tips in US dollars was some of the best-paid work in Cuba.

For example, our tour guide, an economist, had resigned a position in the finance ministry, telling us that in a good week he could earn a month's pay in tips alone. A similar situation exists for persons working in the hotels and other places reserved for tourists. This was our first impression of racism in Cuba—all of the persons in this relatively well-paid industry were white or mulatto. The only persons we saw working in the hotel with dark skins were in the kitchen.

On the first day of our official tour we were lucky to run into an elderly black man who spoke fluent English, having lived in Detroit for more than decade where he worked in the auto industry. He told us, "Come with me, I know more than he [the tour guide] does." The next day he met us at the hotel, we had lunch at Floridita (Hemingway's famous hangout, known for its great daiquiris), and then he took us on what might be described as an "Afrocentric" tour of the city. While sipping a beer and talking in the hotel bar, Ricardo said he was reluctant to visit in the hotel since in general it was reserved for tourists, and throughout our conversation he spoke in a quiet voice, fearing our conversation was being monitored by a nearby dark-skinned security agent. Later during lunch Ricardo discussed racism and socialism in Cuba, telling us that Fidel did for blacks in Cuba what Lyndon Johnson did for blacks in the United States. That is, the revolution, while removing overt and odious forms of racism, did not destroy what Dr. King called the monster of racism itself. He said Afro-Cubans were still denied equality based on their skin color, especially in employment and access to government offices. Like everyone we spoke to in Cuba, he praised the equalitarian character of Cuba's housing, health, and educational opportunity structures but complained that since the "government owns everything, you can't shop," implying that ordinary Cubans would be better off under a more market economy.

Ricardo's attitudes about racism were echoed in conversations with a young black woman (when I use black, I am referring to people with dark skin not just Afro-Cubans) at the Cuban American Friendship Institute. We had brought a "friendship package" of toiletries and other items. When we delivered the package, we discussed the situation of Afro-Cubans. When we asked if there were any groups like the NAACP to protest racism, she said no and added that Afro-Cubans were only allowed to express themselves culturally; since the regime claims racism has been destroyed in Cuba, therefore, racial group political expressions are "counterrevolutionary."

While sitting at a bar at the Havana airport awaiting departure to Nassau (since we could not fly directly to Cuba, we traveled to Nassau in the Bahamas then on to Cuba), we ran into an American who was married to a Cuban and had lived on the island for a decade. We had both graduated from Berkeley in 1970 and enjoyed the deliciousness of two 1960s Berkeley radicals bumping into each other twenty-five years later in—where else—a Havana bar. We reminisced about People's Park and the antiwar protests that closed the campus, and then we discussed the state of the revolution. He described himself as "one disillusioned socialist," arguing that since the collapse of the Soviet Union the revolution in Cuba had become a caricature of itself, and that its real achievements in education and health were now little more than masks to shield a corrupt, unresponsive regime wedded to an outmoded Marxist-Leninist model of central planning. When I asked what he thought was the degree of support for Fidel and whether the revolution would survive Fidel, he responded, "It is impossible to know." As we were waiting in the airport, my briefcase was stolen (nothing of value in it); my former Berkeley classmate said five years ago such a thing was unheard of in Havana, but now it happened frequently. We encountered a good bit of begging on Havana streets, mainly young boys, but nothing like the streets of San Francisco or other major

US cities. My impression was that while the people of Havana were poor, there was no culture of poverty.

Although we saw a few white Americans in Cuba, we encountered only one black American, a professor from SUNY New Paltz, doing research on comparative Cuban-Brazilian race relations. He said he was struck by the official line that there was no racism in Cuba when it was plain to see. For example, he thought it an indicator of racism that at the officially sponsored panels on race relations in Cuba there were no Afro-Cubans. For the last leg of our trip, we spent a couple of days in Miami Beach visiting with my old Howard colleague Jean-Claude García-Zamor. Jean-Claude, who did development work in Africa, pointed out that one of the by-products of the enormously successful Cuban system of higher education was it produced a surplus of well-trained professionals who were sent by the government to Africa, providing much needed health, engineering, and other services to many African countries.

Slavery was not abolished in Cuba until 1886. In 1959 Fidel became the first Cuban leader to openly and unequivocally denounce racism and pledge to eliminate it. Undoubtedly, progress has been made, but also undoubtedly the monster is still alive and well. In my view this is partly because the monster of racism is so deeply ingrained in the white psyche and culture that it transcends economic and political structures. Our twenty-fifth wedding anniversary holiday in Cuba was an education in racism, socialism, and the struggle for black liberation. I suppose it is accidental, but the only countries I have visited (except for a brief visit to England for my nephew's wedding) are communist Cuba and communist China. I have never wished to visit Europe, but next year Bird, Jessica, and I plan to visit Ghana, which will be my first visit to the motherland. (The place I most wished to visit was Palestine, to walk where Jesus walked—the River Jordan, Mount of Olives, the Dead Sea, Garden of Gethsemane, Jerusalem. But I would not visit as long as the land was occupied by Israel.)

As I indicated in a previous chapter, I have had a long interest in the liberation struggle of the Palestinian people. Like Du Bois and most black leaders in 1945, I likely would have supported the creation of the Jewish state in Palestine in the wake of the German genocide, and because of the historic attachment of the Jewish people with the land of Palestine. That is, in spite of the injustice to the indigenous Palestinians, I think the UN resolution dividing the land between the two peoples was an act of balancing of historically just claims. For biblical reasons this was probably the view of many blacks; as my sister Thelma puts it, "God gave that land to the Jews." More secular blacks like Du Bois and Ralph Bunche saw the creation of Israel as a reasonable compromise for the two people. This black consensus was shattered in the late 1960s as radical blacks embraced an anticolonial, anti-imperialist perspective, which led them to view Israel as a white Western settler colony akin to Rhodesia or Algeria. In 1972 the National Black Political Convention called for the abolition of the Israeli state (Stokely Carmichael referred to Israel as the "Zionist weed"). While not the view of the mainstream black establishment (it modified the 1972 convention resolution to call for the preservation of Israel and the creation of a Palestinian state), but even the establishment black leadership by the 1970s was calling for Israeli withdrawal from the West Bank and Gaza (Palestinian territories it seized in the 1967 war) and the establishment of Palestine as a nation-state. Thus, my views were well within the mainstream of black political and intellectual thinking. My views of the situation became increasingly sympathetic toward the Palestinians as a result of Israel's establishment of settlements in the occupied territories in flagrant violation of international law and UN resolutions, and its increasing repression of the Palestine resistance. As Israel's repression of the Palestine liberation movement became more violent and brutal, I began to search for ways I could more actively protest. One way was to try to get NCOBPS to go on record in opposition to Israeli oppression and in support of the BDS (Boycott, Disinvest, and Sanctions) movement.

In 2014 I tried unsuccessfully to get NCOBPS to adopt a resolution condemning Israel's invasion of Gaza, where one of the world's most powerful militaries assaulted the poorly armed people of that small enclave, killing hundreds, wounding thousands, razing homes, displacing families, and damaging or destroying schools, mosques, and health facilities. I considered Israel's invasion and seemingly nearly unrestrained war against civilians to border on war crimes and proposed that NCOBPS adopt a resolution to that effect. The executive council, however, refused to act on the resolution without the approval of the general membership, so the resolution could not be adopted in a timely manner.

In 2013 the American Studies Association adopted a resolution to boycott Israeli academic institutions to protest the oppression of the Palestinian people. Subsequently, similar resolutions were adopted by the American Literature Association, the Association of Asian American Studies, the National Association of Chicana and Chicano Studies, the Native American and Indigenous Studies Association, and the Critical Ethnic Studies Association. As is clear, most of the scholarly groups supporting BDS are ethnic studies associations. Therefore, as the first of these ethnic scholarly organizations, it seemed appropriate NCOBPS become a part of this broad coalition of academics of color.

Tiffany, my friend and former San Francisco State colleague, joined me as a cosponsor. At the 2016 meeting of the conference we formally introduced the resolution and it was overwhelmingly adopted. Those who expressed concern were less bothered about the substance of the resolution (one member did privately raise a biblical reservation, contending God had given all of Palestine to the Jews) and more about possible sanctions against them (denial of travel funds), because several state legislatures were considering imposing sanctions on members of organizations participating in BDS.

The resolution Tiffany and I wrote included eight clauses beginning with:

> Whereas the National Conference of Black Political Scientists is committed to the pursuit of equality and freedom for all peoples, to the struggle against all forms of racism, including anti-Semitism, xenophobia, discrimination and to solidarity with oppressed peoples in the United States and around the world; whereas the apartheid-like conditions of the occupation have been funded by robbing Black Communities of desperately needed reparations, funding Israeli militarism to the tune of $150 billion of US expenditures over recent decades which has hamstrung the Palestinian economy causing premature deaths and mass incarceration; whereas there is growing solidarity between Black Lives Matter and Palestinian activists because of the harassment, stop and frisk, killings and mass criminalization and incarceration of young peoples in America both sides have a joint grievance, symbolized by the slogan "When I see them, I see us"; whereas NCOBPS believes that, given the hegemonic military power and the unwavering diplomatic and military support of the United States for its illegal occupation, oppression and repression, that the only way to require the Israeli government to comply with international law is through sanctions, disinvestment and boycotts by the international community; and we are not unmindful that it was partly because of international sanctions that the hegemonic apartheid regime of South Africa was brought into compliance with international law and conventions on human rights; it is therefore resolved that the National Conference of

Black Political Scientists endorses and joins with the American Studies Association and other American scholarly associations in honoring the call of Palestinian civil society for a boycott of Israeli academic institutions.

In his statement accompanying the press release announcing NCOBPS's support of BDS, Todd Shaw of the University of South Carolina, the conference's president, said:

> NCOBPS stands in solidarity with the Palestinian people's struggle for human rights and self-determination as they contest the inhumane and brutal treatment the state of Israel has inflicted upon them in the West Bank occupied territories, and within Israel. . . . The purpose of the resolution is not to boycott the Israeli people. Its purpose is not to boycott peaceful efforts by the government of Israel to negotiate a lasting settlement to the Palestinian-Israeli conflict, which preserves the sovereignty and integrity of both states. The resolution, however, raises concerns that, as many world leaders, human rights advocates, scholars, and other public figures have previously asserted, this treatment is analogous to the apartheid system of South Africa.

The resolution received hardly any attention, but I was pleased NCOBPS is on record in support of the just struggle of the Palestinian people, and the part I played in making it happen.

When I left undergraduate school at Berkeley, I had clear objectives—to become a scholar of black politics and try to use knowledge to contribute to the black liberation struggle, and to become recognized as a top scholar of black politics. Although my formal training was in political science, I thought of myself as scholar in the new discipline of black studies. By the time I completed the doctorate in political science, the political science discipline's long history of racism and indifference to the oppression of blacks had come to an end, and more than a few white political scientists were beginning to publish on the subject. However, from a black perspective much of this work appeared biased, approaching the subject from the perspective of system maintenance rather than black liberation. Moreover, mainstream political science tended to view its work as objective, value-free, nonideological, while black studies was unapologetically ideological committed to the development and use of knowledge to contribute to the empowerment and liberation of black people. As Ron Walters told us again and again at Howard, "dispassionate scholarship was somebody else's luxury."

The overarching theory or frame of reference guiding my work was developed from Mack Jones's 1969 essay "A Frame of Reference for Black Politics," published in Lenneal Henderson's *Black Political Life in the United States*. In the essay Jones postulates that as a result of the violent imposition of a system of racial oppression, whites in America occupy a "superordinate" or dominant position in relationship to blacks that they seek to maintain, while the "subordinate" blacks seek to alter this relationship to secure their liberation. The study of black politics is therefore about power, the asymmetrical power struggle between whites and blacks. Asymmetrical because whites have a near monopoly on the "hard" power bases of wealth, knowledge/technology, violence, and size/population, while blacks have had to rely on the "soft" power bases of "God," morality, and appeals to the nation's democratic, equalitarian ethos. In order to fully understand black politics, Jones argued one had to go beyond this simple power dynamics of group conflict and focus also on the ideological base of the conflict, which is that whites justified or rationalized the subordination of blacks on the basis of the institutionalized ideology of white supremacy or black inferiority. Power, racism, and the ideology of white supremacy are thus the central variables in black politics research. The work of the black liberation political science scholar was to carefully identify manifestations of these phenomena politically (but also in some instances socially, economically, and culturally) and explain their interactions systemically. This kind of scientific work is the first step in the development of ideas and strategies of liberation.

In doing this work of black studies in political science I thought it was necessary to publish in both traditional social science journals and journals of black studies to gain the approbation of colleagues in both disciplines. Over the years I published articles and reviews in *Political Science Quarterly*, *Social Science Quarterly*, *American Political Science Review*, and *Western Political Quarterly*, as well as the *Journal of Black Studies*, *Phylon*, *Journal of Negro Education*, and the *Western Journal of Black Studies*. My articles, reviews, and books dealt with multiple areas of black politics: racism and white supremacy, black-white opinion differences, the Black Power movement, black political culture, black ideologies, black leadership, conservatism and its relationship to racism, and the presidency and race, including studies of the Obama and Kennedy presidencies and the role of race in the polarization of the presidency and American politics.

At the invitation of the New York reference house Facts on File in 2003 I published the *Encyclopedia of African American Politics*, the first in the field and a revised, updated editions in 2016 and 2021. Encyclopedias, handbooks, and textbooks are important in establishing the parameters of a new field and the codification of knowledge. As I indicated I also coauthored (with Hanes Walton) an undergraduate textbook, *American Politics and the African American Quest for Universal Freedom*, first published in 2000 and now in its ninth edition. Colleagues describe it as a "landmark text," "the preeminent text in the field," and "the definitive text in the field." I also wrote an introduction to political science textbook. Unhappy with the standard comparative politics approach in virtually all introductory texts, Eric Stano of Longman Publishers approached me to design a completely new and different text. The text "Families, Groups and Governments: A New Introduction to Political Science" viewed politics as a ubiquitous phenomenon manifested in all sustained, ongoing relationships from the interpersonal to the international. Using comparative liberal, Marxist, and feminist approaches, the text identified 8.5 power bases (money, knowledge, God, morality, size/solidarity, charisma, authority, violence, and the .5 status) that might be employed in the interpersonal politics of everyday life, marital politics, group conflicts, and politics among nations. The manuscript was favorable reviewed and Stano liked it, but Longman elected not to publish because, while the reviews were favorable substantively, most also said that the text was so radically new and different that few professors would likely adopt it because it would require retooling of how they taught the class. Faculty adoption being the bottom line in textbook production, publication was canceled, a decision I understood and accepted (I was allowed to keep the several-thousand-dollar advance). In retirement, I reworked the text, turning it into a monograph, *Power, Philosophy and Egalitarianism: Women, the Family and African Americans*, published in 2020 by Routledge.

When I retired in 2018 after forty years as a professor, I had authored, coauthored, or coedited seventeen books (including the encyclopedia and the African American politics textbook), more than one hundred conference papers and articles, and had an established reputation as a leading scholar of African American politics. The breakthrough books were *Racism in the Post–Civil Rights Era: Now You See It, Now You Don't* and *We Have No Leaders: African Americans in the Post–Civil Rights Era* published in 1995 and 1996 in the SUNY series in African American Studies. Originally intended as a single big book, these two volumes, tracing the course of racism and white supremacy, and the incorporation or co-optation of blacks into the system in the post–civil rights era, solidified my status as a top-rank black politics scholar. Both sold well for academic books, each selling more than three thousand copies (typically an academic book sells less than five hundred). Both won awards (the racism book was awarded the Gustavus Meyers Prize in 1996 for outstanding book on human rights, and *We Have No Leaders* the NCOBPS 1998 Outstanding Book Award), chapters from each were reprinted in volumes edited by other scholars, both are often cited in the literature, and both were adopted for classroom use. Of *Racism in the Post–Civil Rights Era*, Joe Feagin, perhaps the leading post–civil rights era scholar of racism—certainly the most prolific—wrote:

> In this insightful book Robert C. Smith has no reservations about using the "R" word (racism) as the most accurate label for the still-extensive system of white generated oppression facing African Americans. Providing careful, systematic documentation, Smith examines the expressions of the centuries-old framework of white supremacy in contemporary white attitudes, individual white racist actions, institutional patterns of societal racism and black responses to racism. It is a downright refutation of the notion, omnipresent in journalistic and scholarly writing over the last decade, of a "declining significance of race" in the United States.

Of *We Have No Leaders* my friend Dianne Pinderhughes wrote, "This is the broadest view and review of African American politics in the post–civil rights era of which I am aware. This makes for a very rich understanding of the era, and each organization and policy issue Smith reviews. His work is a major contribution to the literature of African American politics."

When *We Have No Leaders* was published, I received a letter from Events Management Services, a publicity firm, offering to publicize the book in a "customized campaign for talk radio and the print media." Unlike most public relations firms, it said it did not charge a monthly retainer, but instead a fee was charged for each radio or television appearance or for each review or interview in national and regional newspapers and magazines. The fee for radio started at $150 but varied by market size and audience of the news organization. Although it is unlikely I could have afforded an extensive media campaign, I summarily rejected their offer of services. I at that time had never heard of scholars hiring publicity agents, which appeared more Hollywood than Howard (when I was at UCLA, I recall one of the worst things said about a faculty colleague was that he was "popularizer"). Looking back, assuming I could have afforded it, I think I should have considered the firm's offer of services; there is nothing wrong with a scholar, particularly one writing about politics, having his work publicized in order to attract a larger audience than his peers. This came home to me when *Conservatism and Racism, and Why in America They Are the Same* was published in 2010. After *We Have No Leaders*, I consider this my most important book, but it was not reviewed, received little notice, and relatively few copies were sold. The book, however, was noted in the conservative blogosphere, where it was dismissed as the typical rantings of a left-wing San Francisco professor; but, as one commentator wrote, there was no reason for concern because "he has no audience."

In 2020 in the wake of the police murder of George Floyd and the subsequent nationwide uprising, George Washington University listed the conservatism and racism book, among more than a hundred others, on what it called a "Solidarity Resource Syllabus." The university's Diversity Office said the syllabus would help students "actively and effectively" combat racial prejudice. Conservative students on campus protested the book's inclusion, claiming it suggested they were racists. The president of the campus Republicans cited its inclusion on the syllabus as an example of liberal bias and indoctrination. In addition to the *Washington Times*, the story was reported by other conservative media including Fox News. For several days I received hate emails from angry conservatives. After about a week of student protests by campus conservatives, the university removed the book from the syllabus. As a result of the controversy, the book received national attention and there was a brief uptick in sales.

Although I did not retain the services of a professional publicity firm, from the time of my arrival I was aggressively promoted by San Francisco State's public relations office. Within weeks of my arrival, I was on the local NPR station (KQED) discussing the legacy of Huey Newton in the aftermath of his murder. I became a frequent guest on KQED, and was often interviewed by local television, radio, and print media. Within a decade I was also interviewed by BET, NPR, and other national and international media. In 1999 I was cited by the central university administration as the most quoted faculty in the twenty-three-campus California State University system. Initially, I liked doing this media work—being on television and radio and seeing my name in the paper—and it is a role of scholars to bring background and context to media discussion of issues in their areas of expertise; but as time passed, I increasingly found the media work tedious, often trivial and annoying, especially the television "soundbite" interviews (I recall doing a television interview for five to ten minutes where exactly three words were used in the broadcast: "She is an extremist," referring to California Supreme Court Justice Janice Brown, then a nominee for the District of Columbia appeals court). Partly because of the publicity of the media work and perhaps because of my reputation as a black scholar of note, I was asked by Geoffrey Cox to join Blacks for Schwarzenegger in the governor's 2006 reelection campaign. I declined.

In 2006 Ronald Dellums returned to Oakland and was elected mayor. Dellums did not wish to be mayor. A year before the election, he was a guest speaker at our local NAACP's annual Martin Luther King Day celebration, where he told us at breakfast that under no circumstance would he run for mayor. In the end, however, he succumbed to pressures of Oakland's black establishment, who viewed him as the only hope for blacks to regain the mayor's office. During his tenure as mayor, I became for the Bay Area media the go-to scholar for comments on his administration. Looking back over the clips, my quotes from the outset were uniformly critical of his lackadaisical approach to the job. As I told the *San Francisco Chronicle* at the midterm of the administration, "He's been reluctant to govern. He ran as visionary leader who would make Oakland the model city. He's not even been a good routine mayor, let alone a visionary one. He didn't seek the job. The job sought him. Perhaps he was unprepared. The next two years will be like the past two. It's his personality and character." After he left office, Dellums became the first fellow in residence at the Ronald Walters Policy Center at Howard, where in a discussion he told us becoming mayor was the worst mistake of his career.

Although I was less than enthusiastic about media work as time went on, there was one story—the impeachment of Bill Clinton—that I was happy to engage. I abandoned my usual neutral, objective approach to discussing issues in the news and became an active partisan calling for Clinton's resignation or impeachment during the Monica Lewinsky scandal. This not only made my comments more newsworthy for the Bay Area, but it put me at odds with my San Francisco State political science colleagues, except Kay Lawson, and most of my black colleagues around the country. I never liked Clinton, viewing him as a lowlife and "Slick Willie," who had skillfully played the race card by disparaging black people in order to win the support of white racists yet nevertheless winning and retaining the overwhelming support of black leaders and voters, even after signing antiblack legislation such as the welfare reform and crime bills. As Malcolm would have said, "he ran a con game" and I resented it. But even if I had been a supporter or admirer, I would have favored his impeachment. First, I thought the underlying offense—oral sex with an intern young enough to be his daughter—constituted, given the age and power differentials, sexual harassment and abuse. This behavior disgraced and brought the office of the presidency into disrepute and merited impeachment. Second, he committed two felonies or "low" crimes—perjury and obstruction of justice—which merited impeachment. Finally, he committed a high crime, violation of his oath as president to "take care that the laws be faithfully executed." Not only did he not faithfully execute the law, he willfully broke the law by lying under oath and obstructing the investigation of his behavior. I repeatedly made these points in every media venue available, and as I said disagreeing with most of my colleagues and even President Corrigan, who quietly chided that I was too harsh on Clinton.

As a result of my scholarly productivity, the university continued to compensate me reasonably well. Cost of living increases were rare, given the state's perennial budget problems, but the occasional merit increases based mainly on publications resulted in substantial salary increases. On one of those occasions, department chair Richard DeLeon in a letter to the provost wrote, "Smith continues to be the department's most active and productive scholar. . . . The department's scoring system cannot adequately reward Robert Smith's record of research and publications. He deserves a substantial raise beyond what the department's scoring system projects. I would ask the President to consider making additional awards out of discretionary funds to Smith . . . because of his high quality of nationally recognized publications in an important area of political science." Although I could have earned more if had left for other places, Bird and I were generally satisfied the salary was adequate, which in the last years was about $150,000. I occasionally earned a bit of money from lectures, and from royalties for my books and editing the SUNY series. The African American politics textbook in its multiple editions earned more than a bit of money, usually about $50,000 per edition.

After more than a decade living on the East Coast, my California dream came true and I was able to return and work in America's most beautiful and progressive city, and my ambition to become a nationally recognized scholar of black politics was realized. Did my scholarly work contribute to the liberation of black people, which was also an ambition? Not in any way I can discern, but who knows? All I know is that in addition to documenting the continuing significance of racism and white supremacy, I urged the increasingly co-opted and comfortable black leadership elite to embrace more system-challenging ideas in order to enhance black power and leverage in the system. This might have made my work appear too radical for the men and women doing the day-to-day practical business of black politics. In 1992 Hanes Walton asked me to coauthor an article about Martin Kilson, political scientist and the first black tenured on the Harvard faculty, focusing on his abrupt embrace of conservatism and the Republicans when Ronald Reagan was elected president and his equally abrupt shift back to liberalism during Clinton's presidency. In the somewhat cheeky article, published in Henry Louis Gates's *Transition*, we wrote, "This abrupt U-turn in Kilson's thinking or more precisely his writings is puzzling. How can a man deny himself, or worse his children? Kilson has not explained these sudden shifts in his stance. Indeed, in his 'Anatomy of Black Conservatism' article he, like a deadbeat dad, does not even acknowledge his role in the creation." In his response Kilson wrote:

> Robert Smith and Hanes Walton share what might be called apocalyptic radicalism; this creed posits that if opponents of the American establishment remain outside its day-to-day agencies long enough—bellowing resentment of its racist, sexist exclusivism and plutocratic greed long enough—the establishment will, like Humpty Dumpty, come tumbling down, to be replaced with sugar and spice and everything nice. Robert Smith has been a proponent of this black variant of what Lenin might have called infantile leftism for a decade or more, while Hanes Walton— whom I thought was a pragmatic and freethinking progressive rather like myself—is a new recruit.

When I first read Kilson's characterization of me I was surprised that he or anyone familiar with my work would have this view—"apocalyptic radical," "infantile leftist"—who me? But thinking about the observation years later, I concluded perhaps Kilson was on to something. One can never know how one's work will be perceived by others. I do know in the context of the time the work was radical and left because this is what the fight for the liberation of black people required.

CHAPTER 10

The End

After the publication in 2018 of my *Ronald Walters and the Fight for Black Power, 1969–2010*, I accepted an invitation from the Wichita, Kansas—Ron's hometown—NAACP to give the keynote address honoring his legacy at their ninety-ninth annual freedom fund dinner. Shortly before the dinner started, I tripped across a wire on the ballroom floor and shattered the femur in my right hip. The pain was excruciating—the worse that I had ever experienced. The injury from the fall was likely made worse because several months before the hip had been injured as a result of a dog biting me while I was taking my morning walk. Surgery was performed in Kansas; the hip was repaired; and, joined by Bird and for a time by my son-in-law Jesse, I spent three weeks in a Wichita rehabilitation hospital. As a result of the multiple drugs administered during and after the surgery, I lost much of my appetite and more than fifty pounds, dropping from 176 to at one point 123 pounds. When I returned home, I went through months of at home and outpatient physical therapy before I was able to walk and drive again.

While being treated for the hip injury, I was diagnosed with lung cancer. Having smoked a pack of cigarettes a day for almost fifty years, I was not shocked by the diagnosis, nor was I sad or depressed. At the time I was seventy-two and for those years I had never had a serious illness or injury. In that sense, I had lived a privileged life, and after a half century of smoking I could hardly be surprised or upset. It was a risk that I had fully accepted, and I was emotionally, if not physically, prepared to accept the consequences, although I was annoyed that the hip injury and the cancer occurred at the same time. I began chemotherapy several weeks after the diagnosis. The results were encouraging although the prognosis was that I would likely be dead in three or four years. This prognosis did not depress or sadden me (as fate would have it, my brother Buddy and niece Brenda were diagnosed with cancer at about the same time). My mother, who lived to be 103, often quoted scripture, Psalm 90: 10: "Our days may come to seventy years, or eighty, if our strength endures; yet the best of them are but trouble and sorrow, but for they quickly pass, and we fly away." Enough said.

The medical care I received for the hip injury and the cancer was excellent, and it was paid for entirely by Medicare and the supplemental insurance provided by the university to retirees. I did not take this for granted, as I came to know cancer patients who did not receive the quantity or quality of care I received because they had less comprehensive insurance coverage (for example, I received the drug Neulasta, which Medicaid and some private insurance plans did not cover). This alternately angered and depressed me because it was a reminder of the inequalities, cruelties, and immorality of the American health system, which provides Cadillac care for some and barely a PT Cruiser for others.

When President Kennedy was killed at age forty-three, one of his friends remarked that at least he would not have to endure the indignities of old age. At seventy-two those indignities were a part of life—the loss of my teeth, the routine aches and pains, the fading of memory, and most distressing for me the loss of sexual capacity. As one who rejoiced in the 1960s sexual revolution and enjoyed a joyous sex life with Bird, this was indeed an indignity. In my late fifties I was gradually adjusting to a less joyous sex life. I tried Viagra and Cialis, but they did not help very much and were prohibitively expensive. Yet another example of the rip-off marketing of drugs in the United States by the pharmaceutical industry, which the government allows with near impunity.

Before the cancer diagnosis, I had cut back on cigarette smoking because California voters had imposed a two-dollar-per-pack tax. Prior to the tax Bird and I each smoked about a pack a day, which came to about $500.00 a month. This was crazy; literally, burning thousands of dollars a year to slowly kill ourselves, in addition to the dangers secondhand smoke did to our children and grandchildren. Recognizing this was stupid, we nevertheless continued to do it. I suppose we were addicted; however, we never really tried to stop because we enjoyed smoking, at least we thought we did. The new two-dollar tax, however, would simply do much damage to the wallet; while not quitting, I reduced my use to about a couple of packs a week. After the cancer diagnosis I briefly considered quitting and likely would have if Bird had quit, but she did not so, figuring the damage was done, I continued to smoke about a couple of packs a week. We both smoked Kool's and were inclined to quit when most of the cities and towns in our area banned the sale of menthol cigarettes. Menthols are the preferred cigarettes of African Americans, and the cities enacting the ban expressed concern to protect our health (the Food and Drug Administration during the Obama administration considered a ban of menthols out of a similar concern). The local ban made it difficult to obtain Kool's so we smoked less.

From my college days until my late fifties I smoked marijuana daily, along with drinking multiple beers. Until I was arrested for DUI I regularly drank and drove (on long trips I would drink and smoke a joint). My DUI arrest was public and somewhat embarrassing. The American Political Science Association was in town and I gave a party for a small group of friends in town for the meeting. Most of the afternoon I spent drinking (by now Jack Daniels) and listening to the Temptations. When I drove to the train station to pick up friends, I was high and was stopped by the police for turning into the wrong station entrance. The smell of alcohol was obvious; as my friends watched I attempted to walk a straight line and recite the alphabet (I missed Q). I spent most of the night in jail. The party went on and I was told a good time was had by all. The penalties for DUI in California were substantial, including a fine of a thousand dollars, suspension of the driver's license, and either a weekend in jail or picking trash on the freeway (I spent the weekend in jail). The auto insurance also went up substantially. I learned my lesson and never drank and drove again.

Sometime after my fiftieth birthday I quit smoking marijuana (I consider the legalization of weed in California and elsewhere in the United States a belated, major victory for the 1960s generation). Many of my friends and colleagues smoked, but after decades I no longer enjoyed the high, although I continued to smoke occasionally and kept a stash for guests. For marijuana I substituted Jack Daniels, which was no improvement either for my health or for the wallet since I drank every afternoon. I never got drunk and found a drink an afternoon delight after a morning of study or writing. After the hip surgery, I, regrettably, lost the taste for alcohol and for the most part stopped drinking, except for the occasional sip with friends at lunch or dinner. Although I drank and smoked excessively, except for the cost it never bothered me. I considered both part of the joys of living along with good food and sex.

Like most people I suppose, I found growing old unpleasant, missing the vigor and joys of youth and the satisfaction of the middle ages, if one was lucky enough to be doing satisfying and fulfilling work. In retirement with little to do or wishing to do, one reflects on the past that has no future. Except, the past does have a future and if one is lucky it is all around in the presence of children and grandchildren. I once was skeptical when persons in prominent positions said they were retiring because they wanted to spend more time with their grandchildren. But I found that to be one of the pleasures of aging and retirement. Another joy was even more the company of Bird. Marrying her at the young age of nineteen under the circumstances that brought us together—and memories of our good life together for almost a half century—brings daily joy that my beautiful Bird did not fly away. The months I was incapacitated as a result of the hip surgery and working with me doing the cancer treatment brought us closer together in the bond of lasting memories and affection. If Bird were to die before me—which I fervently hope she does not—I would kill myself, because I would not wish to live without her. It would be pointless.

And then there are the daughters. I always wished to have girls I guess because I have been mostly around women all my life and always enjoyed the pleasures of their presence. In old age I was graced by three daughters who were always around; Blanch lived with us and Jessica and Scottus were both just a short ride on the freeway away. Although they grew up in predominantly white neighborhoods and attended largely white schools, our daughters were consciously reared in blackness by Bird and me. The house was adorned with African and African American art; black literature was read and discussed; *Jet* and *Ebony* were in the house; black music was constantly heard; photos of Malcolm and Martin were on the walls, as were pictures of parents, grandparents, and in one case a great-grandparent; speeches by Malcolm and Martin were played at home and on road trips. When they were young, we took them to Baptist churches for appreciation of that crucial aspect of blackness, and I would sometimes play gospel music and preach to them. We encouraged our daughters to link their fate to the brothers and sisters in the "hood" and to never look down on poor black people. Most of their friends and playmates in elementary school were white, but by junior high, or high school for sure, they were all black. We urged them to date and marry black. Bird and I look back with sober satisfaction in the most important work of our lives—three strong competent black women who are taking on the responsibility of care of their aged parents.

Although intellectually impaired, Blanch is the best she is able to be, working full-time in a sheltered workplace; she is a responsible and good person. Her disability is the greatest disappointment of my life, and I often think if only things had been different, she would have been just like her daddy. As I watch her as she approaches middle age, it is a daily pleasure to see what a thoroughly decent person she is as she copes with the misfortunes of her life.

My middle daughter Jessica is in temperament probably the least like her daddy. Strong-willed and opinionated like Bird, she is supremely self-confident and independent, the one most likely to say what she thinks (Scottus says in the 1960s she would have been a Black Panther). She dates, but I have never met a boyfriend, and against my will she says marriage and children are not for her. Once I quipped that I hoped she was not a lesbian; she snapped that she was not but if she were, she would be a proud one. I had wanted her to go to Howard, get a PhD, and become an English professor. Instead she graduated from San Francisco State and teaches literature in the local school district after living for a time in Los Angeles. She teaches at a nearby high school and often stops by in the mornings and afternoons. She is beginning to assist in routine housework as we start to age out of it.

My youngest child, Scottus Charles, named after Bird and me, is perhaps my sentimental favorite, probably because she is the youngest, was unanticipated, and maybe because without her I would not have her grandchildren (my grandson Greyson Robert Rutland was born in 2015). My sister Cleo said early on that of the three daughters Scottus would give us the most trouble. She was discerning. Scottus was often inattentive to her schoolwork, more frequently disobedient, hung around with the wrong crowd, likely began sex early, and did the worse thing a young girl—especially a young black girl—could do: she became pregnant before she completed her schooling or was married. In the US, unlike the European social democracies, there is little support—Bill Clinton during his presidency shredded what little there was—for women and their children. Unless there is extensive family support, the woman and her child are likely to live in poverty. I did not wish this fate for my daughter and my first grandchild. So, I urged my daughters to refrain from pregnancy until they were married or until they had finished school. Scottus did not. But not only did she get pregnant without completing college, the father of the child was a "bad boy." Daniel, the father, was Mexican American; that did not bother me, but he was a high school dropout who engaged in petty crimes and misdemeanors that kept him in and out of jail. Given this, I urged Scottus to get an abortion.

I am ambivalent about abortion. I know I would not like to have been aborted, although I suppose my mother at her age, poor and single, might have considered aborting what was probably an unwanted pregnancy. I am pleased she made the decision not to get rid of me and raise her thirteenth child as a single parent. Yet, I do not think governments should have the authority or power to force women to have children every time they become pregnant. In any event governments—at least democratic and humane ones—cannot prevent women from having abortions. All they can do is make them more expensive. Wealthy women wishing an abortion can simply vacation in Paris or someplace where they are legal and have the procedure. Middle-class women for a price—a relatively high price since the procedure is illegal—can find a doctor willing to perform an abortion. But if the woman is poor, then she is in trouble, having to attempt to self-abort, go to a poorly equipped midwife, or into the back alleys for a costly and unsafe procedure. Thus, making abortion a crime is unwise public policy. Nevertheless, I think abortion is tantamount to murder, the willful taking of a human-life-to-be. Bird and I had an abortion when we were at Purchase, and I still feel bad about it; particularly when I consider the baby might have been my only son.

In any event, Scottus did not take my advice and gave birth to my first grandchild, Karysa Rae. As one might expect, the first time I saw Karysa I was joyful Scottus rejected my advice. And I feel shame knowing she will one day learn that if her grandpa had his way, she would not be here— aborted—dead. For several months Scottus and Daniel lived together. She got a job as a medical receptionist at a local hospital and Bird and I provided child care. Within a year or so Daniel and Scottus went their separate ways and several years later he was arrested for murder and imprisoned. Karysa, now a teenager, is a strikingly beautiful young lady, an excellent student, and because of her looks already has a career as a model—and she has appeared in minor roles in movies. In appearance she is clearly mixed-race. People often ask her, "What are you?" Although she might most accurately respond, "Blaxican," to reflect her Mexican American and black lineages, for some time Bird and I insisted she identify as black. Bird still does. But I changed my mind and told her that while it was up to her to choose how to ethnically identify, in my opinion she should identify as mixed-race and acknowledge her Mexican American heritage. Why, I ask Bird, should Karysa identify herself on the basis of the discredited racist and white supremacist so-called one-drop rule?

A couple of years after Daniel and Scottus went their separate ways (Daniel provided child support when he was able to do so until his arrest for murder), Scottus began to date Jesse Rutland. Jesse was the near opposite of Daniel. He was black, a police officer, and one of the most intelligent, level-headed, empathetic, and responsible young men I have encountered. I am thoroughly pleased he is my son (in-law)—the son I never had. Several of my San Francisco State colleagues expressed concerns about having a policeman in the family. I found this ridiculous; the all-too-typical negative attitudes liberal professors have toward cops. In fact, some professors see cops as necessary evils rather than as persons who perform a service to the community as important as professors, and one we should encourage decent and intelligent young people to enter. Jesse is somewhat conservative and holds attitudes about police use of deadly force that are perhaps typical of his colleagues. This means we argue when—as is all too frequent—the police kill unarmed black people. He almost always argued the killings are justified while I often thought they constituted murder. Nevertheless, I have learned and learn from him about how the job is done. I think he also learns from me. Planning to retire from police work in his early fifties, he is studying for the master's so he can teach criminal justice at a junior college.

Jesse and Scottus had two wedding ceremonies, one in the wedding chapel of San Francisco's ornate City Hall, where couples from all over the country are often married. And then a second on a beach in Hawaii. I thought the second ceremony was a waste of money (a lot of it mine), especially since they also honeymooned in Italy. Also, I did not like going to Hawaii because I viewed it as a typical overpriced tourist destination, which it was. What further annoyed me about Hawaii once we arrived was that there were few Hawaiians in Honolulu. "Hawaii without Hawaiians" seemed anomalous (Indigenous Hawaiians are about 10 percent of the islands' population). Even in such supposed authentic Hawaiian traditions as the expensive luau we purchased, there were no Hawaiians. This brought home the fact that the state was a conquered, occupied territory forcibly incorporated into the United States. While there I read *Hawaii's Story by Hawaii's Queen*, Liliuokalani, her 1898 plea to the international community for restoration of her throne. I also read literature of the small Hawaiian nationalist movement, which fights for the liberation of Hawaii and the restoration of the monarchy. Reading their literature was melancholy, reminding me of brother Obadele at Prairie View and the Republic of New Africa's fight for an independent black nation in the southern United States.

I found the election of Donald Trump to the presidency inexplicable. After reading the political science research on the election I still found it hard to understand how one of the world's most advanced democracies could select a person so manifestly intellectually, temperamentally, and morally unfit to be president (I am writing a book trying to make sense of the madness). Moreover, Trump is the first president in a hundred years to openly espouse white supremacist and racist views. It was continuously distressing that enough of my fellow citizens would elect and continue to support Trump as he conducted the most reckless presidency in the history of the nation. My distress was reinforced as the political science research revealed Trump won by mobilizing the still-substantial racist vote, those whites of all backgrounds who are "racially resentful" and upset about the "browning" of America and the perceived loss of white power. These Trump voters interpreted his "Make America Great Again" slogan as "Make America White Again." Coming of age during the time of the intelligent, inspiring civil rights reform presidency of John Kennedy and contemplating ending with Trump affirms my abiding pessimism about the prospects for a racially equalitarian society, the kind of society that would make America great for the first time.

The distress and pessimism after Trump's election were tempered by the Democratic Party's shift to the left in reaction to Trump's triumph. The proportion of racially liberal whites in the party increased, and increasing numbers of white liberals, partly as a result of Bernie Sanders's insurgent democratic socialist campaigns for the presidency, embraced socialism. In the near term the prospects are for two racially and ideologically polarized parties, battling for a majority of the electorate. On the outcome of this battle I repair to the wisdom of brother Bob Dylan and shall not prophesize because the answer is blowing in the wind. I have mentioned Barack Obama only in passing in this manuscript, because although he is the first black president and I, like most blacks, rejoiced in his election, he contributed hardly anything to the black liberation struggle. He was the most intelligent and rhetorically gifted president since Kennedy. But for blacks he was just a grand historical symbol (in order to celebrate the historic symbolism, Bird ran unsuccessfully to become an Obama delegate and we attended the Democratic Convention in Denver). I wrote a book, *John F. Kennedy, Barack Obama, and the Politics of Ethnic Incorporation and Avoidance*, showing how this was necessarily the case. I compared Obama's election and presidency to Kennedy's, showing how both ignored—avoided—issues of concern to their ethnic groups. I argued this was necessary if they—as the first of their ethnicity to be elected president—were to win and successfully govern. I did not expect much from Obama, and he did not deliver much. But as I told the *Christian Science Monitor* on the eve of his departure from office, "I would say he did the best he could on race, given the resources at his disposal, the political climate, public opinion and Congress."

In 2006 I was invited by Reverend Jefferson Parramore Rogers to deliver the tenth annual Howard Thurman lecture at Stetson University. Located in Central Florida between Orlando and Daytona Beach, Stetson is a small undergraduate college founded in 1876. Reverend Rogers earned a master's in theology from Howard, where his mentor was Thurman, the first dean of Howard's Rankin Chapel. An influential theologian, Thurman wrote on nonviolence and the emancipatory message of the teachings of Jesus, writings that helped to shape Dr. King's civil rights philosophy. Reverend Rogers was an advisor to Dr. King and for a time head of the Washington office of King's Southern Christian Leadership Conference. At Stetson he headed the Center for Community Service. In 1996 he inaugurated the annual Thurman lecture. Among those invited to give the lecture were Stokely Carmichael, Taylor Branch, Derrick Bell, and John Lewis. As we used to say back in Louisiana, to be included among this group was to stand in some tall cotton.

Reverend Rogers invited me to give the Thurman lecture because of his admiration for *We Have No Leaders*, telling me he had studied it over several readings and thought it was the best book on why the civil rights movement declined after Dr. King's death. In inviting me to give the lecture, he asked that I take stock of the book's pessimistic conclusions ten years after its publication. During my visit to Stetson, Reverend Rogers was ill, but we nevertheless spent several hours over lunch discussing Dr. King, the civil rights movement, and what he saw as the decline of "Kingian" black leadership since the movement shifted from protest to routine electioneering, lobbying, and officeholding. Since this was a major thesis of *We Have No Leaders*, he asked if I thought things had changed in the decade since the book was published. When I said no, he asked me to make sure to drive that point home during the lecture, that it was necessary to hold the leadership accountable because we are still "blind and led by the blind," and it was the role of those who gave the Thurman lecture to be the "voice of justice and speak the truth." Because of his health, Reverend Rogers was not able to attend the lecture, but he prepared a beautiful introduction, which someone read and gave me a copy of: "A brother in the battle for justice in the tradition of indigenous, anti-colonial intellectuals, with the courage to humbly tell the truth and fight for the liberation of the oppressed." Reverend Rogers and I stayed in touch after the lecture, as we made arrangements for me to assist him in writing his memoir. He thought he would be able to arrange funds for me to travel to Stetson to review his papers and conduct interviews with him and other persons in the movement that he would assist in setting up. Unfortunately, he became too ill while making the arrangements to work on the project. Although he lived several more years, for much of the time he was incapacitated by illness and old age. He died in 2014 at the age of ninety-seven.

For most of my life—more than fifty years since I was in undergraduate school at Cal State, LA—I have devoted time to reading, thinking, talking, and arguing about American politics, hoping that intellectual work could contribute to the liberation of African Americans. In most of my writing and talking I have reached rather pessimistic conclusions about the prospects for post–civil rights era breakthroughs in the liberation struggle. My pessimism derives from several sources, my knowledge of the persistence of racism and the tenacity of the ideology of white supremacy, to certain undemocratic features of the US Constitution, to the relative powerlessness of blacks in relationship to their white adversaries, to the relative powerlessness of their white allies and their tendency to often betray black interests, and to the failure of the black leadership group to effectively leverage the little power we have because of its tendency toward elite integration and accommodationism. African Americans were a central part of the great 1960s generation that propelled more liberation movements than any other generation of Americans. Most of these movements—women's liberation, gay liberation, sexual liberation, and the drugs and music; and the great assistance we provided to the Vietnamese in their liberation struggle—were in the long run more successful than the black struggle although it was the model and inspiration for some of the other movements.

When I returned to Shreveport and Benton in 2015 for the fiftieth anniversary of my high school graduation, I found the places had been transformed to the degree where there was little difference between them and similar places in the North. The old order of segregation and legal subordination was no more. Blacks still lived in separate places, were disproportionately poor, and maintained separate religious and to some extent cultural institutions, although the once-vibrant commercial, entertainment, social, and recreational life of Shreveport that emanated from the old segregationist order has for the most part disappeared. In this way the civil rights movement had radical, profound, and enduring liberating consequences that made the lives of all black people in Benton and Shreveport better because they are less burdened by the old white supremacy ideas and direct racial subordination that were present when I was growing up.

In the political life of Benton and Shreveport, blacks vote at rates nearly equal to whites, and they hold offices on the governing bodies proportionate to their share of the population. In Shreveport the mayor and a majority of the city council are black, and blacks are fully integrated into the city's elite political and civic life. When I returned in 2010 for my sister Bernice's funeral, my nephew Lynn, a prominent businessman and behind-the-scenes political operative, hosted a reception at his home (located in an affluent, nearly all black lakeside development) where the guests included the mayor, a US district judge, a US marshal, the editor of the city's major newspaper, a state senator and representative—all African Americans. This power and status of blacks in Shreveport was not imaginable when I was growing up and is reason for celebration of the strides toward freedom of the last fifty years. Yet the status and power of Shreveport's black elite, as elsewhere in the country, coexists with the poverty and dispossession of the impoverished, so-called underclass, a label for the black poor I have always considered a slur. Meanwhile, whatever the label, the black poor in Shreveport, as elsewhere, is ignored and often disparaged by the elites of both races. Thus, in Shreveport as elsewhere there is little cause for optimism if one is concerned about the well-being of the black poor. Beyond the plight of poor black people—on whose well-being rests the liberation of all of us—the black community in the United States today in terms of home ownership, employment, and mass incarceration is worse off than it was when I was graduated from high school.

In the last half century my work documented the critical ideological, material, and structural constraints that confine blacks as collectivity to a subordinate position in America. The Black Power movement was a heroic effort on the part of my generation to confront these constraints. I must at the end of our time confront the grim reality that between the co-opted black elite and the beleaguered masses, without significant structural changes and reparations the African American collectivity's subaltern status will endure for a long time. How a relatively powerless group such as blacks can bring about structural changes has always been the Achilles heel of the black fight for freedom. The major contribution of my generation to this long fight for liberation was in the realm of scholarship, the creation of programs in black studies. With black studies, we irreversibly changed the American university, turning it into a site for documentation of Western subordination of peoples of color, for unmasking the power relations that subordinate colored people, and a place to develop theories and strategies of liberation. Clearly, this work is incomplete and is the unfinished work of the next great generation.

By the early twenty-first century, black studies, born in student protests and opposed by the white academic establishment as well as the NAACP and the civil rights intelligentsia (Kenneth Clark, John Hope Franklin, Bayard Rustin, Rayford Logan, Ralph Bunche), was institutionalized in the American academy. It is available as a major at most leading research universities and elite liberal arts colleges. About a thousand professors (two-thirds black) are employed in black studies, with most holding joint appointments and fifteen universities offering the PhD. As a result of black studies and similar programs, the Eurocentric perspective of the traditional curriculum became multicultural, bringing about a radical transformation of higher education and an increase in the knowledge base of power of blacks, other minorities, and women. This transformation of the university inevitably led to a reaction from the old guard academic establishment, reflected for example in best-selling books declaring multiculturalism in the academy and society was contributing to the "disuniting of America" and the "closing of the American Mind." These reactionary responses are longing for a past that has no future.

Meanwhile, black studies was undergoing significant changes, incorporating feminism and intersectionality into a discipline that at its origins was masculinist and heterosexist. Young black studies scholars also increasingly employ postmodern epistemologies and methods in study of liberation struggles of peoples based on the intersection of class, gender, sexuality, and race. I initially viewed these changes in black studies as retreat from the centrality of race and racism but came to see this view too represented a past that has no future.

I have ended most of my books pessimistically. For example, the 1995 book *Racism in the Post–Civil Rights Era: Now You See It, Now You Don't* ended pessimistically, suggesting racism is likely an immutable feature of American society. Two of the three anonymous reviewers objected. One wrote, "Rather than end the book on a pessimistic note, the author might point to specific policies that could work—at least to diminish racism—if tried and the way to mobilize coalitions in support of these policies." The second wrote, "Has Mr. Smith just thrown up his hands, given up and in essence accepted the fact that blacks will always be the victim of racism, or can he offer a few ideas or suggestions about changing the status-quo?" I have argued that there is little prospect for the kind of structural changes necessary to move toward full liberation of the black collective. But rather than end my autobiography with this woeful conclusion, I shall end with a story I told at the beginning. In 1963 my mother forbade me to join in the civil rights protest when Dr. King came to town to inspire and rally the Shreveport movement. As I wrote in chapter 1 she said something like, "That boy King is going to get himself killed along with a lot of other people, and nothing is going to change." Within two years the great civil rights revolution was written into law, changing Benton and Shreveport almost overnight. I am not singling out my seventy-year-old, seventh-grade-educated mother for myopia because if you had asked the leading scholars of race in 1963, they likely would have been as myopic as my mother. This shows how little I or any other scholar knows about what is coming next, and when.

Notes

Introduction

3   *It is safe to say:* Leonard Steinhorn, *The Greater Generation: In Defense of the Baby Boom Legacy* (New York: St. Martin's Griffin, 2006), 26.

Chapter 1

24   *Integrationist impulse . . . achieve equality in its own right:* Harold Cruse, *Plural but Equal: Blacks and Minorities in America's Plural Society* (New York: William Morrow, 1988), 67.

24–25   *Left it at that . . . racial achievement might have been achieved:* Cruse, *Plural but Equal*, 33.

29   *President Kennedy is referred to . . . as a "bystander" on civil rights:* Nick Bryant, *The Bystander: John F. Kennedy and the Struggle of Black Equality* (New York: Basic Books, 2006).

Chapter 2

32   *LA was so barren:* Magnificent Montague, with Bob Baker, *Burn, Baby! Burn! The Autobiography of Magnificent Montague* (Urbana: University of Illinois Press, 2003), 85.

38   *Rioting mainly for fun and profit:* Edward Banfield, *The Unheavenly City: The Nature and Future of Our Urban Crisis* (Boston: Little, Brown, 1970), 211.

39   *Malcolm X fathered no legislation:* Bruce Perry, *Malcolm: The Life of a Man Who Changed Black America* (Barrytown, NY: Station Hill Press, 1991), 380.

40   *This paper became my first article:* Robert C. Smith, "Black Power and the Transformation from Protest to Politics," *Political Science Quarterly* 96, no. 3 (1981): 431–443.

42   *The five-stage Negro to black conversion process:* William Cross, "The Negro to Black Conversion Process: Toward a Psychology of Black Liberation," *Black World,* July 1971.

42   *Those "who were darker than blue":* Song by Curtis Mayfield, "We the People Who Are Darker than Blue."

48   *Mao's* **Little Red Book** *and its teachings on the "Pitfalls of Liberalism":* *Quotations from Chairman Mao Tse-Tung* (Peking: Foreign Language Press, 1966), 245–249.

Chapter 3

72   *Any attempt to analogize black oppression with the plight of the American white woman:* Linda La Rue, "The Black Movement and Women's Liberation," *The Black Scholar* (May 1973): 26.

74   *Noticed that during the course of the last few years, revolution:* Robert A. Dahl, *After the Revolution? Authority in a Good Society* (New Haven: Yale University Press, 1970), 3.

Chapter 4

79   *We argue that there is a malaise not just in the political science department at Berkeley:* Political Science Graduate Students, UC Berkeley, "Political Science at Berkeley: An Invitation to a Discussion," 10.

82   *My first published work, a comparison of Marx and Fanon's theories:* Robert C. Smith, "Beyond Marx: Fanon and the Concept of Colonial Violence," *Black World* (May 1973): 23–33.

Chapter 5

95   *This is precisely the type of decision making that is suited to the technologies of modern organization:* Daniel P. Moynihan, "The Professionalization of Reform," *The Public Interest* (Fall 1965): 12.

95   *Policy analysis is an activity faced with an essentially hostile environment. . . . the activity is most likely to flourish:* Jacob B. Ukeles, "Policy Analysis: Myth or Reality?," *Public Administration Review* 37, no. 3 (May–June 1977): 225.

99   *I wrote a long theoretical paper based on the project:* Robert C. Smith, "Sources of Urban Ethnicity: A Comparison of Alternative Explanations," *Race and Ethnic Relations* 5 (1988): 159–192.

Chapter 6

101   *The first systematic case for transforming traditional "Negro" colleges into "black" institutions:* Charles Hamilton, "The Place of the Black College in the Human Rights Struggle," *Negro Digest*, September 1967.

101   *A black university "that would deliberately inoculate a sense of racial pride and anger in black students":* Hamilton, "The Place of the Black College in the Human Rights Struggle," 6–7.

102   *Any time one moves from recitation of facts into the realm of meaning:* Ronald Walters, "The Meaning of Black Studies," 1969 paper prepared for Syracuse University School of Education.

105   *This resulted in my first article in a peer-reviewed journal:* Ronald Walters and Robert Smith, "The Black Education Strategy in the 1970s," *Journal of Negro Education* 48, no. 2 (1979): 156–170.

107   *I also revised parts of it for journal publication, eventually publishing three chapters in journals:* "The Black Congressional Delegation," *Western Political Quarterly* 34 (1981): 203–221; "Black Appointed Officials: A Neglected Category of Political Participation Research," *Journal of Black Studies* 14 (1984): 139–147; and "The Political Behavior of Black Presidential Appointees, 1960–1980," *Western Journal of Black Studies* 8 (1984): 139–147.

Chapter 7

112   *In 1977 he secured a contract with the prestigious Academy of Political and Social Sciences to edit a special issue of its* **Annals** *on urban black politics:* John R. Howard and Robert C. Smith, eds., *Annals of the American Academy of Political and Social Science* 439 (1978).

114   *The privatization of education. . . . In this sense Purchase fits neatly:* Henry Etzkowitz and Joseph Fashing, "Ideology and Educational Utopias: SUNY at Purchase," *Liberal Education* 62, no. 4 (December 1976): 566.

114   *Rather than serve an exclusive clientele:* Etzkowitz and Fashing, "Ideology and Educational Utopias," 557.

114   *Take the college to the people. . . . potential EOP students from other parts of the state are automatically excluded from attending Purchase:* Etzkowitz and Fashing, "Ideology and Educational Utopias," 553.

126   ***National policy makers should be sensitive to these kinds of variations:***
       Robert C. Smith, *Equal Employment Opportunity: A Comparative
       Micro-Analysis of Boston and Houston* (Totowa, NJ: Allan Held, Osmun
       & Co., 1982), 92.

Chapter 8

130   ***Rick and I wrote multiple papers and journal articles in this kind of
       collaboration:*** Richard Seltzer and Robert C. Smith, "Color Differences
       in the Afro-American Community and the Differences They Make,"
       Journal of Black Studies 21 (1999): 279–286.

131   ***We published the paper in the new* AIDS and Public Policy Journal:**
       Robert C. Smith and Richard Seltzer, "Racial Differences and Interracial
       Racial Differences among Blacks in America in Attitudes toward AIDS,"
       AIDS and Public Policy Journal 3 (1988): 31–35.

133   ***In 1985 I coedited with Walters a special issue:*** Ronald Walters and Robert
       C. Smith, eds., *Reflections on Black Leadership*, special issue of the *Urban
       League Review* 9 (1985).

134   ***Arguably [Hanes Walton] was one of the greatest political scientists of
       his generation:*** Quotation is from the back cover of Robert C. Smith,
       Hanes Walton, Jr., Architect of the Black Science of Politics (New York:
       Palgrave Pivot, 2018).

135   ***Race . . . is the most important cleavage in American life:*** Hanes Walton,
       Jr., Robert C. Smith, and Sherri L. Wallace, *American Politics and the
       African American Quest for Universal Freedom* (New York: Routledge,
       2017), xx.

138   ***John Garcia of the University of Arizona and I prepared an article for
       political science:*** John A. Garcia and Robert C. Smith, "Meeting the
       National Need for Minority Scholars and Scholarship: What Professional
       Associations Might Do," *PS: Political Science and Politics* 23 (March
       1990): 62–63.

139   ***The only living person on the list, he came in ahead of Ida Wells-Barnett,
       Fannie Lou Hamer, and Adam Clayton Powell:*** Robert C. Smith,
       "Rating Black Leaders: The NCOBPS List," *National Political Science
       Review* 8 (2000): 124–138.

139   ***Reed must be faulted for his consistent lack of restraint:*** Dianne Pin-
       derhughes, "The Jesse Jackson Phenomenon: The Crisis of Purpose in
       Afro-American Politics by Adolph L. Reed, Jr.," *American Political Science
       Review* 81, no. 1 (March 1987): 292.

139   ***Reed's emotionality renders him unable to deal seriously with the phenomenon of Jesse Jackson:*** Kenneth Clark, *New York Times*, July 6, 1986.

141   ***I am very disappointed with him:*** Robert C. Smith quoted in Peter Slevinson and William Claiborne, "Jackson Admits He Fathered Child," *Washington Post*, January 19, 2000.

147   ***In 2000 I wrote an essay about him which included a rare interview:*** Robert C. Smith, "Imari Obadele: The Father of the Modern Reparations Movement," *Africana.com*, June 1, 2000, available at http://www.hartford-hwp.com/archives/45a/312.html.

Chapter 9

150   ***He also sought to recruit "top rate" faculty, citing my appointment in 1989 as an example of the university's success in this effort:*** "San Francisco State Aiming to Restore Some of the Luster of Its Past, *San Francisco Examiner*, October 15, 1989.

152   ***Like the transformation of black music:*** Robert C. Smith, "Recent Elections and Black Politics: The Maturation or Death of Black Politics," *PS: Political Science and Politics* 23 (1990): 161.

161   ***The* Chronicle *story by Denise Magner:*** Denise Magner, "Push for Diversity in Traditional Departments Raises Questions about the Future of Ethnic Studies," *Chronicle of Higher Education*, May 1, 1991.

161   ***The* Times *ran two stories:*** Anthony DePalma, "Hard Won Acceptance Spawns New Controversies around Ethnic Studies," *New York Times*, January 2, 1991; "Learning While Doing," *New York Times*, January 6, 1991.

162   ***Dreary, tyrannical politicization of the campuses:*** Mona Charen, "Growing Resistance to Campus Thought Police," *Orange County Register*, December 6, 1990.

166   ***There is nothing mysterious. . . . Soul, a creative force, activates research:*** Molefi Kete Asante, *Kemet, Afrocentricity and Knowledge* (Lawrenceville, NJ: Africa World Press, 1990), 108–109.

168   ***The campus paper ran a story on its front page with my comments:*** Deana Cunningham, "Poly Sci Professor Sparks Debate, Smith Says Women Should Look for Husbands, Not Jobs," *Golden Gater*, October 3, 1991.

168   ***The* Chronicle *ran the story on the front page below the fold with a photo of me:*** Perry Lang, "Black Women Advised to Pursue Men, Not Jobs," *San Francisco Chronicle*, October 10, 1991.

168   *Preoccupation with sensationalism:* Deana Cunningham, "Smith Criticizes Media, Professor Claims Front-Page Story Was Sensationalism," *Golden Gater*, October 17, 1991.

169   *Giving Brother Smith the benefit of the doubt:* Julianne Malveaux, "Black Women Target of Everyone's Ire," *San Francisco Examiner*, October 31, 1991.

169   *What Smith suggested is a horror for all women:* Sandra Powell, "Love, Marriage, Race and Sexism," *Golden Gater*, October 29, 1991.

170   *Professor Smith should be fired:* Lee Heller, letter the editor, *San Francisco Chronicle*, October 29, 1991.

170   *While these renditions make news:* David Kirp, "A Professor's Right to Speak His Mind," *San Francisco Examiner*, October 21, 1991.

171   *Smith largely ignores other state policies:* Hugh Davis Graham, "Review of We Have No Leaders," *Ethnic and Racial Studies* 21 (1998): 804.

172   *To fold the African American position into the position of whites:* Kwasi Cobie Harris and Robert C. Smith, "No Way In," *Newsletter of the California Black Faculty and Staff Association* 20 (1990): 4.

173   *Conflicting interests of the two exploited groups—low wage immigrants and displaced black workers. . . . a coalition animated by such arrogance and self-righteousness:* Harris and Smith, "No Way In," 4.

174   *With a reasonable degree of confidence:* Steven Shulman and Robert C. Smith, "Immigration and African Americans," in *African Americans in the U.S. Economy*, edited by Cecilia A. Conrad, John Whitehead, Patrick L. Mason, and James Stewart (Lanham: Rowman & Littlefield, 2005), 200.

175   *Memory matters:* Manuel Pastor, "Somewhere Over the Rainbow: African Americans, Unauthorized Mexican Immigrants and Coalition Building," in *The Impact of Immigration on African Americans*, edited by Steven Shulman (Piscataway: Transaction, 2004), 133.

175   *The damage to African Americans has been done:* Michelle Garcia, "A Bronx's Tale," *Nation*, June 19, 2006, 15.

176   *I was asked to do the paper on the NAACP:* Robert C. Smith, "The NAACP in the Twenty-First Century," in *Black Political Organizations in the Post–Civil Rights Era*, edited by Karin Stanford and Ollie Johnson (New Brunswick: Rutgers University Press, 2002).

187   *An example of liberal bias and indoctrination:* Douglas Ernest, "Conservatism Is Racism Claim Promoted by George Washington University Diversity Office," *Washington Times*, July 16, 2020.

188   *He's been reluctant to govern:* Christopher Heredia, "At Midterm, Dellums Faces Growing Criticism," *San Francisco Chronicle*, December 29, 2008.

190   *This abrupt U-turn in Kilson's thinking:* Hanes Walton, Jr., and Robert C. Smith, "U-Turn: Martin Kilson and Black Conservatism," *Transition* 62 (1993): 210.

190   *Robert Smith and Hanes Walton share what might be called apocalyptic radicalism:* Martin L. Kilson, "The Gang That Couldn't Shoot Straight," *Transition* 62 (1993): 217.

Chapter 10

198   *I would say he did the best he could on race:* Linda Feldman, "Was Barack Obama a Transformative President?," *Christian Science Monitor*, January 18, 2017.

202   *"Disuniting of America" and the "closing of the American Mind":* Arthur Schlesinger, Jr., *The Disuniting of America: Reflections on a Multicultural Society* (New York: W. W. Norton and Co., 1998), and Allan Bloom, *The Closing of the American Mind: How Higher Education Has Failed Democracy and Impoverished the Souls of Students* (New York: Simon and Schuster, 1987).

Index

Malcolm X (Malcolm Little), 39–40,
46; autobiography of, 49; MLK and,
39, 160
Malveaux, Julianne, 169
Mandel, William Marx, 63
Mao Zedong, 74, 154, 155; *Little Red
Book*, 48–49, 64
Marcuse, Herbert, 60, 63, 74–75
Marshall, Ray, 125
Marshall, Thurgood, 122–123
Martel, James, 153–154
Marx, Karl, 60, 63, 103; Fanon and,
82; Hilbourne's seminar on, 104
Mason, Jackie, 151
Mason, Larry, 12, 36, 59–60, 69–72,
88; on spirituality, 151–152, 155
Mayfield, Curtis, 17–18, 45–46
Mazzolini, Tom, 144
McCarthyism, 61, 63, 69
McClain, C. C., 28
McClain, Paula, 106, 108, 144, 145,
166
McCloud, Emma Jean, 107
McCone Commission, 82
McCormick, Joseph, 130
McGee, Dean, 159
McGee, Philip, 156
Michaux, Lewis H., 94
Micheaux, Oscar, 111
Miles, Pocahontas, 9
Million Man March (1995), 44,
175–176
Mills, Billy, 33, 47
Moore, Michael, 152
Morris, Milton, 137
Morse, Wayne, 69–70
Motown music, 17–18, 35, 37, 45, 68
Moynihan, Daniel Patrick, 95, 98, 170
Mugabe, Robert, 103
multiculturalism, 4, 161–164, 202
Munoz, Carlos, 55–56
Myrdal, Gunnar, 176

n-word, 27, 119
NAACP, 163, 176; education
committee of, 91; "integrationist
impulse" of, 24–26
Nation of Islam, 39, 94, 175–176
National Coalition of Blacks for
Reparations in America, 146–147
National Congress of Black Faculty,
142
National Labor Relations Board, 121
National Research Council (NRC),
141–142
Native Americans. *See* Indigenous
Peoples
"Negro" versus "black," 40, 42, 44,
101
Nehru, Jawaharlal, 155
Nelson, Dale, 98–100, 119–120
New School for Social Research, 92,
94–97, 100
Newton, Huey P., 41, 49–50, 64, 187
Niagara movement, 26
Nixon, Charles, 143
Nixon, Richard, 41, 73, 76, 132; on
affirmative action, 121–122; "war on
drugs" of, 96
non-Western philosophy courses, 63,
82, 151
Norton, Eleanor Holmes, 133
Nyro, Laura, 18, 68

Obadele, Imari, 146–147, 197
Obama, Barack, 132, 140, 193, 198
Obatala, Jomo Kenyatta, 43–44, 47
O'Connor, Kathy, 118, 120
Omar X (Omar Davidson), 38–40, 42,
53, 55
O'Neil, Thomas, 176
Open Mind (organization), 138, 162
Osher Lifelong Learning Institute
(Olli), 2
Ottinger, Richard, 120